JOURNAL FOR THE STUDY OF THE NEW TESTAMENT
SUPPLEMENT SERIES
151

Sheffield Academic Press

Narrative Art and Act
in the Fourth Gospel

Derek Tovey

Journal for the Study of the New Testament
Supplement Series 151

For Lea and Anna

Copyright © 1997 Sheffield Academic Press

Published by Sheffield Academic Press Ltd
Mansion House
19 Kingfield Road
Sheffield S11 9AS
England

Printed on acid-free paper in Great Britain
by Bookcraft Ltd
Midsomer Norton, Bath

British Library Cataloguing in Publication Data

A catalogue record for this book is available
from the British Library

ISBN 1-85075-687-2

CONTENTS

Part I
THE DYNAMICS OF ART AND ACT

PREFACE

This book is a slightly revised version of a thesis presented to the University of Durham at the end of 1994. It represents the culmination of a four-year exploration, both of the Fourth Gospel and the critical study of narrative, or narratology as the literary critics call it. Though few of the results of the research are new, it offers, I think, new ways of putting old questions. To this extent I hope to make a contribution to the ongoing discussion of the Gospel and the perennial problems it poses. I have decided against any substantial revisions for two reasons. First, I intend this work to be a methodological prolegomenon to further explorations, and a framework against which further research may be set. Second, an adequate defence of those aspects against which critique may be directed would require more attention than might be provided by a footnote here or a paragraph there. The result would be a different book: more probably, another book.

One aspect of this study, however, calls for particular comment. I have described the beloved disciple as having the authority of an eyewitness. Those who examined the thesis encouraged a presentation of this in a more nuanced form. They felt, I think, that I was in danger of giving the impression that most of the material in the Gospel was an almost direct transcription of events from the ministry and life of Jesus. I do intend to mean that the beloved disciple was a contemporary of Jesus, who knew Jesus personally and upon whose witness the Gospel claims its authority. I do not intend to suggest that everything recorded has necessarily been directly witnessed by the beloved disciple. I did consider whether I should try and find another form of words to describe the beloved disciple's role and function, for instance, 'witness contemporary with Jesus', or 'first generation witness'. In the end, I decided to let the matter stand. It seems to me that there is a growing consensus among scholars that such a witness stands behind the Fourth Gospel, whatever else may need to be said about the Gospel's prehistory. However, I would hope that anyone reading to the end of my study would be aware that even to talk about 'eyewitness testimony' does not, thereby, necessarily secure 'factual historical data' in the Gospel. It is testimony refracted through a retrospective and personally committed viewpoint. Even to speak of 'factual historical data' requires care, given the nature of historical discourse as reconstruction. One of the aspects of this study that I would like to take further is the question of the way in which the Fourth Gospel may be a 'theological elaboration' on an historical substratum. What is required is another work in the shadow of C.H. Dodd's *Historical Tradition in the Fourth Gospel*, but taking up some of the methodologies outlined in this book. I attempt in this book also to raise questions against what I see to be somewhat facile distinctions between 'history' and 'fiction', and 'history' and 'theology'. This too calls for more work.

Since completing my study, a book has appeared that makes a fresh attempt to identify the beloved disciple. In his book, *The Beloved Disciple: Whose Witness Validates the Gospel of John?*, James Charlesworth makes a case for understanding that the author intends the reader to associate the beloved disciple with Thomas. The argument is cumulative and cogent; it is both circumstantial and speculative, drawing upon evidence taken from tradition and ancient literature, both Christian and otherwise, and based upon the literary indications of the Gospel itself. If the beloved disciple is to be identified with one of the named characters in the Gospel, then the case for Thomas is, on literary grounds, a strong one, as Charlesworth shows. It is, I am persuaded, as strong as any on offer. Yet I remain among those convinced that, while the beloved disciple is a real historical figure, the implied author did not intend to make clear any connection with one of the named disciples. The identity of the beloved disciple is effectively lost to us, though it may have been known to the first readers, or at least to the writer's community. If an association with a given, named disciple was intended, it may simply have been a commonly known fact against which the Gospel was read, and which the implied author took for granted; but the writer has given later readers no clear indication of this. I would meet a number of Charlesworth's arguments for Thomas with some of the points, *mutatis mutandis*, which I advance against Lazarus (see below pp. 123-24). Some of his arguments drawn from the presentation of Thomas in the Gospel, become arguments for the identification of the beloved disciple as Thomas on the basis of a prior association of the two. These, and other arguments, require more attention than can be given in the process of revising this study. Other of his conclusions do not depend upon identifying Thomas with the beloved disciple. In the end, Charlesworth admits that final certainty on his proposals cannot be reached, as the implied author does not make the connection between Thomas and the beloved disciple 'pellucidly' clear.[1] To this extent, his work does not run counter to my observations on the beloved disciple. Some of his proposals I would wholeheartedly endorse.

More people than can be mentioned here have contributed to the genesis of this book by their encouragement and support, and the stimulus of their advice. Professor Tony Thiselton and Dr Stephen Barton supervised my research and to each I owe a special debt of gratitude. Tony helped to set my course, and guided my reading and research for which this study is the richer. When he departed for Nottingham, I came under Stephen's supervision. He had already been my mentor during my preliminary Master's degree, and many of his ideas on the Fourth Gospel have deepened and enriched my understanding of it. I was glad he shared an interest in a literary approach to the Gospels. I shall always be grateful for his friendship, his perceptive and wise oversight, and the careful attention to my work which rescued it on many occasions from slackness of thought or infelicity of expression. Neither he nor Tony can be held responsible for deficiencies that remain. My debt to other scholars, some of whom I have been privileged to meet in person, will be obvious, I trust, in what follows. I have appreciated the stimulus of interchange with members of the Biblical Studies faculty at Durham, and fellow research colleagues; this has continued among colleagues and students within the Auckland Consortium for Theological Education. Special thanks are due to Michael Fraser for his patient advice and willing assistance in handling computer technology. My thanks to Mrs Lois Anderson and Mrs Sunny Yang for help with the illustrations.

I wish to record here my thanks to the Trustees of the Christ's College Tripp Travelling Scholarship, the Dorothy Maclean Trust and members of the parish of Methven for some initial financial support. Ongoing financial assistance was received in scholarship funding, and other forms, from the University of Durham, the St John's College Trust Board and the College of the Southern Cross, the F.N. Davey

1   J.H. Charlesworth, *The Beloved Disciple: Whose Witness Validates the Gospel of John?* (Valley Forge, PA: Trinity Press International), pp. 431-34.

Memorial Trust Fund (SPCK), and St Augustine's Foundation. I should like to thank the Tyndale House Council for granting me a period of study at the Tyndale House Residential Research Library, Cambridge. My very sincere thanks to friends in St Nicholas' Church (Durham), to Drs Andrew and Marian Coleby and to Mrs Irene Earl for their generous and timely assistance.

Last, but by no means least, my deepest appreciation goes to my wife, Lea, and daughter Anna, who journeyed with me, helped make this work possible and shared in the challenges and joys that accompanied it. It is with love and gratitude that I dedicate this book to them.

ABBREVIATIONS

BDF	F. Blass, A. Debrunner and R.W. Funk, *A Greek Grammar of the New Testament*
BETL	Bibliotheca ephemeridum theologicarum lovaniensium
Bib	*Biblica*
BJRL	*Bulletin of the John Rylands University Library of Manchester*
BSac	*Bibliotheca Sacra*
CBQ	*Catholic Biblical Quarterly*
ConBNT	Coniectanea biblica, New Testament
ET	English translation/translator
EvQ	*Evangelical Quarterly*
ExpTim	*Expository Times*
JAAR	*Journal of the American Academy of Religion*
JBL	*Journal of Biblical Literature*
JSNT	*Journal for the Study of the New Testament*
JSNTSup	*Journal for the Study of the New Testament*, Supplement Series
JTS	*Journal of Theological Studies*
Neot	*Neotestimentica*
Nestle-Aland[26]	Nestle-Aland, *Novum Testamentum Graece*, 26th edn, Stuttgart: Deutsche Bibelgesellschaft, 1988
NovT	*Novum Testamentum*
NovTSup	*Novum Testamentum*, Supplements
n.p.	No place of publication given
NTG	New Testament Guide
NTOA	Novum Testamentum et Orbis Antiquus
NTS	*New Testament Studies*
PMLA	*Publications of the Modern Language Association of America*
RB	*Revue biblique*
REB	*The Revised English Bible*, Oxford University Press/ Cambridge University Press, 1989
RevExp	*Review and Expositor*
RSR	*Recherches de science religieuse*
RSV	Revised Standard Version
SBL	Society of Biblical Literature
SBLDS	Society of Biblical Literature Dissertation Series
TBT	*The Bible Today*

TToday	*Theology Today*
TynBul	*Tyndale Bulletin*
UBSGNT[3]	K. Aland *et. al.*, *The Greek New Testament*, 3rd edn, United Bible Societies, 1975
WUNT	Wissenschaftliche Untersuchungen zum Neuen Testament
ZNW	*Zeitschrift für die neutestamentliche Wissenschaft*

Chapter 1

INTRODUCTION

'The Johannine Christ speaks differently from the Christ of the Synoptics; he speaks John's language', stated Franz Mussner thirty years ago, in *The Historical Jesus in the Gospel of St John*.[1] He then asked this question: 'To what extent is the Johannine Christ "identical" with the historical Jesus of Nazareth? Should the *Vita Jesu* which the fourth evangelist presents not rather be termed (even if in an elevated sense) a novel about Jesus?'[2] In statement and in question, Mussner articulated what many readers of the Fourth Gospel have perceived and pondered down the centuries. He also highlighted issues that are at the heart of the present study. The problem that Mussner raised and sought to address is that of the Johannine 'voice' and the Johannine perspective Mussner chose to call the 'mode of vision'.[3]

This book is concerned with what may be broadly called the Johannine point of view. Put simply for the moment, this is the way in which the evangelist presents his story of Jesus, the attitude he takes towards his subject and the standpoint from which he writes. The way the story has been told has thrown up many questions that have puzzled readers and exegetes. Why, for instance, in John 3 does the discussion with Nicodemus become a monologue from Jesus that resonates with the Johannine voice? Should this monologue be understood as the words of Jesus or of the evangelist? The problem is compounded when, in the latter part of the chapter, John (the Baptist) also speaks in Johannine language. Throughout the Gospel there are disjunctions and apparent dislocations in the discourse. These cry out for explanation and have given rise to many theories of textual dislocation or have

1. F. Mussner, *The Historical Jesus in the Gospel of St John* (ET: W.J. O'Hara; London: Burns & Oates, 1967, German edn, 1965).
2. Mussner, *Historical Jesus*, p. 7.
3. Mussner, *Historical Jesus*, p. 8.

been attributed to the way in which putative sources have been redacted. We shall not, of course, be able to look at every instance of dislocation, nor examine all the many exegetical conundrums the Gospel contains, but I hope to demonstrate that attention to the way in which the narrative is mediated, the structuring of the discourse and the narrative art of the implied author in his use of a variable narrative situation, may cast these problems in a new light. An understanding of the implied author's narrative strategies may explain the seeming sutures and rifts that puzzle readers.

The standpoint and attitude to his subject of the implied author raise other questions of a more referential nature. Is he close to or distant from the time of his story? What is the motivation for his story of Jesus? How does he stand in relation to other Christian tradition, for example the Synoptic tradition? Is he faithful to tradition or does he feel able to reinterpret it freely? I shall attempt to consider these questions not only in terms of narrative mediacy but also with regard to the kinds of claims made by the discourse.

'Point of view' is a term that derives from literary critical discussion of narrative texts. This study, therefore, adopts an approach that is literary in orientation. In this chapter, I shall consider some of the implications of a literary approach to the study of the Gospels and provide a brief overview of some specific instances of literary studies of the Fourth Gospel. Then I shall turn to the definition of 'point of view', and of narrative. Included in the latter will be a consideration of the reasons for and implications of reading the Fourth Gospel as a narrative. Finally, I shall provide an overview of the book as a whole. But first I shall consider how point of view correlates to traditional concerns of Johannine scholarship and the 'Johannine problem'.

The 'Johannine Problem' and Point of View

In their study of the Fourth Gospel, scholars have, in a sense, always been concerned with questions of point of view, though the matter would not have been expressed in those terms. To begin with, Johannine scholarship has been interested in the question of the authorship of the Fourth Gospel; that is, the source and *authori*ty of the narrative. The traditional approach has been a straightforward enquiry as to the identity of the real author. While this is still of continuing interest (most commentaries, for example, include a survey of this in their introductions)[4] discussion is now more often directed to the issue of the situation out of which the Fourth Gospel is written, and that to which it is addressed. Thus attention is given to the tradition history of the Gospel's sources, the nature of the Johannine community from which it is said to have sprung, and its *Sitz im Leben* in the late first century CE. Included in this are questions to do with source and redaction, the relationship of the Fourth Gospel to the Christian tradition (most especially as found in the Synoptics) and to the wider intellectual milieu of Judaism, Hellenistic Judaism and the Graeco-Roman world, as well as Gnosticism and other ancient Near Eastern religious and philosophical systems.

Beyond questions of authorship and the ambience within which the Gospel was shaped, the idiosyncratic nature of its material (when compared with the Synoptics) has raised the question of its relationship to the life and death of the Jesus of Nazareth whose story it undertakes to tell.[5] Is this story historical in any sense, and how much of it is reliable or accurate as an account of the historical Jesus, as opposed to mostly 'theology'? Widely divergent views have been expressed. On the one hand, one finds expressed a skepticism about the historical reliability or worth of the Gospel, and a rejection of any historical interest on the part of the implied author. Such a position is well illustrated by A.T. Hanson's *The Prophetic Gospel*, where it is argued that the Gospel's worth as a source for history is subsumed under, and obviated by, the implied author's theological purposes, shaped under his use of Scripture.[6] On the other hand, J.A.T. Robinson, in *The Priority of John*, argues for Johannine 'priority' in terms of a connection to an independent and early strand of tradition and reliable witness to the historical Jesus.[7] Many scholars attempt a mediating position that affirms reasonable historicity for much of the narrative's detail

4. See M. Hengel, *The Johannine Question* (ET; trans. J. Bowden; London: SCM Press, 1989), for a recent book-length study.

5. Similarities and points of contact with the Synoptics also raise questions about possible borrowings by the Fourth Gospel from the Synoptic tradition, or at least of the existence of a shared tradition which is early.

6. A.T. Hanson, *The Prophetic Gospel: A Study of John and the Old Testament* (Edinburgh: T. & T. Clark, 1991), pp. 2-7, 50, chapter 17 (especially the summary on p. 318).

7. J.A.T. Robinson, *The Priority of John* (ed. J.F Coakley; London: SCM Press, 1985), pp. 23-33, and chapter 2.

while stressing the theological, essentially suprahistorical nature of the overall intent.[8]

Finally, attention in Johannine scholarship is directed towards what, under modern literary approaches to point of view, might be called the Fourth Gospel's ideology, or, in more traditional terms, the fourth evangelist's theological and ecclesiological purposes.[9] Here, scholarship explores themes relating to the evangelist's presentation of christology, pneumatology, eschatology, ecclesiology and the Gospel's understanding of faith and discipleship.

All these areas of Johannine study, I suggest, may be subsumed under the broad issue of the Johannine point of view. They concern the perspective which forms the author's attitude to Jesus and the historical standpoint from which he wrote. They examine the context from which he wrote, his purposes in writing, and the audience for whom the Gospel was intended. Although I contend that these areas of enquiry may be subsumed under point of view, it is not my intention to deal with them all here. That would be impossible. Rather, I shall attend to the dynamics by which point of view is established in the narrative.

At the beginning of his magisterial book, *Understanding the Fourth Gospel*, John Ashton outlines 'four circles of enquiry within which all conceivable questions must fall'. These are (1) content, (2) author, (3) readers and (4) the work itself. He then proposes a schematic representation of this as follows:

> [T]he *work itself* occupies the centre of the page, with *author* and *readers* on either side. Arrows pointing from both author and readers towards the work indicate that the nature of the work is determined from two directions. The fourth circle, *content*, may be placed anywhere on the periphery of the page. In a three-dimensional model it would probably cover the surface of the sphere, with the work itself at the centre.[10]

8.   See e.g. the discussion in R.E. Brown, *The Gospel according to John I–XII* (Garden City, NY: Doubleday, 1966), pp. xli-li (especially Part C of this section). Cf. J. Marsh, *The Gospel of St John* (Harmondsworth: Penguin Books, 1968), pp. 17-20 (where he offers an interesting attempt at an examination of what is meant by 'history') and pp. 48-59.

9.   Cf. here, R.A. Culpepper, *Anatomy of the Fourth Gospel* (Philadelphia: Fortress Press, 1983), p. 33.

10. J. Ashton, *Understanding the Fourth Gospel* (Oxford: Oxford University Press, 1991), p. 4 (italics his).

The removal of content from the work itself is curious. The content of a work is anything but peripheral to the work itself, which is defined by its content. This is supported by the fact that the questions posed by Ashton under content, might well be posed of the work itself and, indeed, to some extent cover the same ground.[11] The alternative three-dimensional model offered, that is that content is the surface of a sphere of which the work is the centre, is revealing in that it suggests a viewpoint that is fundamental to traditional approaches to the 'Johannine problem' and affects not only questions of content but the other areas of enquiry as well. It is that answers to the problems posed by the discourse are found with reference to factors extrinsic to the Gospel itself: in the background against which it is to be read, in the circumstances in which it arose, in the influences under which it was formed. In other words, the *context* of the Gospel's production is what is important.[12]

The perspective and methodological framework on which this present study is based contrasts with this extrinsic approach. It starts from Ashton's perceptive observation that 'the nature of the work is determined from two directions', that of the author and that of the reader. Indeed, the *primary context* from which meaning arises is the interaction between author and reader, realized in the text. The text is the locale where the author has encoded his meaning by the way he tells the story and structures its various parts (plot, themes, settings, events, characters and so forth). But this meaning is recovered by the reader who must decode and interpret the author's 'code'. The Fourth Gospel's 'encoding' activity took place *circa* the late first century CE, and is found in the medium of a narrative in *koine* Greek. Decoding is done by real readers, in this case readers in the late twentieth century CE. The text is the arena where the ancient encoding and the modern decoding activities meet: and where both ancient and modern contexts must be held in tension.

The Gospel, then, is a dynamic literary communication situation through which the reader's understanding is formed by the narrative choices and strategies of the author. In the first part of this book we focus upon these strategies, in particular, by examining the narrative situation(s) from which the story is told and how it is structured. We

11. Ashton admits the overlap that exists among the circles of enquiry.

12. Ashton's schema would be improved, I think, by making *context* one of the four circles of enquiry and subsuming content under the work itself.

shall also consider what intentions and effects are achieved by what is said and how it is said. However, the meaning of a narrative is also determined by expectations which the reader brings to the act of reading. These expectations may be shaped and reshaped by the dynamics of the discourse, but they themselves also, to some extent, predetermine how the discourse is received. Meaning, then, is 'taken' as well as 'given'. In the second part of this book we will consider some of the aspects of narrative discourse and conventional expectation which determine how a narrative is taken.

The Literary Approach to the Gospels

The application of techniques and methods drawn from modern literary criticism to the study of the Gospels, along with theoretical underpinnings from literary-critical methodologies, has been something of a growth industry in the past twenty years. Treatment of the Gospels as narratives has been particularly indebted to the recently developed disciplines of narratology, rechristened 'narrative criticism' by biblical scholars,[13] and reader-response theory. The history of this development has been well documented elsewhere and I shall not take time to cover it here.[14] I will, however, make some general observations on aspects of the convergence with, and more especially divergence from, the older forms of biblical criticism of these newer approaches, particularly regarding the question of point of view. In the section following this, I shall then survey some of the monographs which take up a literary approach to the Fourth Gospel.

It must be recognized, of course, that the literary approach to the Gospels is by no means a homogeneous or unified discipline. Rather it encompasses a broad range of theoretical constructs and methods ranging from those whose roots lie in a formalist approach to litera-

13. S.D. Moore, *Literary Criticism and the Gospels* (New Haven: Yale University Press, 1989), p. xxii; cf. M.A. Powell, *What is Narrative Criticism?* (Minneapolis: Fortress Press, 1990), p. 19.

14. See here especially R. Morgan with J. Barton, *Biblical Interpretation* (Oxford: Oxford University Press, 1988), chapter 7; Moore, *Literary Criticism*, and, for a brief overview of narrative criticism, M.W.G. Stibbe, *John as Storyteller* (SNTSMS, 73; Cambridge: Cambridge University Press, 1992), pp. 5-12. For a survey of the development of various schools of modern literary criticism see M.A. Powell *et al.*, *The Bible and Modern Literary Criticism* (New York: Greenwood Press, 1992), pp. 3-19.

ture to those whose indebtedness is to philosophies of linguistics and communication such as semiotics and speech-act theory. The turn to a literary mode of analysis, then, encompasses a wide range of methodologies such as formalism, structuralism, post-structuralism, deconstruction, narratology, and reception (reader-oriented) and feminist theories. The literary approach to gospel study prefers a synchronic perspective as opposed to a diachronic one. Thus attention is focussed upon the final form of the text as we have it today, and not on the prehistory of that text.[15] From this fact derive three general tendencies.

First, literary readings presuppose an holistic approach to the text as against a tendency to atomize it into units of earlier material and sources. This does not preclude readings which attend to segments or isolatable patterns within the total framework, as literary interest in chiastic structures within the Fourth Gospel testifies. But it does mean that stress is placed on the overall coherence of the narrative, and meaning is found in the relationship of parts to the whole. Along with this goes an understanding of gaps, lacunae and fissures in the text as purposefully conceived, to be understood and resolved in terms of the rhetorical strategies and ploys of the implied author, or as textual signals inviting the implied reader to actualize the narrative reality or obtain meaning by testing hypotheses and imaginatively filling the gaps. The literary text, on this perspective, becomes 'a dynamic system of gaps'.[16]

Here, then, is a conception of the text as intentionally created and having an overall purpose and unity fundamental to its creation. In a very real sense, the development of redaction criticism, with its interest in the editorial activity of the evangelists, may be seen as a stage on the way to this understanding (as witnessed by the fact that 'composition criticism' grew out of redaction criticism). The work of redaction critics is generally premissed upon a similar presumption of purpose on the part of the editors and redactors. It is true that a radically 'deconstructive' source criticism, and even a reductionist redaction criticism might well conceive of the Gospel texts as more or less haphazard collections of disparate materials randomly patched together.

15. Most narrative critical approaches to the Gospels specify the particular edition of the gospel text being read but this does not preclude reference to issues raised by the critical apparatus.

16. M. Sternberg, *Expositional Modes and Temporal Ordering in Fiction* (Baltimore: John Hopkins University Press, 1978), p. 50.

But, it would seem, most biblical critics have operated with some sort
of conception of the intentionality of a Gospel's implied author (or,
the editors and redactors) giving an overall coherence to the text. In
his commentary on John's Gospel, Bultmann, despite his interest in
differentiating source from redaction and holding that the text requires
a good deal of reordering, nevertheless conceives of a purposeful
activity on the part of the evangelist, as is shown by these comments
selected at random. 'The Evangelist repeats this argument here, because
he *wishes to bring the discussion back* to the text of the source... to
which the Evangelist has *added his own gloss*.' 'Here as elsewhere the
Evangelist is concerned to attack this apocalyptic conception of
salvation.' 'The motif has a definite place in a miracle story, but the
Evangelist *gladly adopts* it.'[17]

Second, there is a recognition of the role of the reader in the
reconstruction of the meaning of a text. Meaning is conceived as the
outcome of a creative interchange between the author of a text and its
readers. A corollary of this is that the meaning of a text is not fixed,
but may vary amongst readers and different readings. Thus a text may
give rise to multivocal readings. It is a truism to say that biblical critics
have always offered different readings of a Gospel text, or have given
varied interpretations. But it is perhaps the literary approach that
most clearly demonstrates, and welcomes, diversity of interpretation.
There is, however, a more substantive point to be made here. It is
that, in a literary study, attention is fixed upon the rhetoric of the text,
and upon the way it shapes the act of reading: and beyond that, upon
the nature of meaning not so much as content to be excavated from the
text as an event created by the implied author's narrative strategies
and the reader's responses.[18]

A third feature of the literary approach has been the tendency to
bracket out issues and considerations of an historical–critical nature.
This is a direct result of the more synchronic interests of the discipline. Some scholars have welcomed the break up of the hegemony of
the historical critical paradigm which has resulted from the arrival of
this newer paradigm,[19] others see in it the chance for a repristination

17. R. Bultmann, *The Gospel of John* (ET: G.R. Beasley-Murray; Oxford: Basil
Blackwell, 1971), pp. 353, 355, 398 (italics mine).

18. See here R.M. Fowler, *Let the Reader Understand* (Minneapolis: Fortress
Press, 1991), pp. 2-3.

19. See, for instance, Fowler, *Let the Reader Understand*, p. 1.

of the historical mode.[20] Others have embarked upon the literary study of the Gospels with scarcely a backward glance, making little or no attempt at a rapprochment between the two. More recently, however, and as far as the study of the Fourth Gospel is concerned, there has been an attempt in the work of M.W.G. Stibbe and Margaret Davies to bring together issues of literary and historical criticism. It is a move to be welcomed and one which I will attempt to continue. Johannine studies cannot escape the question of the Gospel's relation to history. It is important that narrative-critical approaches do not wholly abandon the issue.

Literary Study of the Fourth Gospel

To my knowledge, a comprehensive survey of the development of the literary study of the Fourth Gospel has yet to be made. A brief sketch is given by Stibbe in the introduction to *The Gospel of John as Literature: an Anthology of Twentieth-Century Perspectives.*[21] Something of the range of methods which gather under a literary approach to the Gospel may be appreciated by the nature of the articles collected in this anthology. Structuralism, deconstruction, reader-response and speech-act theory, narrative criticism and feminist interpretation are all represented here. The selection is also intended to illustrate the point that interest in a literary perspective upon the Fourth Gospel has a history which reaches back into the early decades of this century. A recent collection of essays which illustrates the variety of perspectives to which a literary approach to the Gospel gives rise is the fifty-third issue of *Semeia*, edited by R.A. Culpepper and F.F. Segovia, entitled *The Fourth Gospel from a Literary Perspective.*[22] Here I will briefly survey five monographs which, with the exception of the last, fall within the category of narrative critical approaches to the Fourth Gospel. All of them are concerned with the Johannine point of view from a literary perspective.

---

20. N.R. Petersen, *Literary Criticism for New Testament Critics* (Philadelphia: Fortress Press, 1978), pp. 9-10.

21. M.W.G. Stibbe (ed.), *The Gospel of John as Literature* (Leiden: Brill, 1993). See further the bibliography in that volume. Cf. also J.E. Botha, *Jesus and the Samaritan Woman* (NovTSup, 65; Leiden: Brill, 1991), especially pp. 30-39.

22. R.A. Culpepper and F.F. Segovia (eds.), 'The Fourth Gospel from a Literary Perspective', *Semeia* 53 (Atlanta: Scholars Press, 1991).

The first of these, R.A. Culpepper's *Anatomy of the Fourth Gospel*, published in 1983, is widely regarded as having blazed the trail in narrative critical approaches to the Gospel. Culpepper's broad brush analysis of the Gospel text deservedly occupies pride of place in any survey of narrative approaches to the Fourth Gospel. His work is solidly based upon the then contemporary theoretical development of narratology, especially in his use of Gerard Genette, Seymour Chatman and Boris Uspensky. Yet the use of the word 'Anatomy' in the title suggests an emphasis upon the *construct*(ion) of the Fourth Gospel, and a consequent implicit indebtedness to older formalist categories. Nonetheless, point of view comes to the fore in his work as he examines the strategies and devices by which the Gospel's 'whispering wizard' imparts his conception of Jesus to the implied reader. His analysis of the narrator and point of view, particularly in his use of Uspensky's categories, provides an insightful summary of the author's retrospective, memory-based, scripturally-informed understanding of Jesus.[23]

As this study will seek to show, I believe Culpepper's analysis of the relationship between the narrator and the beloved disciple can be refined. His reading of 21.24, seeking perhaps to retain the contours of a critical 'orthodoxy', unnecessarily proposes a 'three person theory' of identity between the beloved disciple, implied author and real author. In fact, the relationship between these requires only a one-, or two-person theory; and it might be argued that one form of the two-person theory, that 21.24-25 (we might add 21.23) is 'the work of an editor who identified the gospel's real author, the Beloved Disciple', is to all intents and purposes but an extension of a one person theory.[24] Furthermore, Culpepper recognizes that the way the narrative is mediated logically implies either 'a sophisticated ploy by an individual author' or arises from some other motivation. He states that it 'probably came about... as a result of the idealizing of the Beloved Disciple and the comment of an editor' but also identifies narrative artistry as a factor.[25] He hints at but does not confirm the possibility that it stems

23. See especially Culpepper, *Anatomy*, pp. 20-34.

24. See Culpepper, *Anatomy*, pp. 45-49; cf. here J.L. Staley, *The Print's First Kiss* (SBLDS, 82: Atlanta: Scholars Press, 1988), p. 13.

25. Culpepper, *Anatomy*, p. 48. Cf. n. 63 which refers to comments made by R. Scholes and R. Kellogg, *The Nature of Narrative* (New York: Oxford University Press, 1966), pp. 246-47, on 'the use of authority-establishing techniques in antiquity'. It should be noted that many of the instances Scholes and Kellogg cite here

from a close personal relationship in historical actuality between real author and beloved disciple, the position this study will adopt.

Culpepper's exploration of such aspects as the relationship between Jesus and the narrator, the use of narrative time, plot development, characterization, and implicit commentary, furnishes the reader with a basic sketch map of the implied author's ideological stance which, to date, in my opinion has not been bettered. While future research will no doubt need to reach greater depths of analysis, or provide a more nuanced presentation of particulars, *Anatomy of the Fourth Gospel* provides a clear and coherent outline of the Gospel's 'literary design'.

J.L. Staley's dissertation, published in 1988 as *The Print's First Kiss: A Rhetorical Investigation of the Implied Reader in the Fourth Gospel*, is, as the title indicates, a specifically reader–response orientation on the Johannine point of view. He explores the various rhetorical levels and strategies of the Gospel to discover how these create or 'evoke' the implied reader. In particular, he is concerned with the way in which the implied author 'victimizes' the implied reader. The effect of this is not only to make the Gospel's text a vehicle for the implied author's message, but makes the experience of reading itself a 'rhetorical–theological strategy' which draws the implied reader into a learning experience and along a journey of faith.[26] The thesis argues that the theology of the Gospel is best discovered from the perspective of the reader who is implied within the text.

The merit of Staley's study lies in his grasp of the reader-response theory upon which he builds, and to which he brings some useful insights of his own. The 'implied reader', for instance, is for Staley not merely the *kind of reader* suggested by the text, e.g. one who reads Greek and hence understands the pun on ἄνωθεν and πνεῦμα (3.3, 8), or requires the translation of foreign (i.e. Aramaic) words. The construct also denotes the *kind of reading experience* structured by the implied author's narrative strategies. Thus the implied reader 'falls for' the implied author's traps; he is surprised by unexpected reversals in the discourse, led astray and brought back onto the right path by

---

of 'eyewitness' account and 'fictional representation' are from authors who are c. 2nd CE or later (Augustine, Xenophon of Ephesus, Longus, Achilles Tatius). The implied correlation of the motivation for these techniques with that which informs the Fourth Gospel must be treated with caution.

26. See Staley, *First Kiss*, pp. 94, 98, 107, 110, 116-17.

the implied author.[27] The argument is somewhat strained at times in the interests of the theory. For example, he makes too much of the purported ironic tension between the portrayal of John in the prologue and that in 1.19-28.[28] The latter amplifies and depends upon what is said in the prologue, rather than contrasts with it as Staley suggests. And he overdoes his stress on the linearity of the reading process and the rhetorical effects achieved by this as he does not allow for a reader's capacity for understanding a narrative's implicit messages.[29] But this does not detract from the genuine gains his study provides for a fresh insight into how the discourse invites a response of faith, and tests that response.

John as Storyteller by M.W.G. Stibbe adopts a structuralist approach to the narrative. More precisely, by a four-fold examination of the narrative's surface structure and its deep generic structure (which includes both the literary and the social context of the Gospel's genesis), Stibbe explores the 'narrative Christology' of the Fourth Gospel. 'Practical criticism' (analysis of the elements of which the narrative is constructed) combines with a sociological reading and a so-called 'narrative-historical' approach to the Gospel's 'pre-text' (i.e. the story's referential foundation in the life of Jesus). The work seeks in this way to create a synthesis of synchronic and diachronic issues in Johannine study.

In part one, under the heading of 'practical criticism of John's narrative', Stibbe outlines the narrative strategies and 'dynamics' by which the implied author develops and gives overall coherence to his narrative christology. Then he examines, using structuralist categories, the genre of the Gospel. In part two, he identifies the passion narrative as having the plot-structure of tragedy, and as showing affinities with the myth of Dionysus. Stibbe follows Martyn, Brown and others in identifying the social context in which the Gospel arose as being a community in 'severe controversy with Judaism'.[30] Finally, in the first part, he defines the Fourth Gospel as narrative history. It is a narrative which draws upon accounts of Jesus' ministry which derive from an eyewitness, and which were collected in a 'Bethany gospel'. This

27. Staley, *First Kiss*, pp. 37, 41; chapter 5 *passim*.

28. Staley, *First Kiss*, pp. 76-77.

29. Cf. his handling of the Cana miracle, especially pp. 84-85; and cf. on 'implicature', below p. 76-77.

30. Stibbe, *John as Storyteller*, p. 61.

source provided a 'pre-text' for the Johannine storyteller, together with 'a collection of Galilean signs/miracles'[31] and possibly Mark's Gospel.[32] These were creatively refigured to provide the 'poetic history' which is the Johannine story.[33]

The second part of the book provides an analysis of John 18–19 where, having analyzed the surface structure of the passion narrative and identified its deep structure as that of tragedy, Stibbe describes the social function of the narrative as providing 'a legitimation of the present family life of Johannine Christians';[34] and, we may suppose, deriving from the Gospel's depiction of an elusive Christ, some rationalization for the need for a strategy of communal secrecy.[35] He illustrates the way in which the Gospel has refigured history by examining and sifting, under a charge, response motif, the narrative's connection with historical facts.

The value of Stibbe's analysis here lies not so much in the sifting of detail in the passion narrative to determine which items may be historically reliable (cf. pp. 169-76), nor in identifying a possible passion source (following Fortna) upon which the evangelist drew (cf. pp. 182-87). It lies rather in showing how the Gospel's passion narrative redescribes historical event to make the christological nuances explicit, and in suggesting the evangelist's motivation for the theological emplotment by which human event becomes the moment of divine disclosure. In particular, Stibbe shows how the evangelist's historical redescription is governed by 'time shapes', some of which outline the progress of chronological time, and give the narrative its sense of causality and logic (a function of its status as historical discourse), and others which indicate the theological significance of the events.[36] Thus he contributes to an understanding of the kind of historical discourse found in the Gospel, from which the historical critic can determine how the narrative may be used for historical reconstruction.

Margaret Davies, in *Rhetoric and Reference in the Fourth Gospel*, seeks to bring to bear on the narrative insights from structuralism and reader-response criticism, while at the same time attending to ques-

---

31. Stibbe, *John as Storyteller*, p. 84.
32. Stibbe, *John as Storyteller*, p. 85.
33. Stibbe, *John as Storyteller*, p. 196.
34. Stibbe, *John as Storyteller*, p. 165.
35. See here Stibbe, *John as Storyteller*, pp. 91-92.
36. Stibbe, *John as Storyteller*, pp. 192-96.

tions important to the more traditional disciplines of historical and source criticism. Her indebtedness to Genette, Iser and Sternberg, while not always overtly stated, is apparent in her use of concepts such as focus, gaps, retrospection, repetition, tempo and narrative time. The narrative is written from the perspective of an omniscient narrator, and provides a temporal sweep which takes in eternity. The discourse betrays features which show that the story is already familiar to the readers[37] and '[t]he whole Gospel is a preparation for the correct theological understanding of Jesus' crucifixion'.[38] Generically, the Gospel, like the Synoptics, is a theodicy.[39] Davies examines the influences of other forms of literature in shaping the Gospel's own form. The foundational influence was provided by the Jewish Scriptures. Parallels with other forms of Jewish literature, such as the Dead Sea Scrolls, Rabbinic writings, *Joseph and Aseneth* or Philo, derive from the fact that all draw upon a shared Scripture. Non-Jewish materials, such as the Corpus Hermeticum or Philostratus' *Life of Apollonius of Tyana*, provide only tenuous parallels, but sufficient, perhaps, to open 'the Gospel to Greek readers ignorant of the Johannine Scriptures'.[40]

The second part deals with the themes and metaphors by which the Gospel's message is conveyed. The third and final section looks for clues to the identity of the implied author and implied readers in the Gospel's language and style, in its characterization, and in references to the geography, flora, climate and socio-cultural aspects of first-century Palestine. In all this there is much interest in the historical accuracy of the detail, and as a corollary, the possible sources for this detail. Much of it Davies maintains could have been derived from the Synoptics, the Jewish Scriptures, or inherited Christian traditions. The tenor of the argument shows a rootedness in the traditional historical-critical approach; and there is much interaction with questions of traditional concern within Johannine scholarship. The book bears witness to the fact that a literary approach need not thereby eschew the consideration of issues to do with the historicity of the material. Davies also seeks to marry this newer discipline with older methods of criticism. For example, her treatment of the Gospel's unity shows a marked

37. M. Davies, *Rhetoric and Reference in the Fourth Gospel* (JSNTSup, 69; Sheffield: Sheffield Academic Press, 1992), p. 30.

38. Davies, *Rhetoric*, p. 31.

39. Davies, *Rhetoric*, pp. 89, 108.

40. Davies, *Rhetoric*, pp. 90-104.

divergence from the position usually adopted in a literary treatment of the Fourth Gospel. Whereas most stress that it be taken as a unity, she upholds the view that it is the result of redactional activity, and the final text remains in fundamental need of editorial revision.[41]

Finally, J.E. Botha has given us a speech-act reading of John 4.1-42 in his monograph, *Jesus and the Samaritan Woman*. While this study is founded upon the application of speech-act theory to the narrative, it nevertheless retains an interest in, and a dependence upon, categories drawn from modern narratology and reception theory. Thus Botha attends to the nature of the communication between the implied author and the implied readers, analyzes the speech-acts of the narrator and the characters, and relates the categories and functions of speech-act theory to the study of the Fourth Gospel as a literary speech-act. The intention throughout is to correlate features of speech-act theory with aspects of narrative criticism and reader-response criticism.

Furthermore, while the thesis is presented as a study of the style of the Fourth Gospel, it may very easily be subsumed under the rubric of studies concerned with the Johannine point of view. This is because his definition of style is that it is a '*contextually determined* phenomenon' which 'has to do with the *choices* available to users of language'. It is an exercise in 'the *successful communication* of texts in contexts' and calls for the study of 'every aspect of language which facilitates the process of communication'.[42] This chimes with an understanding of point of view which sees it as the contextually determined stance of an implied author towards a narrative which is conveyed to the reader by the choice of certain narrative strategies and ploys. The comprehensive context within which he sets the study of style to 'include aspects such as phonology, vocabulary, syntax and grammar, [and] more comprehensive aspects such as text and discourse structure, semantics, social, literary and other concepts, and aspects pertaining to genre, intertext and the reception of text'[43] shows that at root Botha's 'style' may be taken as another term for 'point of view'. I believe that Botha is entirely right to recognize in speech-act theory a methodology, based in linguistics and language use, that can be adapted to the study of narrative. Applied to the literary speech situation, it affords a method for dealing with issues of point of view at many levels, from the wide

41. Davies, *Rhetoric*, pp. 262-65.
42. Botha, *Jesus*, p. 53 (italics his).
43. Botha, *Jesus*, pp. 53-54.

context of a description of a text's genre to the specific analysis of a given stretch of discourse.

In concluding this section it may be helpful to outline briefly some points at which the concerns of this present study converge with those surveyed above, and where some of the significant differences lie. Together with Culpepper, Staley and Botha (and, implicitly, Stibbe and Davies), I find Chatman's communicational model of the narrative text as an interaction between implied author and implied reader through textual entities such as the narrator, narratees, and characters, useful as a basic model of narrative transmission. However, as I shall explain in more detail later, I find that the model of a typological circle of narrative situations, developed by Franz Stanzel, offers a more flexible way of analyzing the surface structure of the Fourth Gospel's narrative. In particular, it provides important insights into the way in which the implied author has manipulated the narrator's point of view.

While Staley approaches the Gospel's narrative from the perspective of the implied reader, my attention is focussed more upon the role and activity of the implied author. In so far as the implied author is the 'image' of the author derived from the text by the reader, it has its basis in reader–response theory. The reverse of this is that because the implied reader is evoked by strategies within the narrative, the implied author (who is the textual evocation of the real author's narrative choices) is also important to Staley's thesis. It is a matter of emphasis: the privileging of one item in the construct over the other.[44] But my interest in the implied author also stems from a sense that there is a purposefulness and intent which can be inferred from the structure of the Fourth Gospel, and for which the concept of the implied author serves as a signal. In determining this purpose, speech-act theory furnishes useful tools of analysis. My use of speech-act theory is more general and eclectic than is Botha's. I am not as concerned as he is to analyze the speech-acts offered in the Fourth Gospel in great detail. Furthermore, my interest is in the application of the theory to an

44. See here S. Chatman, *Coming to Terms* (Ithaca, NY: Cornell University Press, 1990), pp. 74-75. W. Martin, *Recent Theories of Narrative* (Ithaca, NY: Cornell University Press, 1986), p. 29, provides a useful diagram which places different theories of narrative along a number of axes, one of which is the axis: 'authors-narrator-narrative-reader'. My study concentrates mostly on the 'author-narrator' end of the spectrum, in the first part at least; in the second, more attention is given to the narrative-reader end.

understanding of the nature and description of the literary speech situation.

With Stibbe and Davies, I share a concern to relate an examination of the Johannine point of view to the issue of its relationship to the events of history. In this I incline toward the stance taken by Stibbe and share many of his insights. But I attempt to provide a more precise analysis of the relationship between fictional (and 'poetic') and historical discourse. I wish to define more clearly the nature of the Johannine discourse: and to provide a model by which the discourse may be described. Part of this includes a discussion of the Gospel's genre, but here my interest is directed more towards providing a flexible model of genre into which the specific gospel type might be placed, and in suggesting a modern definition of the genre, drawn from the application of speech-act theory to literary discourse, by which the Fourth Gospel may be described. Like Stibbe, Davies and Botha, I attempt to provide a synthesis of a number of methodologies and theoretical constructs: in the case of this study the synthesis is of narrative criticism with speech-act theory.

Point of View Defined

Stephen Moore, in a glossary definition of 'point of view', states that it is 'the rhetorical activity of an author as he or she attempts, from a position within some socially shared system of assumptions and convictions, to impose a story-world upon an audience by the manipulation of narrative perspective'.[45] This study, then, seeks to examine the rhetorical activity of the Fourth Gospel's implied author by analyzing the way the narrative is told ('the manipulation of narrative perspective') and the position from which it is told.

Alternatively, we might say, to adopt a term suggested by Wesley Kort, it attempts to recover the 'tone' of the Fourth Gospel. By tone we mean the function undertaken by the 'author' in selecting the material presented, the 'voice' or style adopted for the presentation and the attitude taken towards the material. The position adopted by the teller towards the material, Kort suggests, is a complex one involving both a narrative point of view and an evaluative one.[46] The narrative point of

45. Moore, *Literary Criticism*, p. 181.
46. W. Kort, *Story, Text and Scripture* (University Park: Pennsylvania State University Press, 1988), pp. 16-17. Kort speaks of a 'physical' point of view. I have

view concerns the narrator's voice and the perspective from which the story is narrated; that is, whether omniscient or limited, told in the first person or third person. The evaluative point of view relates to the attitude of the author to the material presented as suggested by the narrative's norms and speech-acts.

As this study draws upon the insights of literary criticism, it must be acknowledged at the outset that the term 'point of view' is an extremely slippery one, capable of many meanings and uses. Definitions and discussions of it abound amongst the literary theorists.[47] However, despite the ambiguity of the term, I wish to retain it in a comprehensive sense, and, in view of the range of issues which attach to the term, a certain breadth of usage is to be welcomed. 'Point of view' encompasses both ideology and technique (I follow Susan Lanser here): for one's attitude (viz. ideology or evaluative point of view) has everything to do with the way one expresses something.[48] The 'way one expresses something' comes down in a narrative to the mode of narrative transmission used, or the narrative situation adopted. Literary critics have often restricted the term 'point of view' to this latter aspect. If bringing attitude and manner of expression together, appears to the literary critic to collapse distinctions carefully drawn as between, for example, 'mood' and 'voice' (Genette) or 'point of view' and 'narrative voice' (Chatman),[49] I would respond by saying that it seems to me (to state a point of view!) that such matters often run together anyway both in analysis and in readers' reception of texts.[50]

---

adopted the term 'narrative' rather than 'physical' in order to avoid the suggestion of some sort of corporal stance.

47. See here S. Chatman, *Story and Discourse* (Ithaca, NY: Cornell University Press, 1978), pp. 151-58; G. Genette, *Narrative Discourse* (ET: J.E. Lewin; Oxford: Basil Blackwell, 1980), pp. 186-89, 213; and *Narrative Discourse Revisited* (ET: J.E. Lewin; Ithaca, NY: Cornell University Press, 1988), pp. 64-65; S. Rimmon-Kenan, *Narrative Fiction: Contemporary Poetics* (London: Methuen, 1983), pp. 71-72; W. Martin, *Recent Theories*, chapter 6; S. Lanser, *The Narrative Act* (Princeton: Princeton University Press, 1981), pp. 13-19.

48. Lanser, *Narrative Act*, pp. 16-17.

49. See Genette, *Narrative*, p. 186; Chatman, *Story*, p. 153.

50. See Genette's own admission that '[a] narrating situation is a complex whole within which analysis, or simply description cannot *differentiate* except by ripping apart a tight web of connections among the narrating act. . . ' (*Narrative*, p. 215; emphasis his). Cf. Martin, *Recent Theories*, p. 147: 'We experience narrative not as a compendium of categories but as a total movement, the parts of which are perhaps

This is not to say that there is not an important distinction to be made between 'who sees' and 'who speaks' (or between perspective and narration).[51] Clearly a narrator can tell the story as he/she sees it or can tell the story as seen from the perspective of a character. Thus who is speaking and whose perception is being conveyed in the narration may not be one and the same. It is to preserve the critical awareness of this distinction that Genette proposes the use of the term 'focalization' (as he puts it, in correspondence to Brooks' and Warren's formulation 'focus of narration').[52] However, variations in the 'focus' through which the narration is given, or the variety of perceptual points (points of view) from which the implied author may choose to tell the story, is most adequately described and analyzed by paying attention to the *situation* from which the narration proceeds. Where and in what relation to the story is the narrator situated in the telling of it? Thus the model of narrative situations provided by F.K. Stanzel, which I take up in this discussion, seems to me preferable (despite, and even because of certain imprecisions) to Genette's more abstract schema.[53]

In summary, 'point of view' remains useful, both as a term and as a concept, to encompass issues to do with the way in which a story is told (the narration or enunciation of the narrative) and the perspective, or perspectives, from which it is told. Here the study will particularly address the nature and shape of narrative transmission or mediacy. In its ideological aspect, 'point of view' also takes up the purpose for which a story is told, and the standpoint and attitude of the teller with reference to the story narrated. Here the insights of speech-act theory will be important.

The Fourth Gospel as Narrative

Narrative theory and criticism provide the tools for approaching questions of the Johannine point of view for two reasons. First, both in theory and practice, a literary critical approach to narrative offers terms and methods useful precisely for discussing issues of point of

best characterized by the phrase "point of view. . . " '

51. Genette, *Narrative*, p. 186; cf. Rimmon-Kenan, *Narrative*, p. 71.

52. Genette, *Narrative*, pp. 186, 189.

53. Stanzel's method is dealt with in chapter 2, pp. 52-58. D. Cohn, 'The Encirclement of Narrative', *Poetics Today* 2 (1981), p. 158, points out that Stanzel's approach anticipates Genette's distinction between 'who sees' and 'who speaks'.

view. Second, the Fourth Gospel is a narrative. In spite of its many differences from the Synoptic Gospels, in this one respect it is alike: it purports to tell the story of Jesus, the Messiah/Christ. Much of its material, and indeed large tracts of the Gospel, for example, the prologue and the discourses of Jesus, might seem such as to remove it from the category of narrative. Yet this very material has itself been worked up into a narrative framework. And, while not entirely free of the episodic character of the Synoptic narratives, the Fourth Gospel shows a more integrated and developed narrative form. Progress from episode to episode is more evenly done. The frequent use of temporal markers (τῇ ἐπαύριον, καὶ τῇ ἡμέρα τῇ τρίτη, καὶ ἐγγὺς ἦν τὸ πάσχα) and connectives such as μετὰ ταῦτα,[54] and the use of flashforward and flashback, give the narrative a chronological and thematic unity.[55] Individual episodes are more extended and complex than tends to be the case in the Synoptic Gospels (see e.g. chs. 4, 9, 11). Where comparison can be made with incidents in the Synoptic Gospels, as in the case of the cleansing of the Temple or the feeding of the five thousand, the Fourth Gospel often shows as much, if not more, of the detail and 'reality effects' associated with vivid narrative.[56] As a narrative, then, analysis of the Fourth Gospel is fruitfully aided by techniques drawn from the theory and criticism of narrative.

The Fourth Gospel is a narrative. But what is a narrative? A narrative may be described (and analyzed) as either an artifact or as an act. That is, we may understand it as an object, an entity or a construct made up of elements such as characters, events and settings. Or we may perceive it as a process, an act by which a message (the story) is transmitted from a sender to a receiver, or an interaction between a teller (an author) and a listener (a reader). In its broadest definition, of course, a narrative is both. As Seymour Chatman puts it, 'each narrative has two parts: a story (*histoire*) the content or chain of events (actions, happenings), plus what may be called the existents (characters, items of setting); and a discourse (*discours*), that is, the expression, the means by which the content is communicated. In simple terms, the story

54. Cf. Jn 1.29, 35, 43; 2.1, 13; 3.22; 4.43; 5.1; 6.1, 4, 22; 7.1, 2, 37; 10.22; 11.55; 12.1, 12; 13.1.

55. See, for instance, the way in which earlier actions ('signs') are recalled in later discourse or narration; e.g. 7.21-24; 12.17, 18.

56. Cf. Jn 2.14,15; 6.9 (πέντε ἄρτους κριθίνους καὶ δύο ὀψάρια); 20.6-7.

is the *what* in a narrative that is depicted, the discourse the *how*.'[57] A story (the message, the construct of characters in settings experiencing events) presupposes a storyteller. And a storyteller presupposes not only the story to be told, but also an interaction between the teller and the audience. A story, then, is a mediated artifact; a narrative is an act of mediation.

By defining narrative as an act, or as a 'performance',[58] and as an interaction between the author and reader,[59] possibilities are opened up for applying speech-act theory to the narrative act. In the use of speech-act theory, particularly in its application to literary discourse, I hope to correlate two aspects of point of view within the Fourth Gospel: the standpoint from which the narrative is told or the 'angle of vision' that the narrator adopts; and the particular attitude the implied author takes towards the narrative and the 'message' he wishes to convey.

Narrative Art and Act in the Fourth Gospel

A word to explain the title of this study is apposite here. The meaning of the Fourth Gospel, the message which the implied author wishes to convey to the reader, is bound up in the way in which the narrative has been structured. The sequence of the events, the plotting of the discourse, gives the story of Jesus a particular slant. Narrative devices and strategies are used to create an image of the author (the implied author) and an image of his audience/readers (the implied reader) which together establish the narrative's norms. In particular, I shall argue, the implied author's point of view is conveyed by a process wherein his voice merges with that of Jesus and his identity with that of the beloved disciple. Understanding the narrative art of the implied author also sheds a new light upon many of the perceived disjunctions, gaps and *aporias* which strike the reader in reading this narrative. Thus foregrounding narrative art provides a key to understanding the meaning of this most enigmatic of gospels.

As well as narrative art, there is narrative act, and not simply in the sense explored above, that is, narrative as an act of narration. We must be concerned also with the speech-acts embedded in the story.

---

57. Chatman, *Story*, p. 19.
58. Cf. R.W. Funk, *The Poetics of Biblical Narrative* (Sonoma: Polebridge Press, 1988), p. 3.
59. See further below pp. 44-47; cf. also pp. 77-78, especially fig. 6.

These take place, as we shall see, both at the 'story world' level of the narrator and the characters, and at the level of what I would call the implied author's speech-acts. These latter have to do with the intents and effects conveyed by the discourse, both at a surface and at a deeper level. In a sense, the sum total of the speech-acts in the narrative's 'story world' produce the total speech-act which is the narrative itself.

Thus art and act come together to produce meaning. Narrative art and act have implications for the Fourth Gospel's theological purpose. But it must not be forgotten that it is *narrative* meaning because the message which the implied author conveys cannot be separated from the Gospel's narrative form. And the theological purpose of the Gospel is contained within its narrative shape.

Narrative and Historical Reference

The Fourth Gospel is a narrative. But narrative as a general category takes in generic types which range from historical, factual accounts to those which are fictional and fantastic. Where is the Gospel to be placed among these various types? What is the relationship of the 'story world' of the Johannine narrative's Jesus to the real world of the life of the historical Jesus? And if, as many readers sense, there are features of this narrative which carry the aspect of fiction, what is the significance of this for an evaluation of the narrative as a source for historical reconstruction? We shall consider, in part two, the question of genre, and examine some of the expectations which help determine generic categories. We shall also consider the nature of narrative as a vehicle for both historical and fictional discourse and, we must add, for theological discourse as well.

Conventions Used in this Study

Already terms and theoretical concepts have been introduced which require further explanation and they will receive fuller treatment in the body of this work. For the moment, I shall make these comments about the conventions used. Much use will be made of the term 'implied author' which may irritate readers unfamiliar with the term, even when its sense has been grasped. Why not refer to the author under conventions more generally accepted by scholarship such as 'John' or 'the evangelist'? But as these conventional appellations attest, in so far as the real author (or authors) of this Gospel is (are) unknown, scholars have operated, in a sense, with the concept of an 'implied author' for a long time. Traditionally, this implied author has been given the name John. (Almost always, in modern scholarship, this convention has been accompanied by disclaimers that the name refers to any particular historical 'John', whether he be John, son of Zebedee, or John the Elder.) More frequently he is designated 'the evangelist'. In a sense, one could read 'the evangelist' for the term 'implied author' in this study. Very often the same entity is in view, namely the hand that has had the major part in shaping the discourse.[60] However, I wish to retain the term 'implied author' to underline the fact that the reader's conception of the author is determined by the text.[61]

The word 'discourse' is commonly used in Johannine studies to refer to the extended speeches of Jesus (including conversations as well as monologues). In narrative theory, 'discourse' refers to the way in which a story is told, a narrative's rhetorical construction, as well as, of course, the narrative itself as the written product of that construction. Although there is obviously potential here for confusion, I think that the context will determine which sense is intended. But, as I have chosen not to make a typographical distinction between the two uses, it is as well that the reader be aware that the word is used in these two ways.

Finally, I use three terms to discuss narrative time: story time, discourse time and time of discourse. 'Story time' refers to the order of events and the length of time (the reader assumes) taken for them to occur in the story world as conceived by the implied author. 'Discourse time' refers to the order of the events as told by the narrator. The order in which events are narrated may differ from the order in which they must have happened in the story world, for the implied author may choose to have them narrated out of chronological sequence.[62] For instance, in John 4, the departure of the disciples to go to the village

---

60. Of course, the evangelist's part in shaping the final work is much debated, and scholarship's conception of the evangelist is influenced by many considerations, such as questions of source and redaction, relationship to the beloved disciple, possible historical referents and so forth. Yet it remains true, I think, that the appellation provides a catch-all for the one whom readers envisage as the 'author' of the Gospel.

61. I use the masculine gender to refer to the implied author as I consider it to be most probable, against the background culture of the day, that the author was male. I have tried to be consistent in not making the same assumption about the readers.

62. Cf. Powell, *What is Narrative Criticism?*, p. 36.

to buy food must have taken place, in story time, before the arrival of the woman to draw water.[63] In the telling of the story, however, the narrator recounts the arrival of the woman and Jesus' request for water (4.7) *before* telling the reader that the disciples are not there (4.8). Discourse time also includes the amount of time taken to narrate an event (that is, the extent of text devoted to the event). In our example, the woman's conversation with Jesus is treated extensively (4.7-26), whereas the two days spent in her village is covered in the space of three verses (4.40-43). In this way the implied author manipulates time for rhetorical and thematic effect. 'Time of discourse' refers to the time when the story is told, the 'point in history' when the narrative text is produced. The Fourth Gospel's discourse makes it clear that time of discourse must be set after the resurrection and the earthly life of the historical Jesus.

Outline of the Work

Part one of the book will examine the dynamic of the Fourth Gospel's narrative art and the nature of its speech-acts. In chapter 2 we shall consider models of narrative transmission or mediacy. In particular, we shall see how F.K. Stanzel's 'typological circle of narrative situations' provides a flexible method by which variations in the narrator's narrative point of view may be described. I shall outline the variations in narrative situation that take place over the course of the Gospel's narrative. Some of the problems this variation brings to the interpretation of the Gospel will be outlined in preparation for further analysis in chapter four.

Chapter 3 will provide a summary of speech-act theory, and examine how it may illuminate both the nature of literary discourse and the analysis of point of view. I shall analyze the speech-acts found at 20.30, 31 and 21.24, 25; these provide an understanding of the direction of the author's total speech-act, the intent of the Gospel as a whole. We shall also see how the structure of the narrative 'works' to establish meaning. Chapters 4 and 5 seek to ground theory in an exegetical examination of selected test passages. In chapter 4, we see how the beloved disciple appears as a character whose narrative point of view merges increasingly with that of the narrator. We examine how the dynamics of narrative mediacy and the operations of the

---

63. The REB preserves story time's order of events by inverting v. 7 and v. 8.

Gospel's speech-acts achieve this dual perspective. These factors suggest a close personal relationship between the beloved disciple and the implied author. In the fifth chapter, we consider the progress of Jesus' discourse with Nicodemus, and the discourse of John as instances of the variation of narrative situations which occurs as the voice of the narrator merges with those of the characters. The theological rationale for this is explored as I draw analogies with Franz Mussner's conception of 'actualizing anamnesis' and consider the 'truth-telling' status of the implied author's speech-acts.

Part two will explore the status of the Gospel as a form of historical discourse through a cumulative argument that first addresses the question of whether there are criteria by which we may distinguish fictional from historical discourse. While we shall find that such distinction is not possible simply in terms of the language used, I shall raise the question whether certain aspects of the Gospel's discourse are accepted by modern readers as marking fictional discourse because of the conventional use of these in modern fiction. In other words, the presence of these features in the Gospel may induce modern readers to read the narrative against a fictional grid.

I shall argue that in the application of speech-act theory to literary discourse, we find categories of description which are important for understanding the Fourth Gospel. First, a fundamental distinction between fiction and non-fiction lies in whether or not the implied author's intentions are perceived to be the depiction of a 'pretended world' where the normal force of assertions is suspended. Second, by providing a description of the Gospel as a display text we may not only moderate a tendency in Johannine scholarship to distinguish 'history' from 'theology', but may also understand the nature of the discourse as a theological elaboration upon an historical substratum. We shall also consider the category of 'natural narrative', that is, spoken, anecdotal reportage, as a source of fruitful illumination of aspects of the Gospel's language and structure. As decisions regarding the genre of the Gospel are important in determining how the discourse is received, we will consider factors which influence such decisions, examining the conventions shared by historical and fictional discourse. I shall also provide a typological circle of narrative genres (adapted from Stanzel's typological circle) that enables a flexible approach to genre and modulates the tension between fictional and historical forms of discourse.

These explorations will then be put to the test in Chapter 7 in an analysis of the Gospel's account of Jesus' Temple act. We shall see that, despite the fact that the implied author takes a certain license with 'history' (meaning in this case events in the life of Jesus as reconstructed by scholarship largely out of the Synoptic Gospels), the Fourth Gospel is not completely worthless as an historical source. Putting the matter in terms more in harmony with the thrust of this study, to describe the Gospel as a theological display text is to say that narrative art is put to the service of theological reflection upon and explication of the significance of the historical Jesus. The discourse, proceeding from the perspective of the implied author's post-resurrection standpoint, might appear to be removed from strict adherence to historical 'fact'. Nevertheless, the material is not thereby made completely vacant of historically valid data. Indeed, I shall argue that the Temple cleansing is narrated in such a fashion that its essential historical significance is brought to the fore, both in its importance for the eventual fate of Jesus and for the post-resurrection understanding of the disciples.

The concluding chapter will provide an overview of the narrative point of view, and the implied author's narrative art and act, and draw out the implications of these for the perspective of the real author vis-à-vis the discourse, and his relationship with the beloved disciple/ implied author. It will also summarize how the particular form of the Gospel's historical discourse relates to matters of historical reference and the stance invited of the reader.

This Study's Evaluative Point of View

In a book dealing with point of view it is appropriate that I conclude the introduction with an account of some of the underpinnings to my own standpoint! Such polemical intent as this study has arises from two presuppositions. First, I am convinced that the Gospel's narrative form is important to understanding its meaning. This form presupposes a structural unity. Thus, there is a bias against reading strategies which seek earlier sources purportedly lying behind the text, or posit dislocations in the narrative. Second, I consider that categories such as 'history', 'fiction' and 'theology' are used somewhat loosely in making judgments on the form of the Gospel's discourse. I attempt to move the debate onto fresh ground by examining the 'ontological' bases of these distinctions. In my opinion, the Gospel has suffered an unwarranted neglect as a source for historical reconstruction and, hence, I seek to redress the balance.

I have sought to draw together a number of methodologies and theoretical perspectives in an eclectic and synthetic manner. At a number of points I have offered my own adaptations of the theoretical models used here. The rationale for this is that, in the first instance, I want the theory to be of service in understanding and illuminating perennial problems in the study of the Gospel, and to be an aid to practical exegesis. So I have attempted to ground the theory in particular aspects of the discourse, choosing specific passages as paradigms for the theoretical framework.

Thus I consider the application of a narrative-critical approach to the Gospel, and the insights which derive from speech-act theory, to have much heuristic value in helping to resolve problems concerning the Gospel's point of view. Therefore, I wish to extend and refine the application of these within the domain of Johannine scholarship. But, beyond this, both narrative theory and speech-act theory raise important hermeneutical issues in terms of the practice of discourse analysis, the understanding of how readers receive texts and the relationship of fictionality and historicity to conceptions of reality and 'truth'. This study seeks so to present the theory that old problems may be put in fresh hermeneutical perspective.

Part I

THE DYNAMICS OF ART AND ACT

Chapter 2

NARRATIVE MEDIACY AND THE JOHANNINE POINT OF VIEW

The Fourth Gospel, as we have seen, is cast in narrative or story form.
Every story presupposes a storyteller, and every tale requires that it
be told. In this chapter we explore the question of the teller of the
Johannine tale and the way in which the story is told. In recent decades
narrative theory and criticism have provided much helpful analysis
and illumination of the process of narrative transmission or mediacy.
Seymour Chatman has called narrative transmission, or the discourse
of narrative, the 'how' of storytelling.[1] His theory of narrative has
been especially important in formulating the thinking of many New
Testament literary critics. In his book, *What is Narrative Criticism?*,
M.A. Powell draws upon Chatman in his description of the communication model of narrative criticism.[2] Chatman's theoretical construct
is the basis, with adaptations and borrowings from other theorists, for
such approaches as those of D. Rhoads and D. Michie, *Mark as Story*
(1982), J.D. Kingsbury, *Matthew as Story* (1988), and R.M. Fowler,
Let the Reader Understand (1991). Studies of the Fourth Gospel which
have drawn explicitly upon Chatman are R.A. Culpepper's *Anatomy
of the Fourth Gospel* (1983) and J.L. Staley's *The Print's First Kiss*
(1988).

In particular, Chatman has provided a model of narrative discourse,
described as a 'structure of transmission', which has been widely
influential amongst biblical narrative critics. His diagram of the
'narrative-communication situation', which draws upon the linguistic
and communication theories of Ferdinand de Saussure and Roman
Jakobson, is reproduced here.[3] S.D. Moore comments that 'Chatman's

---

1. Chatman, *Story*, p. 19.
2. See especially chapter 3.
3. Cf. Chatman, *Story*, p. 151.

narrative communication diagram has subtly yet considerably shaped the way New Testament critics today conceive of the gospel text'.[4]

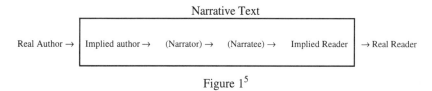

Figure 1[5]

In describing the transaction, the narrative communication which takes place between author and reader, Chatman focuses upon the construction within the narrative text of an 'implied author' and an 'implied reader'. The implied author is the principle of narration, the author's 'second self' who silently oversees the communication process, and through the design of the whole, the particular way in which the story is 'told', determines the outcome of the reading. Thus the function of the implied author is to establish the norms of the narrative. The implied author is 'the locus of [a] work's *intent*', that is, its ' "whole" or "overall" meaning, including its connotations, implications, unspoken messages'.[6] This author is 'implied' because 'reconstructed by the reader from the narrative'.[7]

The implied author is not to be confused with the real author. Indeed, a given narrative may not be the work of a single author, but the collaborative effort of a group of 'authors' or a committee. In *Coming to Terms*, Chatman demonstrates this with reference to the Bible (as in the 'authorship' of the Pentateuch) and by analogy with the production of John Huston's film *The Red Badge of Courage*. This was credited by film critics as the creation of Huston's genius; in reality it was a joint effort which included production managers, the editors and musical director, and members of the film crew.[8] Nevertheless, readers experience narratives, whether literary or other (e.g. film, drama, ballet and so on) as unified wholes. The implied author represents this sense of a unifying agent conventionally imputed to the total

4.   Moore, *Literary Criticism*, p. 46.
5.   Reprinted from S. Chatman, *Story and Discourse: Narrative Structure in Fiction and Film*, p. 151. Copyright 1978 by Cornell University Press. Used by permission of the publisher, Cornell University Press.
6.   Chatman, *Coming to Terms*, p. 74 (italics his).
7.   Chatman, *Story*, pp. 148-49.
8.   See Chatman, *Coming to Terms*, pp. 90-97; cf. his *Story*, p. 149.

narrative by the readers. It is in this sense that the implied author is reconstructed out of the text by the reader. But this is not an arbitrary reconstruction: it derives from 'the patterns in the text which the reader negotiates'. It is the record of the invention (which includes the real author's intention but goes beyond this to include the work's intent) which becomes 'the reader's source of instruction about how to read the text and how to account for the selection and ordering of its components'.[9]

The concept of the implied author is especially appropriate in the study of an ancient text such as the Fourth Gospel where knowledge of the real author (or authors) is lost in the mists of time and tradition, or, indeed, through a deliberate act of suppression on the part of the real author. So, on the one hand, it allows for the fact that the work is essentially anonymous as far as any knowledge of the identity of the real author is concerned. It also encompasses a history of composition which may have been the work of several hands (the editors and redactors of source criticism) and may have taken place within the context of a community. On the other hand, I believe that it is also possible, by paying attention to the textual patterns and strategies from which the image of the implied author emerges, to make some reasonably strong inferences about the probable identity of the real author or authors from whose hands the Fourth Gospel has come to us. These inferences will be outlined below.

If the norms of the narrative are *established* by the implied author, they are *encapsulated* in the 'implied reader'. The stance which the real author wishes a reader to take towards the narrative is determined by the profile of the implied reader. The implied reader represents 'the audience presupposed by the narrative itself'.[10] The real reader may be informed how to perform as implied reader by the presence of a narratee-character, or the stance may have to be inferred on ordinary cultural and moral terms, but acceptance of the readership implied by the narrative is necessary if it is to be understood.[11]

The terms 'narrator' and 'narratee' have to do with the mode of transmission. They are the textual constructs by whom and to whom, and through whom, the narrative message may be transmitted, but

9. Chatman, *Coming to Terms*, pp. 83-84, 87. On the question of 'intention' see the whole of chapter 5 for Chatman's views.

10. Chatman, *Story*, p. 150.

11. See Chatman, *Story*, p. 150.

their presence in a text is optional. Every tale implies both a teller and a listener (or reader), but in the narrative itself such elements may be fully dramatized (an overt narrator/narratee) or hidden (covert) or absent (as in non-narrated forms of narrative such as dialogue[12] or where the reader meets only a 'disembodied' narrator). The implied author and the implied reader, on the other hand, are always present. The meaning of a narrative is obtained with reference to these elements, for meaning is 'encoded' by the implied author and 'decoded' by the implied reader. The narrative transaction may be taken as a communication between two 'interlocutors', author and reader, in the guise of their textual constructs, the implied author and the implied reader.

Discussion of the way in which the narrative of the Fourth Gospel is mediated or transmitted provides a methodological framework for this study for two reasons. First, as Chatman himself states, 'narrative transmission concerns the relation of the time of story to time of recounting of story, the source or authority for the story: narrative voice, "point of view" and the like'.[13] It is with issues such as these that the present work is concerned even though it seeks to explore them on a wider canvas than a simple concern with narrative critical issues would require. Second, while the concerns of this study have to do with the story of John's Gospel and address issues to do with the content of that story (questions, for instance, of the relation of the story world to the historical world) the manner of the story's expression is itself a critical factor for understanding the nature and purpose of the Gospel's theological art and intent. 'Mediation always opens the possibility of interpretation', writes Chatman[14] and hence the nature of that mediation—how, in what manner and mode the story is transmitted—is an important determinant of the interpretation that will follow. Narrative mediacy is a guiding principle for understanding.

Deficiencies in Chatman's Communications Model when Applied to the Fourth Gospel

While Chatman's model has provided a useful starting point for the work of Culpepper and Staley on the Fourth Gospel, each has had to

---

12. However, even in dialogue there may be traces of narration, e.g. 'he said', 'she replied', and so forth.

13. Chatman, *Story*, p. 22.

14. In R. Fowler (ed.), *Style and Structure in Literature* (Oxford: Basil Blackwell, 1975), p. 239.

modify the diagram to suit their purpose when analyzing the narrative.[15] A major reason for this is that, as Staley points out, Chatman's
model is portrayed 'in one dimension' or on one level only.[16] But the
fact that the narrative transmission of a story's norms and themes
takes place at two levels provides an important theoretical justification
for modifying the model.[17]

The surface level at which the narrative transaction takes place is
directly evident to the reader. It is the level at which the interaction
between the narrator and the narratee occurs, the sphere of the story
world where characters interact and events happen. Explicit commentary takes place at this surface level. A deeper level is that at
which the interaction between implied author and implied reader takes
place. It is at this level that the narrative's implicit commentary—
irony, misunderstandings, symbolism and the like—shapes and directs
the implied reader's grasp of the narrative's norms. In this study,
attention to the surface level of narrative mediacy uncovers the Fourth
Gospel's narrative art. It is at this level that the use of a narrative
critical approach is important. The deeper level is where the Fourth
Gospel's narrative meaning resides. In the recovery of meaning at this
level the insights and application of speech-act theory are especially
valuable. The diagram below is my own modification of Chatman's.

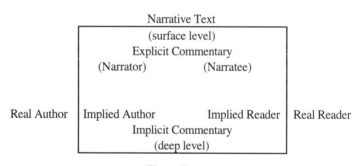

Figure 2

A further difficulty in Chatman's model is that it leads to a failure to
deal adequately with the problem of the narrator, that is the subtleties

15. See Culpepper, *Anatomy*, p. 6; and Staley, *First Kiss*, pp. 21-22.

16. Staley, *First Kiss*, p. 21 n. 3.

17. This reason is in addition to, and aside from, the reasons relating to narrative
levels and reader response cited by Staley which, though cogent and important, are
not central to the present study.

in the implied author's presentation of the narrator, who appears both as omniscient and external to the narrative world and also as one who is internal to that world and whose voice merges with those of characters in that world. A particular difficulty resides in trying to determine the relationship of the beloved disciple to the narrator and to the implied author and hence the relationship that exists among them.

Scholars who have adopted a narrative critical analysis of the Fourth Gospel have failed to give sufficient attention to the different situations from which the narrator narrates. Generally speaking they have been content to describe the narrator as omniscient, speaking in the third person, and standing outside of the story world.[18] At the same time, they have recognized that there are features of the discourse which suggest that the narrator may be conceptualized as 'a character who is both transcendent and immanent to the narrative world'[19] and who is 'finally retrospectively revealed to have been a character in the story he has just finished telling/writing'.[20]

There is, in particular, a certain confusion over the role of the beloved disciple as 'implied author' and as a character who in fact represents an embodiment of the narrator. Staley rightly registers disquiet over Culpepper's statement that 'the narrator dramatically pulls the curtain on the implied author [i.e. the beloved disciple] in the closing verses of the gospel' for in narrative critical terms the narrator is a 'rhetorical device', an invention of the implied author.[21] But Staley's flat assertion here that the narrator presents himself as a character in the story he has just finished narrating begs the question of the relationship between the narrator and the beloved disciple, and between both of these and the implied author. The problem is further compounded when Staley says that the narrator can be none other than the beloved disciple. For he then says that, as 'author/writer narrator' (does he mean therefore, as implied author?) the narrator never intrudes as an 'I' narrator-character in the story.[22] Stibbe for his part

18. See Culpepper, *Anatomy*, pp. 21-26; Staley, *First Kiss*, pp. 38-39; Stibbe, *John as Storyteller*, p. 20, and cf. also his commentary, *John* (Sheffield: JSOT Press, 1993), p. 15.

19. Stibbe, *John as Storyteller*, p. 28.

20. Staley, *First Kiss*, p. 39.

21. Staley, *First Kiss*, p. 13; cf. Culpepper, *Anatomy*, p. 47; and ref. Chatman, *Story*, p. 148.

22. Staley, *First Kiss*, pp. 38-40, ref. especially n. 83. I deal with this particular

implies a confusion between narrator and implied author when he says that 'everywhere the narrator... works to coax the reader round to the point of view or ideological stance which he embraces'.[23] When he later says that the beloved disciple 'is not the actual author of the fourth gospel' and that there is 'a radical distinction between the narrator (the storyteller) and the implied author (the BD)' he surely means that the implied author, through the narrator, *implies* (in 21.24) that the beloved disciple is the author![24]

The problem is that Chatman's linear model is too inflexible a framework by which to analyze the surface level of the discourse. Indeed, it might be noted in passing, that Genette's hierarchical model of levels of narration, with which Staley seeks to modify Chatman, suffers from the same inflexibility.[25] Hence the confusions, actual or implicit, which arise over the roles and functions which relate to the narrator and the implied author, and especially to the beloved disciple as embodiment of narrator and as character. This has implications at the deeper rhetorical level as well. I believe that as a fundamental statement of the Fourth Gospel's rhetoric (which operates at the level of interaction between implied author and implied reader) Culpepper is correct to state, *pace* Staley, that 'there is no reason to suspect any difference in the ideological, spatial, temporal or phraseological points of view of the narrator, the implied author and the author'.[26]

aspect of Staley's thesis in more detail below, pp. 67-68. Granted that Staley is arguing subtle distinctions, I think that his dependence upon Genette here leads to an over-subtlety which falls into contradiction and question whether 'the implied author is always theoretically separable from the narrator', especially where an extradiegetic narrator is concerned (see *First Kiss*, p. 39 n. 79), and if 'real readers tend to identify extradiegetic narrators with real authors' (let alone implied authors) do not the distinctions of theory become somewhat tenuous?

23. Stibbe, *John as Storyteller*, p. 28.

24. Stibbe, *John as Storyteller*, pp. 77-78.

25. This is because structurally they are built on oppositions that are dualistic (and 'dyadic') and tend to render matters as abrupt differentiations. This feature is modified by Stanzel's circular typology. See F.K. Stanzel, *A Theory of Narrative* (ET: C. Goedsche; Cambridge: Cambridge University Press, 1984), pp. 50-51, 60; cf. Cohn, 'Encirclement', pp. 160-61.

26. Culpepper, *Anatomy*, p. 42; cf. Staley, *First Kiss*, p. 13. Staley's objection that 'no flesh and blood author can be omnipresent, but narrators certainly can' betrays a fundamental misunderstanding about the status of a 'flesh and blood' author vis-à-vis the discourse within which the narrator resides. A narrator may be omnipresent as one standing 'outside' the story world of the narrative he is narrating; an author is

It is precisely this unity of points of view to which Culpepper refers which gives rise to the confusions between or among the narrator, implied author and real author which is found in the work of Culpepper, Staley and Stibbe.[27] This is because they work with models and theories which encourage an over-schematized demarcation of these respective narrative categories. The model of a typological circle offered by Stanzel, which I outline below, provides a theoretical framework against which the dynamics of the interrelationship of these roles may be understood, both at the surface level and the deep level, and in the movement from one to the other. This is because it replaces a linear model with a circular one which provides more flexibility in analyzing the surface level of the discourse. Also it suggests a more flexible way of correlating surface level with deep level of narrative mediacy. It allows for a continuum of narrative situations along which the narrative's particular manifestations of point of view can be placed. Put another way, it allows a more subtle hearing of the 'tone' of the narrative.

Before proceeding to a description of Stanzel's model, I must meet an objection which might arise at this point. It is that, given my dissatisfaction with Chatman's approach, why do I not simply jettison it completely in favour of Stanzel's? One reason is, of course, the wide-spread influence of Chatman's model upon the guild of New Testament narrative criticism noted above. This calls for some elaboration of the deficiencies inherent in an application of the model to the Fourth Gospel. These are deficiencies which particularly affect an analysis of the surface level of narrative transmission (but their implications also affect the resolution of issues of deep level transmission). However, in one important respect, Chatman's model merits retention. It provides a clear foundational description of the nature of the interaction inherent in the process of narration. Even while more subtle analysis

omnipresent as the creator outside the discourse itself, that is, both the story world and the text. If a narrator may be 'extradiegetic', an author is 'extra-extradiegetic', to use Genette's terminology. A spatial point of view which is 'omnipresent' vis-à-vis the story world contained in the discourse is one thing (and this kind of omnipresence is shared by a real author with his created narrator); omnipresence in relation to the real world which serves as referent to the story world is quite another.

27. Johannine scholarship which does not follow a narrative-critical approach also wrestles with the same issues and conundrums thrown up by the narrative's manner of discourse though it seeks to resolve them using other hermeneutical categories.

of narrative mediacy calls for modifications of, and supplements to the model, the basic structure of narrative transaction is as Chatman has described it.

Stanzel's Theoretical Model:
The Typological Circle of Narrative Situations

F.K. Stanzel's narrative theory has been little used, and largely ignored by literary critics.[28] For this reason it has not, to my knowledge, been applied to narrative critical studies of the Gospels. His book, *A Theory of Narrative*, offers what is arguably an analysis of narrative trans-mission that is more comprehensive than that of Chatman. Certainly it is the lynch-pin of his methodology, for mediacy is, in his view, 'the generic characteristic of narration'.[29] Foundational to the model is the contention that there are three 'basic possibilities for rendering the mediacy of narration' which he calls 'narrative situations'.[30] These narrative situations are three typical and ideal positions from which the story may be told. They represent the three ideal choices which an author can make regarding the way the narrative will be narrated. They are three typical stances which a narrator may adopt towards the tale being told. They are 'typical' and 'ideal' because they represent 'types' of narration, ideal narrative stances to which particular narra-tives may approximate but of which no one narrative is likely to be wholly or purely characteristic.

Each narrative situation is constituted by a variable set of conven-tions which are characteristic to that situation and thereby set it off from the other two types of narrative situation. They are accepted as constitutive of that situation by a 'tacit agreement between author and reader'. The particular guise a narrative takes on through the narra-

28. For the reasons for this, see Cohn, 'Encirclement', p. 158. Among New Testament critics, Genette and Chatman's theoretical constructs have held the field. For criticism of Stanzel, in addition to Cohn, see S. Chatman, 'The Structure of Narrative Transmission', in Fowler (ed.), *Style and Structure in Literature*, pp. 234-37; and Genette, *Narrative Discourse Revisited*, chapter 17. The complex arguments cannot be entered into here, and the criticisms advanced do not materially affect my use of Stanzel.

29. Ref. Stanzel, *Theory*, chapter 1; and see his *Narrative Situations in the Novel* (ET: J.P. Pusack; Bloomington: Indiana University Press, 1971), p. 6. 'Mediacy' translates the German word '*Mittelbarkeit*'.

30. Stanzel, *Theory*, p. 4.

tive situation adopted leads the reader to expect 'a definite consistency of illusion from the narrative'.[31] That is, the reader will conventionally expect the implied author to maintain a narrative style consistent with the chosen narrative situation and will orient his or her own centre of consciousness vis-à-vis the narrative according to the constraints implicit within the narrative situation.

These narrative situations are constituted by the narrative elements of person, perspective and mode, which themselves appear as three axes of binary opposition. Each of the narrative situations is created by the dominance of one particular axis, and defined by the conventions characteristic of one of the poles of that axis. Thus the constitutive element 'person' appears as a narrative axis with the polarities of 'first-person' narration versus 'third-person' narration. This polarity sets up an opposition between a narrator's identity with the world of the characters (the narration takes place within the story world) against non-identity with that world. It is this identity or non-identity with the story world which is the defining feature of this constitutive element rather than the mere use of the first or third personal pronouns. It is possible to have a narrator using the first person pronoun taking up a position more or less outside of the realm of the characters' existence, while on the other hand a narrator using third person reference may appear to have entered the story world through the device of scenic presentation or free indirect style. But, by and large, the use of the first person pronoun will suggest to the reader that the narrator is part of the story world, while third person narration maintains an aspect of detachment even when the narrator enters a scene as a silent observer.

The element 'perspective' is formed by an axis of which the oppositional polarities are narrative with an internal perspective versus narrative having an external perspective. Narrative with an internal perspective is that in which the narrator recounts the story from a limited point of view, seeing and knowing only what the characters (or a character) see and know, and in some cases the narrator may know less than the characters. An external perspective provides the narrator with omniscience and the ability to range over the topography of the story world at will, now with this character, now with that, and even, if so desiring, to enter into the consciousness of the characters to display or describe their thoughts and feelings.

The third element 'mode' is characterized by an opposition between

31. Stanzel, *Narrative Situations*, p. 21.

a mode of narration where the narrator appears as an overt, dramatized figure, one who takes on the configurations of definite personality
in the mind of the reader, against a narrative mode where the narrator
dematerializes into an impersonal, withdrawn, behind-the-scenes,
ghostly presence, or where the narrative is transmitted through a
'reflector', a character behind or into whom the narrator appears to
withdraw.

These, then, are the oppositions which define the three narrative
situations, each one providing the dominating characteristic of a
particular situation. The three narrative situations are as follows. First,
there is the authorial narrative situation which is dominated by an
external perspective. Here the reader is conscious of the presence of
the narrator, and gains a strong sense of being *told* the story. Nearest
the ideal type of authorial narration, the author himself or herself
seems to enter as narrator, through the alter ego, the implied author.
That is, the textual figures of the narrator and implied author coalesce,
and the identification of implied author with real author is close. As
we shall see, there are many gradations away from a situation where
the authorial presence is felt in an almost tangible way toward the
impersonal, withdrawn, 'figural' medium, or toward an independent
or personalized narrator (who may be thought of as a distinct 'I'). The
dominance of external perspective means that the narrator maintains a
temporal, spatial and psychological detachment from the world of the
narrative and a report-like narration generally dominates.[32]

In the first person narrative situation, the narrator, who may or
may not be the main character, speaks in the first person. This situation is dominated by an identity between the realms of existence of the
narrator and the characters. Here there may be gradations in the
degree of identity with or involvement in that world: for example, the
narrator may tell some other character's story, standing, as it were,
on the periphery of the story world. Where the narrator is the main
character, there may be a distinction between the narrating self and
the experiencing self, as when the narrator recounts his/her childhood

32. See Stanzel, *Narrative Situations*, pp. 23-24. Stanzel uses the term 'authorial
medium' to distinguish the 'actual author' from the 'narrator-figure'. Here we may,
reasonably I think, substitute the term 'implied author'. We must remember that,
depending on the particular narrative situation a narrative occupies, the identity of the
implied author with real author may vary greatly from an implied author whose
persona is more or less identical with that of the real author to one not at all alike.

from a later, adult perspective. In some cases the 'I' narrator may simply appear at the beginning or end of a narrative that proceeds for the most part by third person references. This may be the case with the 'I suppose' of Jn 21.25. It is also possible that the 'we' references in 1.14, 16 and 21.24 are intrusions by the implied author (authorial medium) from the perspective of his time of writing, and the context of his community. Another instance of this self-reference by a narrator who stands outside the story he is telling is found in the prologues to Luke–Acts (Lk. 1.2, 3; Acts 1.1). In the latter part of Acts, of course, we have the interesting, and puzzling, case where the narrator suddenly becomes a character in the narrative (the 'we' passages found from Acts 16.10 onward). As is the case with the authorial narrative situation, so here the first person narrator can withdraw into a more figural type character, or have a presence within the narrative which is 'unmarked' in terms of any sense in the reader's imagination of a tangible presence (as happens in 'stream of consciousness' narrative).

The figural narrative situation arises when 'the reader has the illusion of being on the scene in one of the figures' or is present as an unseen witness to the events.[33] The sense of being told the story recedes, the impression that the reader is on the scene as a silent observer, rather like Scrooge in *A Christmas Carol*,[34] or of seeing things through the eyes of a character, increases. This situation is marked by the dominance of the reflector mode. Another feature is the predominance of scenic presentation, and dialogue is often a technique by which the transition to a figural narrative situation occurs.

Stanzel has schematized his theory of the way in which narrative is mediated in a 'typological circle' of narrative situations.[35]

There are a number of advantages which arise from setting out this triad of narrative situations with their constitutive oppositions in the form of a typological circle. Stanzel himself cites a number of these, among them the more comprehensive description of mediacy afforded by the three constitutive elements of person, perspective and mode. Each narrative situation, as we have seen, is defined by the conventions of one aspect of these elements, but also embraces in a subsidiary manner aspects of the other elements. The secondary constitutive

33. Stanzel, *Narrative Situations*, p. 23.
34. We might rather say that the narrator appears, like the non-speaking Ghost of Christmas Future at Scrooge's side, pointing to the events unfolding before the reader.
35. Ref. Stanzel, *Theory*, pp. xvi and 56.

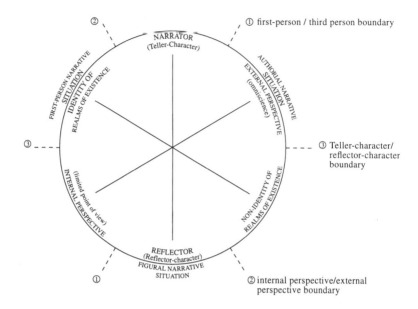

① first-person / third person boundary

③ Teller-character/
    reflector-character
    boundary

② internal perspective/external
    perspective boundary

Figure 3[36]

elements of each narrative situation provide for a way in which the oppositions which define the other two narrative situations can be suspended and resolved. 'For example, in the first-person narrative situation the contrasts in mode and perspective between the authorial [narrator mode/external perspective] and figural [reflector mode/internal perspective] narrative situations are suspended.'[37] An 'I' narrator can, therefore, be either a teller-character or a reflector-character, and may take up a stance internal or external to the story world. By the same token, the figural narrative situation can allow narration in the third person to occur from a position within the story world.

Also, the circular arrangement of the types reveals both the inclusiveness of the system and its dialectic character. Thus, the typological circle operates as an 'inclusive continuum' which incorporates many different variations on the main types of narrative situation and provides for the possibility of modifications away from one type towards either of the other two. Related to this is Stanzel's insistence that the boundaries which separate one narrative situation from another are

36. Reproduced, with modifications, from F.K. Stanzel, *A Theory of Narrative* (Cambridge: Cambridge University Press, 1984), p. 56.

37. Stanzel, *Theory*, p. 60.

open boundaries. Thus the typological circle is intended to furnish a
flexible approach to the description of the process of narration.

This is especially important when it comes to the analysis of the way
in which a particular narrative is narrated. The typological circle may
here provide a model which will account for the narrative's peculiar
character and idiosyncrasies. The narrative features which the work
displays may mean that variations in the way the narrative is told appear
from chapter to chapter, from paragraph to paragraph, or even within
a circumscribed area of text. The flexibility which the circular
schematization of narrative situations affords is very useful in this
context. This is borne out by Stanzel's discussion of 'the dynamization
of the narrative situation' which addresses the way in which the process of narrative transmission may vary over the course of the narration, bringing deviations away from a given narrative situation and
transitions to one of the other two. With this process goes the movement
away from one pole of a binary opposition towards the other pole so
that, for example, a narrative may show a transition from a narrator
(teller) mode of narration to a reflector mode, or from an authorial
narrative situation to a first person narrative stance (as happens in Acts).
By analyzing a narrative's 'profile', that is its sequences of narrative
and dialogue or dramatized scenes (and the ratio of one to the other),
and its 'rhythm', the succession of forms of narration (report, commentary, description, scenic presentation and action report), one can
determine a narrative's basic narrative situation and plot the variations
of this situation and movements towards or into other situations.[38]

As will become apparent in what follows, this possibility of allowing
for the 'dynamization' of the narrative situation, or put more simply,
variations in the way in which the narrative is mediated (often with
consequent changes in the way in which the structure of the narrative
is understood) is most important in understanding the narrative art of
the Fourth Gospel.[39] The schema offers, I think, possibilities of a
more subtle understanding of the artistry of the implied author, an
artistry which bears a rich freight of theological meaning.

38. See here Stanzel, *Theory*, pp. 67-74.
39. See below pp. 62-68.

From Surface to Deep Level of Narrative Mediacy

The typological circle is basically a model for the analysis of narrative transmission, or mediacy, at the surface level (Stanzel calls it the surface structure).[40] However, the interaction between implied author and implied reader is recognized by Stanzel's theory. So how might Stanzel's typological circle be used to help the real reader recover that interaction and the evaluative point of view of the implied author?

To begin with it must be understood that it is the implied author who determines the narrative situation that obtains in a given narrative. The implied author also controls the nature and amount of the movement from one narrative situation to another which will occur within the narrative and is responsible for the creation of the narrative's profile and rhythm. In this way the implied author determines the shape the narrative process will take in the reader's imagination and the way it affects the spatio-temporal location of the reader's 'centre of orientation'. The reader orients not only his or her own relation to the story world, but also that of the implied author, according to the particular narrative situation that obtains at any given point in the narrative. A narrative delivered from the perspective of a first person narrator or a reflector-character, for instance, will suggest an immediate, 'as if we were there' orientation. The implied author may be perceived as existentially involved with the events of the narrative. This will increase a sense of verisimilitude and enhance the 'eyewitness' nature of the narrative. In a first person narrative the relationship between the implied author and the narrator will be a complex one and will either create a sense of shared norms or an ironic distance depending upon the perceived reliability or unreliability of the narrator. An unreliable narrator (one who is self-deceived, ignorant, or immature) tends to be distanced from the implied author. The reader will share the implied author's stance, smiling knowingly and adopting a superior attitude towards the narrator's point of view. In the case of third person narration the transformation of a teller-character into a reflector-character may have the effect of assimilating the norms and values of the reflector to those of the implied author.

On the other hand, a third person narrator will give a retrospective

40. Stanzel, *Theory*, p. 20.

and external perspective to the narration. A greater degree of objectivity will be suggested and in certain types of narrative (e.g. reporting forms such as historical narrative) the closer a narrative remains to an impersonal narrating style (authorial narrative situation), the greater will be the identification of the narrator with implied author, and hence narrator with real author. To some extent, the dynamics of this will depend upon where the reader places a given narrative on the spectrum of possible narratives.[41] Thus, choice and variation of narrative situation in a given narrative forms and determines the implied reader, and hence the real reader's grasp of the point of view communicated by the discourse. This point of view is recovered by giving attention to the type(s) of situation created and understanding the dynamics of this for the narrative's meaning.

The Fourth Gospel and the Typological Circle

Stanzel's typological circle provides him with a model upon which he places examples from the corpus of modern fiction at various more or less fixed points on the circumference of the circle. This he does on the basis of the type of narrative situation which predominates in each instance. Only in one or two cases, for example, those of James Joyce's *Ulysses* or Robbe-Grillet's *Jealousy*, does he permit himself a doubt about the work's position on the circle, or, in the case of *Ulysses*, hint at the variation in the narrative situation which may take place in a single narrative.[42] If I were to attempt to place the Fourth Gospel in this fashion, I would put it somewhere on the circle between an authorial and a figural narrative situation, probably near the 'narrator/ reflector' boundary (or, as Stanzel prefers to call it, the 'teller-character/reflector-character' boundary). This is because, as we shall see, an omniscient narrator periodically becomes part of the story world through the use of scenic presentation; and more importantly, by merging his perspective with that of a character. But it is the way in which the typological circle can illuminate the variations in the types of narrative situation that appear over the course of the narration which proves most fruitful and rewarding in an analysis of the Fourth Gospel. It is by attending to the profile and rhythm of the

41. See below chapter 6, pp. 208-12.
42. Cf. Stanzel, *Theory*, p. xvi.

Gospel and noting how it moves from one situation to another, that we shall best discover the implied author's narrative art and understand something of his theological purpose.

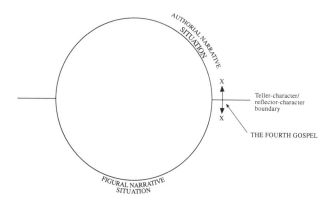

Figure 4

With regard to the Gospel's overall structure, the narrative displays characteristics which show a general movement from an authorial narrative situation towards a figural one, taking place by a process which Stanzel calls the reflectorization of a teller-character. That is, the narrator (a teller-character) changes point of view and voice and becomes a reflector.[43] The stance of the narrator becomes that of a character in the story, or, at least, it is as if the narrator enters the story world, sees with the eyes of a character, and shares the perspective of that character. Note again that Stanzel's theory allows for movement in and out of different narrative situations over the course of the narration. That there are changes and modulations in and among narrative situations is an important consideration, for analysis of the Fourth Gospel's profile and rhythm shows that even while there is general movement from an authorial to a figural situation, the authorial situation can reassert itself quite suddenly and at any point in the narrative. Indeed, analysis of the surface level of the discourse might suggest that the narration never properly leaves the authorial narrative situation even when the narrator appears to withdraw into a reflector-character, or where scenic presentation is dominant. This is perhaps why narrative critics can describe the narrator as being omniscient throughout. However, as the commentaries clearly show, readers

---

43. This process is described in more detail in chapter 5.

find the surface level of discourse ambiguous and indeterminate on this point. Furthermore, it is the dynamics of the interchange at the deeper level and the implications of the theory of variations in narrative situations for communication at this level which make Stanzel's theory so attractive and potentially productive.

The shift from an authorial to a figural narrative situation reflects itself in certain characteristic features described by Stanzel as follows. There is, first of all, '[t]he gradual withdrawal of the person of the authorial narrator up to and including his (apparent) invisibility in the narrative process'.[44] Concurrently, there occurs the 'gradual appearance of a reflector-character (or the reflectorization of an authorial teller-character)' which results in a change in the narrator's, and the reader's, spatio-temporal orientation and perspective from without to within the narrative world.[45] This fading of the narrator and emergence of a reflector takes place through an increase in the use of dialogue and scenic presentation; and also often involves using a free indirect style in which the authorial and figural perspectives combine.[46] The use of adjectival descriptions of a character ('poor X') or 'authorial circumlocutions' ('our hero') which appear to the reader as outside, detached views of a character, are replaced with the simple use of a proper name, and, increasingly, the replacement of a name (or noun) with a pronoun. The greater the incidence of pronouns, the more likely it is that the reader will 'transfer. . . to the consciousness of the character' or enter into the character's situation.[47] Finally, the 'contamination of the narrator's language by the language of the fictional character' or the 'colloquialization of the narrator's language' also facilitates a transfer to a figural situation.[48]

Having noted these characteristics, we may embark on a rapid overview of the Fourth Gospel's discourse to examine and illustrate how

44. Stanzel, *Theory*, pp. 186-87.
45. Stanzel, *Theory*, p. 187.
46. Stanzel, *Theory*, pp. 188, 190-92. Free indirect style is a complex, controversial and much debated literary technique. Basically, it is the mixing of direct and indirect discourse in such a way as to make it neither wholly narrator's discourse nor character's speech or thought. 'Most of the literary explanations of free indirect style today agree in assuming that the essence of free indirect style lies in the dual view of events from the perspective of the narrator and from that of a fictional character' (p. 191). Cf. Martin, *Recent Theories*, pp. 137-38.
47. Cf. Stanzel, *Theory*, p. 189.
48. See Stanzel, *Theory*, pp. 192, 194.

these features are displayed over the course of the narration. Again, the thrust of the argument here is that overall the profile and rhythm of the narrative displays a movement from an authorial narrative situation (as seen in the prologue and chs. 1 and 2) towards a figural narrative situation, via the reflectorization of the teller-character which occurs in ch. 3, and under the increase of extended scenic presentation, as, for instance, in chs. 4, 6 and 9. In chs. 13–21, especially due to the introduction of the beloved disciple, the situation resides, at times, close to the boundary between the figural and first person narrative situations.

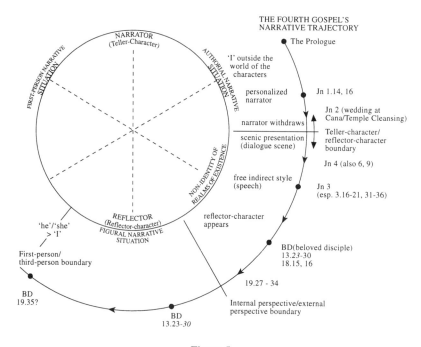

Figure 5

In the prologue and the first two chapters of the Gospel, the narrator appears to narrate mostly from an authorial narrative situation. The perspective is that of one external to the story world and this is increased by the fact that it is also retrospective. The reader's sense of being told a story is strong, and the voice of the narrator is clearly heard: 'In the beginning. . . '; 'There was a man. . . '; 'The next day. . . , the next day. . . , on the third day. . . ' Quite apart from the narrator's clear comments and explanatory statements (giving the time of day,

explaining and translating Aramaic words, giving the reader information about the characters' state of knowledge and so forth), the narrative
begins with some theological exposition on the significance of the
character who is introduced by name at v. 17. The narrator is clearly
both omniscient and omnipresent. He moves freely from vantage point
to vantage point and follows the characters at will. He is with John the
Baptist as the latter engages in discussion with his interrogators, he
follows Jesus with the two disciples and accompanies Andrew to find
Peter and Philip in his search for Nathanael. At the wedding at Cana,
he knows what passes between Jesus and his mother, and between the
steward of the feast and the bridegroom.

There are, of course, the interesting intrusions of the 'we' references at 1.14, 16 which give, perhaps, the merest hint that this narrator has some personal connection with the events he is to recount. But
these are still sufficiently broad in their reference as to include even
his reader and the retrospective perspective suggests that the personal
involvement may simply arise from his connection with a community
in which the traditions of Jesus have circulated. However, the use of
the historical present in a number of instances is also of interest (ref.
1.29, 38, 45). In this context, and because of the retrospective view of
events, these are generally understood as having a past sense (and are
rendered as such in translation). However, according to *BDF* 'the
historical present can replace the aorist indicative in a vivid narrative
at the events of which the narrator imagines himself to be present'.[49] I
shall have more to say on the implications of the historical present in
the Fourth Gospel later.[50] For the present we may note that its use
here suggests a colloquialization of the narrator's language. Arguably,
the manner in which, in the prologue, the narrator intermixes abstract
nouns such as 'the word' and 'the light' with pronouns and the gradual
introduction of proper names (especially that of Jesus at v. 17) induces
in the reader a move from relative detachment to a greater involvement in the characters' world. Even in these early chapters, the use of
dialogue and description begins to draw the reader into the world of
the story.

Chapter 3 marks a transition in the narrative where the disappear-
ance of the narrator is achieved by the merging of the narrator's voice
with that of Jesus and of John the Baptist. The dynamics of this will be

49. *BDF*, p. 167, par. 321.
50. See chapter 6, pp. 176-78, 192-93.

explored in more detail in chapter 5, which also considers some of the implications of this process for claims made for the truth of the narrative.

Jesus' encounter with the woman of Samaria, in 4.7-26, shows a high degree of scenic presentation and contains a lot of dialogue. There is an increase in the amount of incidental detail which lends verisimilitude to the narrative. For example, Jesus' physical condition is described (he is tired), the time of day is noted (4.6), and a seemingly random detail—the fact that the woman leaves her water pot by the well when she returns to the village (4.28)—together with the description of the disciples' puzzlement over Jesus' comment about food (4.31-33), give the sense of immediate, on the spot, narrating. The narrator has become, as it were, the silent, unseen witness to the event (and the reader is drawn into the story world to stand at the narrator's elbow). As this may be described as a 'dialogue scene' (ref. Fig. 5), I place it on the reflector side of the teller-character/reflector-character boundary. Admittedly the narrator retains the stance of an omniscient narrator: he can be both at the scene when the woman arrives back in the village and with the disciples and Jesus at the well. And throughout the story, explicit commentary and transitional statements (e.g. 4.43-45; cf. also 2.23-25; 4.1-4; 5.1-5) return the discourse to an authorial narrative situation. But, at the very least, we can be confident in situating the manner of narration on or near the boundary of the authorial and figural narrative situations where, according to Stanzel's schema, the narrator withdraws, and dialogue scene or scenic presentation predominate. The case is the same for much of the remainder of the narrative. An omniscient narrator moves from scene to scene, commenting the while, but bringing the events vividly to life with deft dialogue and descriptive touches which lend credibility. Periodically he will revert to the historic present. It is little wonder that many readers are taken with the dramatic qualities of this story.[51]

In chs. 13–21, the narrator slips a character into the story whom he refers to as the disciple whom Jesus loved (conventionally known

---

51. There are, of course, the extended discourses of Jesus which, being speech, are essentially non-narrated segments. As far as their situation on the typological circle is concerned, they become subsumed under dialogue scene. Indeed, in so far as the speaker, Jesus, is a character in his narrative, they place the narrator in the situation of communicating via a reflector-character.

as 'the beloved disciple'). The presence of this disciple in the story has provided a conundrum for readers. For here we appear to have an embodiment of the narrator, or more properly the implied author, though this is not made explicit until Jn 21.24.[52] It is certain, at least, that the beloved disciple is brought into some sort of proximity to the narrator. In terms of the particular theory of narrative mediacy that I am adopting, we might describe the narrator as having withdrawn behind the figure of the beloved disciple. The beloved disciple, then, becomes a figural medium and the narrative situation is correspondingly figural.

At 13.21-30, for instance, the perspective becomes that of a narrator who sees things through the eyes of the beloved disciple (or, if we were to put it the other way round, the beloved disciple shares the perceptions of the narrator).[53] The implied author infers that as the beloved disciple leans on Jesus' breast, he sees Jesus dip the morsel in the dish and pass it to Judas, and he watches Judas depart. The statement, 'It was night' (v. 30), which closes this cameo scene, is a classic example of the merging of perspectives. It may be taken both as an observation of the beloved disciple and as a narrative statement by the narrator.

'It was night' is a narrative statement which also has significance at the deep level of communication between implied author and implied reader. Judas' departure is part of the strategy of the 'darkness' in its attempts to overcome the 'light' (cf. 1.50). The narrator (an omniscient narrator at that) betrays his hand in the comment that after Judas had received the morsel, Satan entered into him (v. 27). This might lead the critical reader to ask, is this not simply all the narrative of an authorial narrator? Is it truly the case that here the beloved disciple is a figural medium? It is the peculiarly intimate nature of the exchange between Jesus and the beloved disciple which draws the reader to perceive the event as through the eyes of this disciple. He leans close to

---

52. And, as we shall see, even here there are difficulties in the way of an easy acceptance of the beloved disciple as the implied author, see below pp. 94-95, 142-43.

53. If we were following Genette here, we would say that the narrative is 'focalized' through the beloved disciple, while the narrator is the 'focalizer'. That is, the answer to the question 'who sees?' is 'the beloved disciple': the answer to the question 'who speaks?' is 'the narrator'. But, it does not seem to me as easy as that, for the narrator may be the one who is both focalizer and through whom the narrative is focalized. Nor is it clear how much the beloved disciple really sees.

Jesus as the bombshell about a betrayer is dropped into the conversation. He is in an especially advantageous position to correctly interpret the action by which Jesus makes known the betrayer's identity. It is, in fact, as a response to the beloved disciple's question that Jesus performs the act. He alone among the disciples, the reader would assume, shares with the narrator the knowledge of the true nature of Judas' departure. And yet, how much does the beloved disciple really see and know? If *no one* at the table knows why Jesus says what he does to Judas (v. 28), does this statement include the beloved disciple after all? The implied author teases the implied reader with the interpretative shadows of his narrative.

This, and a further puzzle, will be examined in chapter 4. The other conundrum is the relationship between the beloved disciple and the disciple designated as 'the other disciple' (18.15, 16) and the witness at the foot of the cross (19.35). For the present we may note that, if these figures are to be understood as being one and the same person, as the implied author's narrative strategy would have us believe, then we have here a character of special privilege, not only in his access to the high priest's courtyard and his presence at Jesus' death and witness to his resurrection, but as one who is implicitly the witness to all that the narrator tells the reader in these final chapters.

Finally, we shall close this survey of the narrative situations in this Gospel with the scene at the foot of the cross where stands a witness, so the narrator says, who sees the spear thrust into Jesus' side, followed by a rush of blood and water. The narrator comments, 'He who saw it has borne witness—his testimony is true, and he knows he tells the truth—that you also may believe' (19.35).[54] The reader assumes that this witness is the beloved disciple because of the reference to him in v. 26, but the connection is not made explicit. Indeed, a reader who takes 19.27b literally might think that at this point the narrator makes the beloved disciple depart from the scene.[55]

Whether or not 19.35 is a gloss added to the text at a later date, we may note that here the use of the third person pronoun makes the question of the identity of the narrator with this witness difficult to

54. This, we might note, is the first of two occasions in the discourse where the implied author (through the narrator) directly addresses the implied reader.

55. Cf. Brown, *John*, p. 907; D.A. Carson, *The Gospel according to John* (Leicester: Inter-Varsity Press, 1991), pp. 625-26.

determine.[56] Much discussion has taken place on this point. I shall restrict myself to two observations. First, I place this verse (and thereby the scene to which it relates) firmly in the figural narrative situation (i.e. the narrator is in reflector mode) and positioned near the first-person/third-person boundary (see Fig. 5). Stanzel shows that when a narrative is mediated from this narrative situation, a 'he/she' reference can become an 'I' reference (at least in the reader's understanding if not grammatically). This, I think, reflects the way in which the verse may be read given its context (and in the light of the statement made at 21.24). A glance at the commentaries shows that many accept that it may be read in this fashion.[57] Narrative theory recognizes a distinction between an 'I' narrator who is a narrator-character within the story (as is found in sustained first person narration, e.g. *Robinson Crusoe* or *Great Expectations*, or in an autobiography), and a first-person narrator who is outside the story ('Luke' in his prologues, cf. Virgil or Chariton).[58]

The question is, which of these stances is operative at 19.35? Staley falls into something of a logical inconsistency here. He states that the narrator as an 'author-narrator' is outside the story, 'for although he is finally retrospectively revealed to have been a character in the story he has just finished telling/writing, he never intrudes as an "I" narrator-character in that story'.[59] He cites Gerard Genette who says that 'the real question is whether or not the narrator can use the first person to designate one of his characters'.[60] 'The narrator of the Fourth Gospel', writes Staley, 'never designates himself as such in the story.' But Staley has already claimed that 'the narrator of the Fourth Gospel can be none other than "the beloved disciple"'.[61] He then describes the

56. The verse is omitted by two Latin witnesses: this textual evidence is too slight to allow one to say that it was not originally part of the Gospel (see C.K. Barrett, *The Gospel according to St John* (London: SPCK, 2nd edn, 1978), p. 558; Brown, *John*, p. 936; E. Haenchen, *John 2* (Philadelphia: Fortress Press, 1984), p. 195).

57. Cf. L. Morris, *The Gospel according to John* (Grand Rapids: Eerdmans, 1971), pp. 820-22; Barrett, *John*, p. 557; Brown, *John*, p. 936.

58. Virgil, 'I sing of arms and the man'. Chariton, *Chaereas & Callirhoe*, I.1.i Χαρίτων (κτλ.). . . πάθος ἐρωτικὸν ἐν Συρρακούσαις γενόμενον διηγήσομαι' (G. Molinié, *Chariton: Le Roman de Chairéas et Callirhoé* [Paris: Société d'Edition 'Les Belles Lettres', Guillaume Budé, 1979], p. 50).

59. Staley, *First Kiss*, p. 39.

60. Staley, *First Kiss*, p. 39 n. 83; cf. Genette, *Narrative*, p. 244.

61. Staley, *First Kiss*, pp. 38-39.

narrator, at 19.35, as using a technique of double reference by which
a narrator can move from one level of narration to another (outside to
inside) or refer to himself both in his capacity as character, and as
'restricted author-narrator'. 'The technique of double reference can
more easily be seen', says Staley, 'by simply putting first person pronouns in place of the third person pronouns: thus, "I, having seen,
have borne witness, and my witness is true, and I know that I am
speaking the truth. . . " '[62] Here lies the difficulty: either the narrator
is associating himself with the witness (whom we may take to be the
beloved disciple), in which case I think one can say that he is able to
use the first person to designate one of his characters; or he is referring to the witness as a third party—a reliable, eyewitness source of
information, to be sure, but a third party nonetheless. Staley, and
Culpepper before him, is right to associate the narrator with this
witness. But the 'trick of double reference' is not so that the narrator
can act as though he is omniscient and omnipresent over the major
part of the discourse (as they claim), but precisely so that he can claim
a connection to a reliable witness and a status as an authoritative source
for the words and deeds of Jesus. He is a reliable narrator of Jesus'
story because he himself is, or he has access to, a trustworthy witness.

My second observation is that it is over exegetical conundrums such
as this that Stanzel's narrative theory offers not only helpful insights
but also an advantage over theories which tend to posit sharp distinctions between narrator, implied author and real author (distinctions
which begin to break down when analysis of and application to a particular text takes place). To begin with his approach does not rest on
nor require such distinctions. Rather it offers a model of variable
choices open to an implied author as to how a story will be told. It
also provides a theoretical basis for understanding the merging of
these narrative entities. This is because, on his terms, the question is
that of the particular stance taken in mediating a narrative, and the
possibility of an authorial narrative stance, which is relatively
detached from the narrative, moving by way of first person narration
or narration through a reflector, to a position of greater existential
involvement with the narrative and its world. In chapter 4 we shall
examine further how this takes place in the characterization of the
beloved disciple.

62. Staley, *First Kiss*, p. 40.

Chapter 3

SPEECH-ACT THEORY AND MEANING IN THE FOURTH GOSPEL

'The Gospel of John is a book with a message. The author wants to bring the reader to the point of decision.'[1] These uneqivocal words of Barnabas Lindars may set our course for this chapter. Readers approach the Fourth Gospel with the expectation that it will yield a 'message', and a 'meaning'. It was purposefully conceived and it may be purposefully read. But, as the proliferation of commentaries and studies attests, there is much debate about what that meaning is, where it resides and how it may be found. Does the reader's search for meaning begin with what are conceived to be the author's aims, with the audience for which the writing is intended, or with the (background) situation or context out of which the text springs, or the process by which the text guides and solicits the construction of meaning?[2]

The present study begins with the text of the Fourth Gospel which is seen as the locus of an *active* and *interactive* process of communication between author and reader. Thus the narrative is the primary context for establishing meaning: it is the 'common ground' on which other contexts (context of time of discourse, and reader's contemporary context) meet. It is the dynamic and active nature of the process which is stressed in the theory outlined both in this and the previous chapter.

In recent decades there has been a movement away from understanding a narrative primarily as an artifact, towards seeing it as an

1. B. Lindars, *The Gospel of John* (London: Marshall, Morgan & Scott, 1972), p. 24.
2. For comments illustrative of these different approaches, see Ashton, *Understanding the Fourth Gospel*, p. 9; C.H. Dodd, *The Interpretation of the Fourth Gospel* (Cambridge: Cambridge University Press, 1953), p. 3; and R.A. Culpepper, 'The Johannine *Hypodeigma*: A Reading of John 13.1-38', in R.A. Culpepper and F.F. Segovia (eds.), 'The Fourth Gospel from a Literary Perspective', *Semeia* 53 (1991), p. 133.

act of communication between an author and a reader. In the same way, the use of language may be understood as a performance, or an activity by which meaning is made by what words do as much as in what they are. Thus words are not simply entities within which meaning resides: they are also tools with which a speaker may perform certain actions and achieve certain effects. In understanding the meaning of a literary discourse, the reader needs to attend not only to what the author is saying (i.e. to the propositional content of the discourse) but also to what he or she is doing by what is said. And because a text is written 'speech', it is appropriate to apply methods which will facilitate analysis of what the writer is doing in the discourse. Such methods are available in speech-act theory.

Speech-Act Theory

Speech-act theory is a method of analyzing human language use in terms of the actions and the effects that are achieved by a given utterance. At its simplest, speech-act theory is based on the premiss that to say something is to do something. All human utterance takes place in a context within which certain conditions and conventional expectations operate to invest what is said with meaning. Speech-act theory has been developed by what is known as the 'ordinary language' school of philosophers, of whom the main figures of relevance to the present study are J.L. Austin, J.R. Searle and H.P. Grice.

J.L. Austin, who is regarded as the founder of the 'school', stated that when we say something we are generally doing a number of things, including uttering an intelligible sentence which conveys a particular intention and effects a particular response.[3] To be more precise, he identified the speech-acts performed as falling under three heads.

Locutionary acts (locutions) are basically the production of utterances themselves. As Austin put it, to perform a locution 'is roughly equivalent to uttering a certain sentence with a certain sense and

---

3.   See J.L. Austin, *How to do Things with Words* (London: Oxford University Press, 1962), p. 108; M.L. Pratt, *Toward a Speech-Act Theory of Literary Discourse* (Bloomington: Indiana University Press, 1977), p. 80. See also M.H. Abrams, *A Glossary of Literary Terms* (Forth Worth: Holt, Rinehart & Winston, 5th edn, 1988), p. 240.

reference, which again is roughly equivalent to "meaning" in the traditional sense'.[4]

Illocutionary acts (illocutions) are the acts a speaker performs in uttering the locutions, whether it be that of making an assertion, for example, or promising, warning, commanding, blessing or threatening. An illocutionary act is made up of both illocutionary point and illocutionary force. The illocutionary point is the purpose or end to which the illocutionary act is directed, for example, to get the hearer to do something, as in requests or commands, or to make a representation of how something is, as in a description. As J.R. Searle says, the 'illocutionary point is part of but not the same as illocutionary force'.[5] The illocutionary force is the tone of the locution or the impact which an illocutionary act is intended to have on the hearer. In this sense, illocutionary force approximates to the perlocutionary effect, except that force is perhaps more within the control of the speaker than the effect (but there is, at any rate, an intangible element to the illocutionary force of a locution).

Perlocutionary acts (perlocutions) are the intended effects that locutions are conventionally expected to have or to achieve. One may argue in order to convince, or threaten in order to frighten or warn someone off a certain course of action. It should be noted that a perlocution is the *intended* effect inherent in the locution, or intended to derive from the illocution performed. But the actual effect might be something quite different. A speaker can have no sure control over the effect of a given locution. The actual outcome always, to a degree, resides with the hearer. For instance, I may set out to warn you (the illocution) in order to frighten you or make you change your ways (the perlocution) only to succeed in making you laugh. Or you may choose to understand but ignore the warning.

Austin, followed by Searle, attempted to categorize the types of illocutionary acts which a speaker may perform. Here we shall follow

---

4. Austin, *How*, p. 108.

5. J.R. Searle, *Expression and Meaning* (Cambridge: Cambridge University Press, 1979), p. 3; 'the illocutionary point of requests is the same as that of commands: both are attempts to get hearers to do something. But the illocutionary forces are clearly different.' (Namely, that the force of a request is more conciliatory than that of a command.)

Searle's nomenclature, and his refinement of Austin's taxonomy.[6] Both identified five types of illocution.

1. *Assertives*: illocutionary acts in which the speaker commits him/ herself to something being the case or to representing a state of affairs, whether past, present, future or hypothetical e.g. stating, claiming, hypothesizing, describing, telling, suggesting, or swearing that something is the case.[7]

2. *Directives*: illocutionary acts in which the speaker tries to get the hearer to do something as in e.g. requesting, commanding, pleading, daring.

3. *Commissives*: these are illocutionary acts whose point is to commit the speaker to some course of action in the future, that is, the act of promising, threatening, vowing, etc.

4. *Expressives*: illocutionary acts that express the speaker's psychological state (expressing his/her thoughts and feelings on a matter) e.g. congratulating, thanking, apologizing, deploring, condoling, welcoming.

5. *Declarations*: illocutionary acts which bring into being the state of affairs to which they refer e.g. blessing, firing, baptizing, bidding or passing sentence.

Searle provides a neat summary of these five general categories when he writes: 'We tell people how things are (Assertives), we try to get them to do things (Directives), we commit ourselves to do things (Commissives), we express our feelings and attitudes (Expressives), and we bring about changes in the world through our utterances (Declarations).'[8]

In determining what category of speech-act is being performed we must pay attention to the context in which it is performed. To give an example: the locution 'Would you shut the door' is taken as a request if it is spoken in a mild tone and in an interrogative manner, and as a command when spoken by a superior to a subordinate (both of these illocutions being in the directive category). But spoken with a raised

6.   See Searle, 'A Taxonomy of Illocutionary Acts', in *Expression*, chapter 1. I am also indebted here to Pratt, *Toward*, pp. 80-81.

7.   Searle at first designated this class as 'representatives' (cf. Pratt, *Toward*, p. 80) but states that he now prefers the term 'assertive', 'since any speech-act with a propositional content is in some sense a representation' (*Expression*, p. viii).

8.   Searle, *Expression*, p. viii.

voice and an emphasis on certain words, such as 'would' or 'shut', the locution takes on the aspect of a threat (commissive) with implications of dire consequences to follow if it is not heeded.

Apart from the importance of context (who is speaking, in what manner, in what circumstances, to whom, and so forth) in the understanding of speech-acts, speech-act theory also recognizes that for a speech-act to be successfully performed certain conditions must be met. These are termed 'appropriateness conditions' or 'felicity conditions', that is, conditions which must apply if a speech-act is to be appropriately or felicitously executed. As Pratt puts it: 'They represent rules which users of the language assume to be in force in their verbal dealings with each other; they form part of the knowledge which speakers of a language share and on which they rely in order to use the language correctly and effectively, both in producing and understanding utterances.'[9] These appropriateness conditions will vary depending upon the category of the speech-act being performed. For instance, the appropriateness conditions for questions are that the one asking the question does not know the answer, sincerely wants to know the answer, believes the one asked will possibly know the answer but will not obviously provide the answer without being asked.[10] Searle classifies appropriateness conditions as operating under either preparatory (e.g. the speaker wants to know the answer to the question), essential (the act of undertaking to elicit information from the one asked) or sincerity rules (questioner genuinely wants to know the answer).

The type of speech-act most commonly found in the Fourth Gospel is the assertive as the implied author is concerned to present the implied reader with propositions about Jesus. Thus, the appropriateness conditions which attach to statements or assertions are of most interest to us in our analysis of the Gospel's speech-acts. These are:

1. The essential rule: the speaker commits him or herself to the truth of the proposition being asserted.

2. The preparatory rules: (a) the speaker has evidence for the truth of the proposition (or reasons for believing it), and, (b) it is not obvious

---

9. Pratt, *Toward*, p. 81.

10. Cf. Pratt, *Toward*, p. 82. Rhetorical questions are, in a sense, pseudo-questions as the appropriateness conditions do not apply, or are suspended. They are, in effect, assertives masquerading as directives.

to both speaker and hearer that the hearer knows the proposition (or does not need to be reminded of it).

3. The sincerity rule: the speaker has some reason for wanting the hearer to know, or to be reminded of, the proposition.[11]

Appropriateness conditions, then, are the rules or conventional expectations within which speech-acts operate and which invest them with meaning. They provide the context within which we understand a given locution. The fact that there are these rules and expectations is important when it comes to understanding utterances where the conventions are apparently suspended or subverted. Here, the work of H.P. Grice is significant, particularly that relating to what he calls the co-operative principle and implicature. Part of the general context of a discourse situation, a series of speech-acts, or a conversation, is the understanding and belief (generally implicit) held by the participants in this act of communication that it is a purposeful exercise, a 'co-operative effort' undertaken in pursuit of a common purpose and in a mutually accepted direction. In other words, the communicative act is not random and meaningless but directed towards a given end. What gives the communicative act coherence and continuity is a 'rough general principle' which, other things being equal, the participants will be expected to observe. This is the co-operative principle, which is that a speaker should make his/her contribution 'such as is required, at the stage at which it occurs, by the accepted purpose or direction of the talk exchange in which [he/she is] engaged'.[12]

This co-operative principle is based on a number of conventions which are expected to be in force when the principle is being observed. Grice calls these maxims, and they come under four headings.[13]

1. Maxims of Quantity.

The contribution should be as informative as is required (for the current purposes of the exchange); but not more informative than required.

11. This summary is a conflation of Searle with Pratt, cf. Searle, *Expression*, p. 62; Pratt, *Toward*, p. 82.

12. H.P. Grice, 'Logic and Conversation', in P. Cole and J.L. Morgan (eds.), *Syntax and Semantics. III. Speech-Acts* (New York: Academic Press, 1975), p. 45.

13. Grice, 'Logic', pp. 45-46; cf. Pratt, *Toward*, pp. 129-30.

2. Maxims of Quality.

The contribution should be one that is true, that is, not deliberately false and not one for which there is inadequate evidence.

3. Maxim of Relation.

The contribution should be relevant.[14]

4. Maxims of Manner.

The contribution should be clear, that is, brief, orderly, and avoiding ambiguity or obscurity of expression.

In enumerating these maxims we underscore the fact that speech is a 'rule-governed' form of behaviour (as Searle puts it). But we should also recognize that in much of our speech activity these conventions, or maxims, operate implicitly. Because of the mutual acceptance of the co-operative principle, we are able to depend upon it to aid understanding and communication. For instance, if A says 'I have a headache' and B replies 'I have an aspirin', we understand this not simply as a statement of fact but as an offer of the aspirin to relieve A's headache.[15] Thus the maxim of relevance enables two interlocuters to engage in a type of verbal 'shorthand'. But even more important are cases where one or more of the maxims which underlie the co-operative principle are deliberately breached or flouted. In this case, unless there is some good reason to believe that the speaker is setting aside the co-operative principle, the hearer will normally take steps to decode and to interpret what is said in the light of the assumption that the co-operative principle is still in force. In other words, the hearer will look for what is implied in the locution, and 'will make all the deductions and inferences necessary to maintain the assumption that the speaker is observing the [co-operative principle].'[16]

The act of relying upon the operation of the co-operative principle to make sense of communication exchanges is what lies behind the notion of *implicature*. Implicature involves a process whereby, on the one hand, a speaker flouts the maxims in some way, thereby making

---

14. Grice points out that this seemingly simple maxim hides a number of difficulties as, for instance, how to determine relevance, how a shift in the course of a talk exchange might allow for a legitimate change of topic, and how a seemingly irrelevent contribution might initiate this change.

15. The illustration is Pratt's, see further, *Toward*, pp. 154-55.

16. Pratt, *Toward*, p. 154.

breaches, or gaps and aporias in the exchange, so that something is implied or implicated. The hearer, on the other hand, engages in inference-taking and deduction-making activity in order to discover the implication of what is being said. It is on the process of implicature that much communication depends. It is through implicature that many of the techniques of communication such as irony, symbolism and even metaphor, are created.[17] It is also worth noting here that what is described as 'implicit commentary'—the implied author's silent communication, subsurface signals, nods, winks, 'body language', narrative 'echo effects'—referred to by Culpepper and other narrative critics, is largely achieved by the process of implicature.[18]

There is one further feature of speech-act theory that we should note. This has to do with the relationship of the purpose of a given illocutionary act (what Searle calls the illocutionary point) to reality or to the world. 'Some illocutions have as part of their illocutionary point to get the words (more strictly, their propositional content) to match the world, others to get the world to match the words.'[19] Searle calls the relationship of what is done in the speech-act to the world, the *direction of fit*. A speech-act which aims at describing the world has a word-to-world direction of fit. A speech-act which seeks to effect a change in the world has a world-to-word direction of fit.

In illumination of this feature, Searle provides an illustration borrowed from Elisabeth Anscombe, of a man who goes to a supermarket with a shopping list. He is followed by a detective who makes

---

17. On the use of the term 'implicature' Grice states, 'I wish to introduce, as terms of art, the verb *implicate* and the related nouns *implicature* (cf. *implying*) and *implicatum* (cf. *what is implied*). The point of this maneuver is to avoid having, on each occasion, to choose between this or that member of the family of verbs for which *implicate* is to do general duty' ('Logic', pp. 43-44). Because of the desire to invoke the process of implicature, and establish in the reader's mind what is involved in speech-act terms when something is stated by implication, I shall at times use the somewhat clumsy phrase 'by implicature' rather than writing 'by implication'. I beg the reader's indulgence in this matter, as I also reserve the right to human inconsistency (and the desire to retain some vestige of conventional, grammatical good taste!). At any rate, 'implicature' should be understood as a form of gerundive which subsumes other forms of the substantives of implication under it.

18. Culpepper, *Anatomy*, p. 151; cf. Stibbe, *John as Storyteller*, pp. 27-28, 29.

19. Searle, *Expression*, p. 3.

a list of the items the man selects. Assuming each executes his respective task correctly, the shopper and the detective ought to have precisely the same list. But the purpose or function of each list will have been different. In the case of the shopper it is, as Searle puts it, 'to get the world to match the words'. In other words, his action in the supermarket, what he plucks off the shelves, is to be in accordance with the words on his list. On the other hand, the purpose of the detective's list is to make the words match the world: he notes down words in accordance with the items he observes the shopper select.

> The detective's list has the *word-to-world* direction of fit (as do statements, descriptions, assertions, and explanations); the shopper's list has the *world-to-word* direction of fit (as do requests, commands, vows, promises). . . Direction of fit is always a consequence of illocutionary point.[20]

For each of his five categories of illocutionary act, Searle provides a description of the direction of fit. Assertives have a word-to-world direction of fit. Directives and commissives have a world-to-word direction of fit. In the case of expressives, the direction of fit is suspended. Declarations have a direction of fit which is both words-to-world and world-to-words. This is because of their peculiar character. Declarations attempt to get language to match the world, but they do so neither by describing an existing state of affairs (as do assertives), nor by trying to bring about a future state of affairs (as do directives and commissives).[21] Declarations, by nature, both establish the state of the world and simply declare it to be so, or 'establish' that it is so.

Before we proceed to relate speech-act theory to literary discourse, we might summarize the main points of this section thus. Speech-acts are verbal actions that take place within a context. This context is that of a transaction between a speaker and a hearer,[22] that is governed by certain conventions or rules (we might also say, conventional expectations). Meaning is an outcome of the complex interaction of *act* and *context*. We can represent this in diagrammatic form, thus:

20. Searle, *Expression*, p. 4.
21. Searle, *Expression*, p. 19.
22. Using the singular case to cover instances where the plural might also be appropriate.

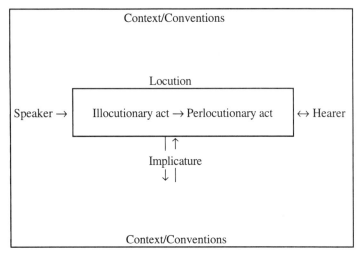

Figure 6

Speech-Act Theory and Literary Discourse

There are a number of advantages in applying speech-act theory to
an understanding of the nature of literary discourse and in applying it
to an analysis of a given literary work. In the first place, as we have
seen in the previous chapter, literary discourse arises out of a communication situation in which the literary work is a transaction
between a speaker and a hearer, or more properly, a writer and a
reader (author and audience) within a given context. A literary work,
as Pratt would put it, comes out of the context of a 'literary speech
situation'. '[L]iterary works, like all our communicative activities, are
context-dependent. Literature itself is a speech context. And as with
any utterance, the way people produce and understand literary works
depends enormously on unspoken, culturally shared knowledge of
rules, conventions, and expectations that are in play when language is
used in that context.'[23]

Second, speech-act theory foregrounds intention in the literary work.
In that respect it shares with recent narrative theory the recognition
that a work of literature is the product of an author who engages in an
act with a purpose. In other words, the work does not simply float
free but must be taken to have been produced in particular circumstances and to a particular end. We may enquire after the illocutionary

23. Pratt, *Toward*, p. 86.

intentions of the author. It is no longer the case that the 'Intentional fallacy' bulks large in literary criticism as it once did, partly because in the use of the term 'implied author', there is a tool which rescues and places in a proper perspective the concept of an intent behind the production of a literary work. Put another way, as Chatman would state it, after 'the real author retires from the text... the principles of invention and intent [yet] *remain* in the text'.[24] Searle somewhat more robustly defends the notion of authorial intention, stating that no critic 'can completely ignore the intentions of the author, since even so much as to identify a text as a novel, a poem, or even as a text is already to make a claim about the author's intentions'.[25]

But, while speech-act theory foregrounds intention, it also provides a way of mediating between the poles of the intentionalist/anti-intentionalist debate, and of recognizing the role of the reader as the respondent in a literary speech situation. For literary speech-acts take place within a context, as do all speech-acts, and this context is broadly speaking the conventional expectations which surround the act. These expectations are as much those brought to the act by the reader as by the author. Or, to put the matter into the terms of 'rule-governed behaviour', rules, conventions, conditions, maxims (or whatever we wish to call them) provide the parameters within which both parties in the literary speech situation operate. Furthermore, when we consider the operations of implicature, we recognize that they arise as much from the inference-taking, deductive activity of the reader, as from the implicative strategies of the author. Indeed, part of the reason why a work takes on a life of its own is that the implicatures derived from the work are dependent upon the background (cultural, linguistic, ideological) out of which the reader makes his or her deductions. The history of the interpretation of any text is in part a history of the changing contexts out of which it has been read.

Context, then, is as an essential part of understanding literary speech-acts as it is for understanding any speech-acts. And implicature is in

---

24. Chatman, *Coming to Terms*, p. 75. But Chatman's comments here also witness to the fact that the debate behind the 'Intentionalist fallacy' has not gone completely. Chatman himself states that he 'stick[s] by the anti-intentionalist view that a published text *is* in fact a self-existing thing' (p. 81). On the notion of the 'implied author' as a compromise rescuing the place of the author in the face of the intentionalist/anti-intentionalist debate, see Lanser, *Narrative Act*, pp. 49-50.

25. Searle, *Expression*, p. 66.

operation at every level of literary speech activity, from the grammatical and syntactical through to the determination of genre.[26] As Lanser points out, not only does implicature provide us with 'a tool for acknowledging, naming, and studying the "gaps" in discourse—the unspoken assumptions and messages upon which meaning depends'— but it also 'expands the boundaries of discourse analysis by expanding the definition of discourse itself'.[27] We must expand the notion of 'text' from a formalist vision of words-on-a-page to the speech-act focus upon a verbal performance whose meaning is determined by having regard to 'co-texts and contexts'. In other words, it is a shift from the literary text to the literary act.[28]

Finally, speech-act theory may help us with the analysis of narrative both at the story level of the narrator's and the characters' speech-acts, and at the level of the implied author's discourse. Thus at the surface level we can analyze the speech-acts of the characters or of the narrator and derive an understanding of their intentions in terms of the nature and point of the speech-acts. At a deeper level, the level of the discourse, and also the sphere of the work's total speech-act communication, the meaning of the text is a function of the interplay between the illocutionary acts (more precisely the illocutionary point and force of the implied author's speech-acts) and their perlocutionary effects.

Speech-Act and Point of View

Point of view in a text arises out of the context of a dynamic relationship existing between an author and the audience, the speech-act itself and its content. As Susan Lanser puts it, 'the manner in which the message is received, interpreted and valued, depends on a complex of factors involving the speaker's relationship to the listener, the message and the verbal act'.[29] She identifies three 'dynamically interrelated aspects of the sender's position vis-à-vis the speech-act' which she terms status, contact and stance. In the production of a literary text, these factors operate 'pretextually' and 'extratextually', that is, they are part of the general context of the communicative situation which precedes the production of the text, and affect both the way in which

---

26. See here Lanser, *Narrative Act*, p. 76.
27. Lanser, *Narrative Act*, pp. 76-77.
28. Lanser, *Narrative Act*, p. 77.
29. Lanser, *Narrative Act*, pp. 85-86.

it is produced and the manner in which it is received by the reader. Traces of these factors of status, contact and stance are embedded in the text on its production and may be recovered by the reader as the communicative situation is reconstructed through reading. The degree to which this recovery is either successful or complete is, of course, affected by the reader's temporal and spatial distance from the 'culture text' ('the particular set of expectations, values, emotional conventions, norms and assumptions dominant or at least acceptable within a given community'[30]) within which the literary text had its genesis. We shall examine each of these factors in turn.

Status concerns 'the relationship of the speaker to the speech act' and encompasses a number of factors which relate to the speaker's status. It has to do with 'the authority, competence and credibility which the communicator is conventionally and personally allowed'. The first of these is the identity of the speaker, which is 'determined by the social hierarchies and roles in a given cultural community'.[31] In modern culture, the authority of a speaker vis-à-vis a given speech-act, or text, may be established prior to the reception of the speech-act or text, as when the speaker is introduced as an expert in the field, or the book's dustjacket identifies the writer's qualifications. In many cases it might be based on prior knowledge by the recipients that this person is a 'leading scholar' or 'well-known novelist'. This identity may go a long way toward securing 'uptake' for a given speech-act or text. But uptake may also be secured through the speaker's credibility in respect of the way in which the speech-act is performed, e.g. by the apparent sincerity and skill shown in conveying the message. As regards credibility Lanser writes: 'Even in the fictional text, statements and events must be motivated and plausible, and textual assertions must be meaningful within the created world: to the degree that these textual assertions posit connections with referential reality, they must be credible in the historical world as well.'[32]

The Fourth Gospel specifically works to secure uptake from its readers by drawing attention to the implied author's status, which it designates as that of an eyewitness, as one of Jesus' inner band of disciples. The credibility of the narrative is stressed by direct assertion; and undergirded by a narrative art which draws the narrator into

30. Lanser, *Narrative Act*, p. 93.
31. Lanser, *Narrative Act*, p. 86.
32. Lanser, *Narrative Act*, pp. 87-88.

proximity with the events being narrated. But, apart from this, for many readers the skill of the discourse has already established the authority of the author as a 'major theological genius'.[33] It is with the Gospel's credibility as regards the historical world that many modern readers have difficulty. This is, in part, the result of a clash of 'culture texts'; a rift between a pre-Enlightenment and a post-Enlightenment world view. We shall explore this in more detail in part two where we shall consider how a combination of conventional expectations and textual signals determine the way in which many modern readers receive the Gospel.

Contact refers to the relationship which a speaker or writer establishes with the audience. In an oral discourse, contact may be made through tone of voice, gesture, physical location. In written discourse, the relationship between author and audience may be reflected in the work itself, in the image of the reader (implied reader) created by the author. 'Contact may be established by direct comments that call attention to the speaker's relationship to the audience; the speaker may even explicitly define his or her presumed readership.'[34] Such a case is clearly seen in 1 John where the writer refers to his readers as 'little children' and 'beloved', thus implying a relationship of a more mature believer to those who are less mature, or under the writer's pastoral care. The author also specifically designates the readers as 'fathers, young men and children' thus making a differentiation in the age or social status of the readers (though 'children' may be an inclusive strategy, again implying that all are under his oversight).

Contact is established both by physical and by psychological means. The actual physical appearance of a text, the size of the print and the arrangement of the text, can affect a book's reception. As an instance, small, densely printed text may suggest 'difficult, scholarly (boring?) material, while large print surrounded amply by "white space" suggests somewhat lighter and easier fare'.[35] We can only guess at what written material would have suggested to many people in the largely aural-oral cultures of the first century CE: perhaps education and wealth; perhaps even, because of its relative inaccessibility to many, a

33. See e.g. Hengel, *The Johannine Question*, pp. 96, 134. He states that two hundred years after his death, the author was given 'the unique honorific title *ho theologos*' (p. 134).

34. Lanser, *Narrative Act*, pp. 91-92.

35. Lanser, *Narrative Act*, p. 91.

certain weightiness of content, so that ἡ γραφή already carried with it an aura of authority. On the other hand, given that texts were generally read aloud, and that the gospels in particular were meant for public reading, factors such as poetic structure, vivid narrative and fluent discourse would have been important techniques in achieving contact.[36]

Psychological means of establishing contact are by such things as discourse register and tone. Here the Fourth Gospel presents the modern reader (and perhaps the first century one, too) with some puzzles. The provision of translations of key Aramaic words such as Μεσσίας and 'Ραββι suggest implied readers for whom Aramaic (or even Hebrew) was not their first language. Also, the constant reference to 'the Jews' appears to put the implied author at some distance from that race. Indeed, it lends to the work a decidedly polemical, anti-Jewish flavour. Yet, at the same time, the Fourth Gospel betrays a very Jewish character. In manner of expression, the implied author seems often to display a semitic turn of mind. He was also, it would seem, well acquainted with Hebrew narrative style.[37]

Stance has to do with the speaker's relationship to the utterance being made. It designates the perspective from which the speaker views his or her subject matter. As Lanser says, '[b]ecause all discourse conveys some stance or range of stances, and because stance is a powerful determinant of what is said and how it is expressed, the way in which a message is received and understood is considerably dependent on the way the stance is presented and the relationship of that perspective to the reader's own, or to the "culture text"'.[38] The analysis of a speaker's illocutionary acts can help to bring an understanding of the stance, which is carried both explicitly by the illocutionary force of the speech-act and implicitly by implicature.[39] At the level of the story—the surface level of the narrator's speech activity—I suggest that the application of Stanzel's theory of narrative situations is helpful for illuminating the stance of the narrator. In the Fourth Gospel, the narrator's stance is also that of the implied author. Below or behind

36. See here P.J. Achtemeier, '*Omnes Verbum Sonat:* The New Testament and the Oral Environment of Late Western Antiquity', *JBL* 109.1 (1990), pp. 3-27.
37. Consider the use of 'type scenes', repetition, '*leitwörter*'. In fact many of the features which Alter explores in *The Art of Biblical Narrative* appear in the Fourth Gospel.
38. Lanser, *Narrative Act*, pp. 92-93.
39. See here Lanser, *Narrative Act*, pp. 79-80.

the illocutionary activity of the narrator, then, is that of the implied author which may be recovered by paying attention to the particular illocutionary point or force of a given illocution, and to the perlocutionary effects of the statements made. The illocutionary point and force of the discourse as a whole is the sum total of the illocutionary acts contained within it.

Lanser also states that '[w]hile *status* most centrally affects the degree to which a message is valued by a receiving community, *stance* co-determines the emotional and ideological response the audience will take from, *and bring to*, the discourse'.[40] This usefully reminds us that stance is something which derives not only from the attitude of the speaker to the locutions performed but also from the attitudes which readers bring to their reading and understanding of those locutions.

Speech-Act Analysis of John 20.30, 31 and 21.24, 25

1. *20.30, 31*

The narrator supplies the reader at 20.30, 31 with the purpose of the Fourth Gospel. It provides a useful starting point for an analysis of the narrator's speech-acts for not only is it a very clear statement of intent, but understanding the illocutionary and perlocutionary acts performed here helps to undergird and confirm the reader's understanding of the status of the speech-acts in the gospel as a whole. In respect of this it is important to remember the close connection that exists between the narrator and the implied author. The narrator is the implied author's mouthpiece and understanding the narrator's speech-acts is a clue to understanding the implied author's intent. (Thus, in keeping with my perception of this relationship I will refer most often to the activity of the implied author.)

The two verses under consideration contain two assertions: (1) that Jesus performed many signs in the presence of his disciples (more than are contained in the book) and, (2) that Jesus is the Christ, the Son of God, belief in whom brings life. But it will be seen that a closer look reveals a complex illocutionary act containing within it several types of illocution.

It will be helpful to take the two verses separately. The assertion in 20.30 may be broken into two subordinate assertions, in order to bring out what is implicit within it (remembering always that in the

40. Lanser, *Narrative Act*, p. 93 (emphasis mine).

actual speech-act no clear distinction is made between the parts; and
that this locution belongs with the next in v. 31):

> Jesus did many signs in the presence of his disciples.
> Many of these signs are not recorded in this book.

The operation of implicature means that from the second of these
assertions the implied reader derives a number of conclusions. The
present text represents a selection of 'signs' from a wider number
available or known to the implied author. This principle of selectivity
is reiterated and underlined by the implied author at 21.25. Also
implicit here is the fact that the selection has been made with a particular end in view. The purpose is made clear in the following verse
to which we shall come in a moment. For the present we should note
that what is also implied is that certain purposes and intents are *not*
in view. Readers looking for a full account of the 'signs' of Jesus will
be disappointed. Moreover, the implied author does not intend to
supply all the details of Jesus' life; nor, perhaps, should the reader
expect that he is governed by considerations of chronological, or
logical, exactitude.

Read in conjunction with the reiteration of this principle of
selectivity (21.25), where the hyperbolic statement is made that 'the
world could not contain the books that would be written', the reader is
encouraged to accept, by implicature, that the scale of Jesus' activity is
such that it bursts the bounds of this world. Not only would the record
of his activity require a superabundance of books, but, in a sense, the
world itself is not big enough to contain him. Thus, just as the book
begins with intimations that its subject matter bursts the bound of
earthly time, so too it outstrips available earthly space. Of course, it
might be that here the implied author has employed a conventional
form of expression. Nevertheless, the illocutionary force of such
expressions is to make large claims for the subject matter.

That Jesus did his signs in the presence of his disciples is one of the
themes of this gospel. We shall see below that it is a claim made both
implicitly and explicitly that this book records signs witnessed by
someone close to Jesus. As the statement made here follows immediately upon the pericope in which Jesus appears to his disciples, including
Thomas, and in the light of Jesus' words to Thomas that those who
have not seen and yet believe are blessed, the implication is that the
resurrection appearance is itself one of the signs.

The implied author's use of the word 'sign' here has occasioned much scholarly discussion about what precisely is meant by the word.[41] In part this arises through the search for a 'Signs Source' but it is also because some commentators are concerned to restrict the reference of the word 'sign' to 'miraculous event' or 'miracle'. This is, I believe, a mistake. There is no doubt that the implied author uses the term σημεῖα to refer to the miracles which Jesus performs and, by extension, the resurrection may be understood as a miraculous event along with the others. But it is far more the implied author's concern to bring to the reader's attention the question of the status and identity of Jesus. In this regard, the signs are by way of identifying marks, indicators, signposts, or tokens of this status and identity. In so far as this is the case, any number of events and acts which Jesus performs may be taken as signs. Indeed, I shall argue below that the Temple cleansing episode is itself a sign (and perhaps the implied author intends this thought to occur to the reader, by implication, when Nicodemus's statement at 3.2 is read). Furthermore, the account of the piercing of Jesus' side, and the flow of blood and water (19.31-37), also functions as a sign to the reader, supported by scriptural texts which corroborate the claims made for Jesus by the implied author and the textual indications of his identity. Thus, in the Fourth Gospel, the term 'sign' is used not to identify a given class of event or action (namely, a miracle), but to serve as a marker, or a question to the reader, requiring him/her to infer what should be understood about the character of Jesus in the light of the event.

Verse 31 supplies the basis on which the selection of signs has been made.

> These are written that you may believe that Jesus is the Christ, the Son of God, and that believing you may have life in his name (RSV).

'These' may refer to the 'signs', or more generally to all that has been written ('these things') about Jesus in the gospel. However, following on from the statement that not all of the many signs Jesus did have been recorded in this book, the ταῦτα δὲ (*'but* these') must suggest to the reader that the implied author refers to the selected signs which are written in his gospel.

41. See here Brown, *John*, pp. 1058-59; R. Schnackenburg, *The Gospel according to St John* (New York: Crossroad, 1990), III, pp. 335-37. The issue is complicated by the reference to 'other signs': which signs are these and are they mentioned elsewhere in the discourse or do they refer to signs not used by the implied author?

3. *Speech-Act Theory and Meaning in the Fourth Gospel*   87

We note that two assertions are made here which we shall distinguish, though again in the mind of the implied author they are inextricably bound together.

> Jesus is the Christ, the Son of God.
> The reader, by believing in him, may have life in his name.

The appropriateness conditions for these two assertions are fully laid out in the narrative which has preceded this illocution. The Gospel has shown the reader what is meant by the statement that 'Jesus is the Christ, the Son of God' and how it is that the reader may have life in his name. Because this study will examine in detail some of the ways in which this is done through the structure of the narrative, we shall reserve a fuller summary of this point to the conclusion. Suffice to say that the signs and the discourses are intended as proofs and explication of these assertions. Thus the discourse as a whole serves to fulfil the preparatory rules, and Grice's maxims of quantity and quality. The role of the disciples as witnesses, and the claims made for the eye-witness status of the beloved disciple in particular, fulfil the essential and sincerity rules, or again in Gricean terms, the maxims of quality. Indeed, implicitly in the narrative (e.g. at 2.17, 22; 19.35) and explicitly here and at 21.24, 25, the implied author is invoking the co-operative principle by assuring the reader that he has good grounds for writing what he does, that he can be trusted (he has his material on good authority) and that it is relevant to the interests of the reader.[42]

As assertives, the two propositions have a word-to-world direction of fit. The Fourth Gospel's implied author seeks to apprize the reader of a state of affairs which already exists. He wants to inform the reader that the Christ has appeared in the world and was known as Jesus, the one from Nazareth. But more than this, this Jesus who was and is the Christ, is also 'Son of God', one who existed with the Father before creation (1.1, 2), who as incarnate Logos identified himself

---

42. If the implied readers are to be taken as being Christians, this relevance will be already accepted; though the implied author may feel they need reminding of it (perhaps in view of their current circumstance) or he may wish to move the relevance on to a higher plane by drawing out for his Christian readers a fuller and deeper significance contained within the statement that Jesus is the Christ, the Son of God, and hence giving them a more acute understanding of their relationship with him and what is entailed thereby. If the implied readers are non-Christian, the relevance is more by way of an invitation to find abundant life by accepting the proposition that Jesus is the Christ, the Son of God, and all that follows from that.

with the Father (5.17, 18; 8.58; 14.9) and made the Father known (1.18; 14.9-11; 17.6), and as resurrected Lord has now returned to the Father, while yet present with his own through the Spirit. Here we may note an important comment by D.A. Carson, who writes: 'Above all, it can be shown, that with very high probability, the *hina*-clause must on syntactical grounds be rendered "that you may believe that the Christ, the Son of God, is Jesus". That means that the fundamental question being addressed by the Evangelist is not "Who is Jesus?".... but "Who is the Messiah?".'[43] This, I think, correctly sets the terms of the question. The narrative seeks to show that the evidence of the signs, which are supported by scripture, all point to the fact that the long-awaited Messiah has arrived in the person of Jesus. Of course, the question 'Who is the Messiah?' might be answered equally by the response, '*Jesus* is the Messiah (or Christ)', as by the response 'the Messiah is Jesus'. The verbal construction of the locution is immaterial in that respect.[44] However, the implied author does not simply wish to establish the fact that Jesus is the Messiah, but also to give the reader a fuller and deeper understanding of what this claim means. In other words, he wishes also to answer the question: 'What is the nature of Messiah? How should the concept of messiahship be understood?'[45]

This deeper understanding of what it means to call Jesus the Christ (messiahship on a 'higher plane'),[46] is presented through an omniscient narrator who from the outset establishes the origins of Jesus as being 'from above', one to whom titles such as Logos, and son of God apply as equally as does that of 'Christ'. He also achieves this through the characterization of Jesus who through discourse and debate with others, notably 'the Jews', seeks to bring his interlocutors to a deeper and greater appreciation of his being and his relationship with the Father. The repeated failure of the Jews to understand who Jesus really is, points to the necessity for a shift in stance if true understanding is

43. Carson, *John*, p. 662.
44. As D.A. Carson shows in 'The Purpose of the Fourth Gospel: John 20.31 Reconsidered', *JBL* 106.4 (1987), p. 644.
45. Here Carson, *John*, p. 662 n. 2, states that the question, 'Who is Messiah' is an identity question rather than a question about the kind of person Messiah would be. I disagree—it is precisely this question which the Gospel seeks to address. In fact, Carson admits as much, see refs. in next footnote. See also J. Painter, *The Quest for the Messiah* (Edinburgh: T. & T. Clark, 2nd edn, 1993), p. 9.
46. See here Carson, *John*, p. 663; and his 'Purpose', p. 647.

to be made possible. The discourse makes clear that this change of stance must be founded upon a willingness to come to Jesus and to believe in him: only from a believing perspective is his true identity seen (cf., *inter alia*, 3.3, 11; 5.39, 40; 6.29, 44, 45; 7.16, 17).

As kerygma and as gospel these assertions also function as declarations in that they seek to bring into being the 'world' which they also assert. In the overall context of the gospel, the implied author wants to bring his readers to share his belief that Jesus is the Christ, the son of God and through this shared belief to enjoy the benefit which flows from it, that of having life in his name. The purpose of his narrative is so to affect their worldview, that they orient their lives in accordance with what follows from accepting his assertions. The illocutionary act is to persuade, the perlocutionary act is to convince and confirm belief. As declarations, then, the assertions have both a world-to-word and a word-to-world direction of fit.

Now the assertions are encompassed within two *hina* purpose clauses. Within the immediate context of the total illocution that is 20.31, then, this world-to-word fit is established by the illocution being both a directive and a commissive. In other words, the illocution is an attempt by the implied author to get the implied reader to do something, namely, to believe. It is also a promise, not as such committing the implied author to do something, but rather committing him to the truth that certain (beneficial) consequences will accrue to the reader in the act of believing.

Let us express the directive like this: 'I (the implied author) have written this that you may come to know and believe that Jesus is the Christ, the Son of God.' In its illocutionary force, this is by way of an invitation (a request even?) or an exhortation. Here the textual evidence has left the commentator (the modern reader) with something of a puzzle, and a quandary which at this distance from the original context of this illocutionary act, may never be entirely settled. It is that the verb in the phrase 'that you may believe' is rendered in the manuscripts both by the present subjunctive (πιστεύητε) and by the aorist subjunctive (πιστεύσητε).[47] Textual support is such that the issue is pretty evenly balanced in favour of either reading. The Committee preparing the third edition of the UBS Greek New Testament 'considered it preferable to represent both readings by enclosing σ

47. Πιστεύητε is read, *inter alia*, by P[66] (apparently), ℵ*, B, Θ. Πιστεύσητε by ℵ[2], A, C, D, f[1], f[13].

within square brackets'.[48] The twenty-sixth edition of Nestle-Aland does likewise.

Barrett provides a nice definition of the difference when he writes: 'The present subjunctive (strictly interpreted) means "that you may continue to believe, be confirmed in your faith", the aorist "that you may here and now believe, that is, become Christians".'[49] The issue raised is whether the implied author is addressing those who are already Christians, in which case his purpose is to encourage them to continue to believe, to remain firm in their belief: and perhaps also to deepen their understanding of Jesus, the Christ in whom they are to have faith. On the other hand, if the gospel is written for non-Christians then the purpose is apologetic and evangelistic. Even a decision in favour of one tense against the other will not entirely settle matters for the implied author is, at times, somewhat loose in his use of tenses. Brown states that the aorist, as well as 'implying that the readers are not yet Christians', may also be used 'in the sense of having one's faith corroborated', and he cites John 13.15 (*sic*) in support.[50]

Given that neither textual witness nor tense can settle the issue, we must look to the total content and context of the gospel to provide an insight into the implied readership. But here too we find puzzles which leave the issue open, for there are features which suggest both types of readership. On the one hand, a non-believing readership seems to be implied, especially as the first twelve chapters are directed towards showing who Jesus is, that is, revealing his 'glory'. The prologue leads up to the introduction of Jesus, who is shown there and throughout the narrative as the revealer of the Father and the one who brings light and life. There is a clear statement of what one must be (and do) in order to receive salvation (1.12, 13). The narrative expands on and explicates this theme and there are paradigms of seekers (unsuccessful and successful) in Nicodemus (ch. 3), the Samaritan woman and compatriots (ch. 4) and the blind man (ch. 9). Jn 12.37-50 provides a kind of summary of the situation in the time of Jesus' ministry: despite the fact that 'all the world has gone after him' (12.19 REB), most in fact

48. B.M. Metzger, *A Textual Commentary on the Greek New Testament* (United Bible Societies, 1971), p. 256.

49. Barrett, *John*, p. 575.

50. Brown, *John*, p. 1056 (the reference should surely be to 13.19, or perhaps 11.15?); see also Carson, *John*, p. 662, Schnackenburg, *John*, p. 338, Lindars, *John*, p. 671.

refuse to believe, though some do believe (even among those in authority) albeit secretly. Jesus, standing as it were on the edge of his 'hour' again issues the challenge of belief in him—salvation for those who believe, judgment for those who do not. It is as if the implied author turns also to the implied reader and asks: 'And you, where do you stand on this question of belief in Jesus?' For Jewish readers here is an apologetic which helps explain why Jesus was not recognized or accepted as Messiah by 'his own'.

On the other hand, the discourse implies a Christian readership. Certainly a readership already familiar with aspects of the Christian tradition, the imprisonment of John the Baptist, for example, and his baptism of Jesus,[51] the 'twelve' (6.67, 20.24) and possibly their names (οἱ τοῦ Ζεβεδαίου mentioned casually as if already known[52]). Also chapters 13–17 would seem to fit well in a book whose purpose was to encourage Christians in their faith; as would the theme of 'abiding' (remaining) in Christ which runs, explicitly and implicitly, throughout the discourse.

Thus we have a narrative, a text, where physical and psychological contact with the implied author is ambiguous. In part this is because the transmission of the text has left us with a locution whose original form is no longer known. We may be certain that the implied author wishes to promote faith in Jesus: again whether his narrative is intended to convert to faith or to confirm in faith is not certain. The discourse implies, as many commentators recognize, that two types of readership are in view: both non-believer and believer. Divorced as we are from the original context of production we cannot know which type is prior. In fact, as we shall see below, the structure of the narrative suggests that neither is to be considered prior. The discourse has a double focus. In the first twelve chapters, the implied author primarily addresses those in whom he wishes to evoke faith. In John 13–21 the

---

51. Ref. 3.24; 1.32-34; of course, the imprisonment of the Baptist may have been a generally known fact. Whether the implied author, and his implied readers, knew the Synoptics is much debated. Obviously, he was in touch at a number of points with a common tradition. Though on 1.32-34, that this implies a knowledge of the baptism of Jesus by John is an inference drawn from the modern reader's post-canonical perspective: it must remain a matter of conjecture whether first-century readers would have made the connection.

52. There is, of course, the problem of whether Nathanael is to be taken as a member of 'the twelve' and if so how this name relates to those on the Synoptic lists.

attention is upon those in whom faith has already been implanted.

The commissive which is contained (at least implicitly) in this statement, we may express in this fashion. '[I promise that] if you believe that Jesus is the Christ, the Son of God, you will (in this act of believing) have life in his name.' Or, '[I promise that] if you continue to believe that Jesus. . . (in the continuation of your belief) you will have life in his name.' Expressing the matter in the form of a commissive captures, I believe, what is the perlocutionary effect intended by the narrative taken as a whole. It is that the reader may be assured that to believe in Jesus is to adopt a stance that is life-giving. Again, this perlocutionary act is possibly directed at a dual readership: believer and non-believer. The intention is both to confirm and build up this life-giving faith, and to convince and convert to this faith.

2. *21.24, 25*

We turn now to the final two verses of the gospel, namely, 21.24, 25. Jn 20.30, 31 are widely accepted as the conclusion of the gospel as originally produced, while ch. 21 as a whole is taken as an added appendix. I do not share this view but as it is only peripheral to our present concern, I have kept the discussion until later (below pp. 109-13). The concept of an 'implied author' does allow for the work of more than one author, as we have seen (see above pp. 45-46), so that we need not rule out under its rubric the possibility that several persons had a hand in the composition of the Gospel. The locution itself identifies the beloved disciple as the author: at the very least this is implied. Even if it is not the case, the locution need only require one author, who was associated with the authoritative source known as the beloved disciple, and who vouched for the reliability of that source on behalf of a wider community of believers (perhaps disciples of the beloved disciple).

It should be noted that the immediate context of these verses is the issue of the eventual fate of the beloved disciple. A rumour has been circulating that the beloved disciple would not die, based on the words of Jesus to Peter and the implied author is concerned to set the record straight. The illocutionary point of the locution has been misunderstood. Jesus never said that the beloved disciple would not die, merely that it ought to be no concern of Peter's should Jesus wish the beloved disciple to 'remain' until he comes. Many have felt that the death of the beloved disciple has occasioned this corrective reminder of Jesus' words, lest the failure of the rumour to hold good should bring disillusionment and loss of faith among the believers. I reserve judgment on this and think it possible that the beloved disciple is still alive at the time of writing and wishes to quash speculation about his fate. And, in any case, the issue here, in the implied author's view, is not interest in the fate of another disciple (be it the concern of Peter, 'the brothers', or the implied reader), but one's own commitment to discipleship. It is well within the bounds of possibility that this most elusive of disciples should couch his language in oblique third person reference. Nothing must detract from his central concern which is to bear witness to Christ. In this respect, John the Baptist's attitude, 'He must increase, I must decrease' (3.30) is the beloved disciple's (viz. implied author's) attitude as well.

I will take this further. What is uppermost in the implied author's mind is not the death of the beloved disciple but his remaining until the Lord comes. It is possible, reading with ℵ*, C² and others that the locution at 21.23 is something like this: '... but Jesus never said that he would not die, but, "If I wish it that he remain until I come..."'.[53] Perhaps, by implicature, the implied author is saying something about the coming of Jesus (the *parousia*), and is hinting or hoping that it may be soon.[54]

This is, of course, speculative. Yet I think that what is uppermost in the implied author's mind in supplying this double ending is the theme of witness: both the validity of his narrative's witness and the continuation of that witness. And, if the reading of 21.23 just suggested is in any way correct, then what is also implied by the statement left hanging ('If it is my wish that he should remain until I come...') is that witness will continue into the future.

With this in mind, we turn to the analysis of the illocutionary act contained in 21.24, 25. Again, it will be helpful to note that this contains three assertions.

53. Nestle-Aland²⁶ and UBS³ enclose the phrase τί πρὸς σέ in square brackets, and Metzger, *Textual Commentary*, p. 257, gives it a {D} reading, which indicates a high degree of doubt as to whether its inclusion is original. The addition of the phrase in ℵ¹ suggests scribal activity in making 21.23 agree with 21.22.

54. That is, the reader is implicitly invited to say 'And may it be soon!' or to ask, 'Might it be soon?' (completing, as it were, the incomplete statement). Cf. Rev. 22.20: Ἀμήν, ἔρχου κύριε Ἰησοῦ. Whether the implied author intends to evoke all that goes with *parousia* expectation in early Christian thought is another matter.

> The beloved disciple is the witness whose authority stands
> behind what is written.
> His testimony is true.
> Jesus did many other things.

These assertions have been put here in a very generalized way in an attempt to state what is, I believe, the heart of the propositions being put forward. This is because, for reasons of textual and semantic uncertainty arising from the phraseology used, the actual locution may be read in a number of different ways, as the commentaries well testify. Nevertheless, the illocutionary point and force is not thereby materially affected. Let us take each assertion in turn.

The beloved disciple is the witness whose authority stands behind what is written. We may leave aside the matter of the confusion of the textual evidence as being scarcely material to understanding the over-all sense of the locution. Again the matter of whether the present participle, ὁ μαρτυρῶν, necessarily signifies that the beloved disciple is still living hardly need detain us. Whether still living or not, it is on the basis of his authoritative witness that this narrative is promulgated. Of course, if he is dead then the question is from whom this illocution derives. At issue is the understanding of the verbs γράψας and οἴδαμεν. On γράψας we may note Barrett's comment that '[i]t is conceivable but perhaps not probable that [this] should be translated "caused to be written", and means no more than that the disciple was the ultimate and responsible authority for "these things"'.[55] The issue largely turns on scholarly conjectures as to the possible identity of the implied author; on whether he might have been an eyewitness (i.e. the beloved disciple) or someone writing at his behest, or merely drawing upon traditions with which the beloved disciple is connected (assuming that the beloved disciple is more that just an 'ideal disciple figure' created by the implied author).[56] Whichever way the issue turns, the point of this assertion, supported by others in the gospel (cf. 19.35), is that the narrative is based upon eyewitness authority, and that this authority is the beloved disciple. Quite apart from this, the gospel evidently draws upon traditions shared by the Synoptics and must, therefore, have some basis in primitive witness. The way in which the implied author's narrative art establishes clear links between the

55. Barrett, *John*, p. 587.
56. John 21.23 surely implies that an historical figure is in view. See also, Charlesworth, *The Beloved Disciple*, pp. 13, 141-42.

authority of the beloved disciple and the status of the implied author will be further examined. The relationship between the narrative and historical reference will also be explored.

His (the beloved disciple's) testimony is true. The actual locution is, 'we know that his testimony is true'. The crucial question raised by commentators, then, is what should be understood by the use of the second person plural form (*we* know).[57] My own view is that this is an inclusive 'we' (used on a number of occasions by the implied author, for instance, at 1.14, 16; 3.11) whereby the implied author includes others besides himself: whether they be fellow eyewitness disciples of Jesus, the community within which this witness operates, or, in fact, the wider group of believers, the 'church'. (Indeed, at 1.16 it almost certainly includes all believers.) But a decision against such an inclusive 'we' and in favour of some other referents, such as the community which publishes this narrative and wishes to corroborate it with an 'imprimatur', does nothing to alter the force of the illocutionary act. It is to vouch for the narrative's veracity and trustworthiness by appealing to its source of authority.

In this regard, what is of most interest in speech-act terms is that taken together these two assertions, or the illocution which contains them (21.24) is a specific instance of the fulfillment of the essential rule and the sincerity rule: that the speaker commits himself to the truth of the expressed proposition (in this case, the 'these things', τούτων, that is, the total narrative) and to a belief in the truth of the expressed proposition. By implication, the illocution also suggests fulfilment of the preparatory rules, or in Gricean terms, the maxims of quality; that is, that the speaker is in a position to provide evidence for the truth of the expressed proposition. Thus the illocutionary point of these statements is to secure the validity of the witness expressed in the gospel.

Jesus did many other things. This third assertion is expressed, of course, in a much fuller locution: 'But there are many other things which Jesus did; were every one of them to be written, I suppose that the world itself could not contain the books that would be written.'

---

57. Brown, *John*, p. 1124, points out that Chrysostom reads 'I know', perhaps taking οἴδαμεν as οἶδα μέν. Brown finds it a problem that a third person and a first person pronoun should be used in quick succession by someone referring to himself. It would be more likely, he feels, that we would find something closer to the form at 19.35, 'He is telling what *he* knows to be true'. What a person would or would not do must, of course, remain at the level of subjective assessment.

Expressed thus, the reader is immediately put in mind of 20.30 and so, in the light of the hyperbole in this statement, understands by implicature that what is found here is but a selection of the information on Jesus available, or known, to the implied author. It is also possible that this concluding statement is of a conventional sort found in other literature of this type.[58]

The phrase, 'many other things which Jesus did' means, most probably, that the implied author has in mind (and makes general reference to) other deeds and events in the life of Jesus contained in the tradition and known to him, and perhaps to at least some of the readers. It, like the 'I suppose' which has much exercised commentators, is very likely just part of the conventional 'throw-away' comment with which he concludes his book.[59] At any rate, the difficulties and the discussion occasioned by the use of 'I suppose' ought to remind us that at this temporal distance from the time of writing, we may analyze the illocutionary acts, and decide upon their illocutionary point and force, with perhaps more surety than we can reconstruct the actual circumstances of the act of production or the speaker of the locution!

What conclusions regarding the nature of the gospel as a whole may be drawn from the narrator's speech-acts at 20.30, 31 and 21.24, 25? We have seen that the implied author is, explicitly and implicitly, guiding the reader to understand certain things about the narrative which he/she has just read. The story is based on the authoritative witness of a source close to the main character, Jesus. This source is the beloved disciple. The purpose for recounting this story is in order that the reader may come to believe certain things about the Christ, namely that he is Jesus, the son of God. The perceptive reader of the narrative will know what depths lie in that claim. The implied author's desire is that, in believing, the reader will have life in the name of Jesus. Again the perceptive, thoughtful reader will now know how

58. See here Bultmann, *John*, p. 697 n. 2; Brown, *John*, p. 1130. On the conventional habit of selectivity and editing in ancient *bioi*, see R. Burridge, *What are the Gospels?* (Cambridge: Cambridge University Press, 1992), pp. 142-43 and *passim* under 'scale', 'allocation of space' and 'topics'. On the Fourth Gospel, cf. especially pp. 224-25.

59. I use the term 'throw-away' in the manner of a modern's assessment of a conventional tag! To the implied author, as to other writers of the time, these were far from being 'throw-away' but were intended to enhance the authority and importance of their subject matter, and their discourse, in the minds of their readers.

believing comes about and what it entails.

The reader will also understand that certain perlocutionary acts flow from these assertions. First, he has been supplied with all the information necessary to come to an informed decision about Jesus. This information rests upon the securest, most trustworthy of authorities. The perlocutionary effect is to convince and persuade. Of course, whether this effect is achieved in reality is not within the purview of the implied author. Readers are at liberty to accept or reject at all levels. They may refuse to acknowledge the authority of the witness. (The implied author, all too aware of this fact, works hard to secure uptake on this point.) They may also reject what is claimed for the narrative's main character. To do this, the discourse warns, is to bring themselves into judgment.

Second, implicit within the principle of selectivity is the understanding that the narrative is directed towards certain ends. It is not intended to be a complete account of the acts of Jesus but has at its heart theological motivations. The implied author wishes to set the deeds of the historical Jesus, those aspects of his life which he chooses to recount, within the context of the wider significance of Jesus' true status. He seeks to persuade the implied reader to a belief in Jesus which is shaped by an understanding of his true nature as presented in the story: it is a theologically motivated historical narrative.

But as an historical narrative, the degree to which the implied author secures uptake of its truthfulness to historical actuality, depends to a great extent upon the 'culture-text' within which it is received. The 'culture-text' established since the Enlightenment, at least in the Western Church, has been one which has led to skepticism toward the historical reliability, or usefulness, of the Fourth Gospel. I will argue that this skepticism is based on dichotomies drawn between 'history' and 'fiction', and between the historical task and the theological enterprise which are no longer useful or sustainable.

The Fourth Gospel's Speech-Acts as Discourse-Act

In the preceding section we examined the specific speech-acts contained in 20.30, 31 and 21.24, 25. Now we must broaden the scope to take in an overview of the speech-act achieved by the Fourth Gospel as a whole. The implied author communicates the meaning of his narrative directly by statements he makes, through the narrator, to the implied reader (such is the case with the verses examined above). He also communicates meaning indirectly through the speech-acts characters make to other characters, as in, for example, Jesus' discourse with Nicodemus, or in the farewell discourses directed at the disciples. Beyond both of these, the implied author communicates meaning by the overall structure of the narrative discourse. That is, the Fourth Gospel itself is a macro speech-act which is the result of the cumulative effect of the individual speech-acts performed in the narrative, and the implicature set up by these speech-acts. For the sake of convenience, I shall refer to the speech-act represented by the Fourth Gospel as a whole as the discourse-act.

The process of understanding the meaning of the Fourth Gospel may be put like this. If we were to enquire after 'the work's intent', to borrow Chatman's phrase, we would recover it as the overall illocutionary stance taken by the implied author and the accumulation of the discourse's perlocutionary effects on the implied reader. The work's intent, the speech-act achieved by the Gospel as a whole, that is, the discourse-act, brings together the implied author's communication with the implied reader both at the surface level (the level of communication between narrator and narratee, characterization and plot) and at the deep level of implicit commentary or communication by the artifice of implicature: irony, symbolism, motif and so forth.

Analysis of the discourse-act, under the aegis of traditional literary criticism, would entail a discussion of the themes of the Fourth Gospel. But it is important to realize that 'themes' arise out of the total act of communication just described.[60] In other words, a 'theme' is what an implied author has put into the narrative through narrative art and act.[61] It is also determined by what an implied reader takes out of the narrative in the process of decoding the implied author's message. Beyond the confines of the text, theme also arises through the understanding and experiences which both real author and real reader bring to the narrative communication situation from life and the general cultural context.[62] The terms 'theme' and 'themes' provide, as it were,

---

60. Cf., on 'theme', Abrams, *Glossary*, p. 111.

61. As well as elements at the surface level of narrative art (characterization, plot, setting etc.) other elements often subsumed under 'theme' (see Abrams, *loc. cit.*) such as *motif*, *leitmotif* or *topos* belong to this creative activity.

62. Important here are the intertextual resonances between the text and other earlier texts.

a convenient shorthand way of referring to the narrative evidence of this complex process.

The Themes of the Fourth Gospel: Textual Indications
The themes of the Fourth Gospel are introduced in the narrative's prologue (1.1-18) and are developed as it progresses. A full discussion of the narrative's themes cannot be entered into here. We are, in any case, not concerned so much with discussing each of the themes to be found in the Gospel, as in examining how the implied author conveys the meaning of the Gospel, and an understanding of its themes, by the way in which he structures the discourse as a whole. However, in order to set the stage for what follows, I must briefly outline what I take to be the narrative's leading themes, and some of the overt textual indications by which these are established.[63]

The first major theme has to do with the status and identity of Jesus as the Christ, the son of God, and revealer, *par excellence*, of the Father. This 'christological' picture of Jesus emerges from the story through a number of narrative strategies. One is the ascription of titles or abstract nouns to the person of Jesus either by the narrator (Logos, Light, son of God), or by a character e.g. John (lamb of God, 1.29, 36), Andrew (messiah, 1.41) or Nathanael (son of God, King of Israel, 1.49). Jesus' status (δόξα) is revealed through the overt claims he makes (3.13; 4.26; 5.17, 19-24; 8.57) or in the images he uses to define his self-identity. The 'I am' sayings are a good example of this latter case (cf. 6.35; 8.12; 10.7, 11; 11.25; 14.6; 15.1). Other statements link Jesus' claims about himself directly with assertions or descriptions of Jesus' significance made by the narrator (12.46, cf. 1.4, 9; 5.26, 7.38 cf. 1.12, 13). The narrator presents Jesus performing miracles (2.1-11) or prophetic acts (2.13-21) which point to his dual role as the one who fulfills scriptural prophecies of the Messiah and also establishes a new 'Israel' constituted upon himself rather than a Mosaic regime of law and Temple.[64] The argument for who Jesus is,

---

63. In a narrative as richly textured as this, readers may readily detect other themes. This survey is not to be taken as exhaustive. Other readers might wish to add other themes and even rank them more highly than these. However, whatever themes might also be perceived as being present in this discourse (themes, for instance, to do with ecclesiology, pneumatology or eschatology) those listed here are unmistakably central.

64. We might describe this as a theme of the 'replacement' of the old Israel founded by Moses by the new Israel founded by Jesus. I use the word 'replacement'

then, is a cumulative one based on the narrator's explicit commentary, the flow of the story itself as it presents Jesus' significance in deeds supported by words and scriptural references, and by implicature.

A second theme is that of witness to Jesus and the authentication of the claims made for him. It answers the implied reader's question: 'How can I know that Jesus is who he is claimed to be?' The events recorded in the story are 'signs' which point to the true signficance and nature of the one performing them. The words of Jesus (often attached as a discourse to one of the deeds) function to amplify and draw out the inner meaning of these 'signs'. Many of the characters serve as witnesses to Jesus: John (1.19-36 and 3.27-36),[65] the Samaritan woman (4.28, 29) and Martha (11.27) to name but three. Witness and validation also comes from God, the Father (3.2, 31-35; 5.17, 19, 30, 31, 37; 8.54; 12.28; 14.10, 11; 17.7, 8). The Paraclete and the disciples will fulfill their function as witnesses in the future beyond the time of the story. Their witness takes place in the time of the discourse, for the story is a selection of the many 'signs' which Jesus performed in the presence of the disciples but which are only fully understood and hence able to be passed on after Jesus has risen from the dead, when the Holy Spirit has been given.

The witness of the Holy Spirit and that of the disciples, then, is introduced into the narrative proleptically. The Holy Spirit will aid the disciples in their witness (by process of ὑπομνησις/ὑπομιμνήσκειν) but the disciples will also be able to act as witnesses by virtue of their having been with Jesus 'from the beginning' (15.26, 27). Note that the words ἀπ' ἀρχῆς, and the fact that the verbs are in the present tense (μαρτυρεῖτε, ἐστε), set up a parallel between the disciples' presence with Jesus from the beginning, and the presence of the Logos with God 'in the beginning' (1.1). In contradistinction to the Synoptic Gospels, the first event in the activity of Jesus sees him gathering disciples, or

advisedly, as the Johannine thought may not be that Jesus displaces or replaces the divine intention for Israel expressed in the Torah but that he brings it to its full and essential completion. In Jesus, 'Israel' as it is truly meant to be is fully realized and in this sense 'all who came before are thieves and robbers' (10.8) and, insofar as the Jews of his day have diverted Israel from its true course by rejecting Jesus, they are 'children of the devil' not children of Abraham (8.39-47) and stand accused even by Moses (5.45, 46).

65. There is some doubt as to whether 3.31-36 represents John's words or the narrator's words. For a discussion of this feature, and its signficance, see below chapter 5, pp. 153-54, 157-58.

having a group of disciples gather around him. Thus his public activity begins in the presence of disciples. Again in contrast to the Synoptics, nowhere in this story is a specific calling of 'the twelve' recounted. In the Fourth Gospel there is no account of the disciples being sent out on a missionary tour during Jesus' ministry, as there is in the Synoptics.[66] In this story the accent falls not so much on their calling or function as apostles, as on their role as witnesses.

A third theme is that of response to Jesus. This theme seeks to answer the implied reader's question: 'What are the implications of this portrayal of Jesus' status and identity for me?' Fundamental to the exploration of this theme is the stark division made between 'light' and 'darkness' (3.19-21; 12.35, 36); between those who 'see' and those who are 'blind' (9.39-41). The implied reader is left in no doubt that there are only two options available in response to the claims made for (and by) Jesus: they may be rejected or they may be accepted. Nothing should be taken for granted, for the story presents the paradox that when the Christ came to his own people, they did not receive him (1.11; cf. 5.39-47).

However, among the individuals who encounter Jesus, the implied author portrays a range of responses which enables him to explore all the ambiguities and nuances of belief in Jesus.[67] These characters represent a continuum of response-types ranging from those who hold to a secret belief or fragile, fallible commitment, to those who progress from uncertainty or skepticism to full confession. Characters may come to a tenuous and faltering belief as does Martha. She confesses Jesus to be the Christ (11.27) yet cannot quite understand that he can be the resurrection and the life (11.39, 40). On the other hand, the blind man represents one who moves from believing that Jesus is some sort of wonder-working prophet to a full and frank worship. Throughout the gospel the ambiguities of response to Jesus are set forth in all their variegated hues. Many believe in him, yet Jesus will not trust himself to them (2.23-25) and he recognizes that for many the response is motivated by little more than a desire for marvelous proofs (4.48; 7.21) or self-interest (6.26). Among the disciples there are those who

66. Although John 4.1, 2 appears to indicate that they engaged in baptizing people (at Jesus' behest?). These verses present something of an interpretative crux. I think this may be an instance of the narrator bringing in an observation on the church's activity at the time of writing.

67. See here Culpepper, *Anatomy*, pp. 104, 145-48.

do not believe (6.64) or who pull back when they find Jesus' teaching too difficult to accept (6.66). Even within the inner core of discipleship there is a 'devil' (6.70). The narrator conveys the impression that throughout the ministry of Jesus, response to him was mixed and ambiguous. He conveys this as much by the juxtaposition of contrary statement (7.25-31; 12.42, 43) as by portraying inner debate amongst the people (7.11-13). Nevertheless, however ambiguous and uncertain the response of many may be, in the discourse of Jesus the issue is clear. Belief in him brings life and the removal of judgment; lack of belief condemns one already to judgment (3.17-21).

Associated with this theme of response to Jesus, is that of remaining in him. It has long been recognized that μένειν (to stay, live, abide, remain, continue) is one of the theme-words of this narrative. It evokes, and associates itself with, many other themes of the Gospel. For instance, the first two disciples to follow Jesus ask him, 'Rabbi, where are you staying?' (῾Ραββί, ποῦ μένεις;). Jesus' invitation to 'Come and see' is also an invitation from the implied author to the implied reader to follow his story and discover where Jesus is truly from. It emerges that he is 'from above' and his true place of abode is with his Father (16.28). This is a closely woven and richly textured theme which gives rise to many of the narrative's subtleties of symbolism and irony. Jesus is the Logos who was with God but who came to dwell for a while among humankind (1.1, 14).[68] He is the one, coming from the bosom of the Father, who has come to make God known (1.18). When Nicodemus (3.2) or the disciples (16.30) acknowledge that Jesus has come from God, do they truly understand what this means? Much of the Gospel's irony is built on the inability of his hearers to understand what Jesus means when he says that he is from the Father.

The theme of remaining is also associated with the idea of having new life in Jesus. Those who have God's word abiding (μένοντα) in them (as the Jews manifestly do not) will come to Jesus and find life (5.38-40).[69] Anyone who keeps Jesus' word will be loved by the Father, and, together with Jesus, he will take up his dwelling (μονὴν) with him or her (14.23). Having eternal life is a matter of being incorporated into Jesus' fold by entering through the door (10.9), and by incorporating Jesus into oneself (in an almost literal sense, the discourse

68. The verb used at 1.14 (ἐσκήνωσεν) is evocative of the dwelling and remaining of the Shekinah amongst the Israelites in the wilderness.

69. Is there an association here with the Logos of the prologue?

suggests; 6.52-58). Thus, the one who eats and drinks of Jesus' flesh and blood abides (μένει) in him (6.56). Eternal life, so gained, begins now, and in the future there is the promise of a dwelling, specifically, in one of many rooms (μοναί) where Jesus is with the Father (14.2).

Not only does abiding in Jesus give an entry into eternal life, but it is also the essence of discipleship (15.1-11). Remaining in Jesus is a prerequisite for continuing as a disciple, and it opens the door to the fruits which discipleship brings (15.4). Among these are the privilege of receiving what is asked for (15.70) and of receiving the gift of the Holy Spirit, who will dwell (μένει) with the disciple for ever (14.16, 17). Remaining in Jesus means bearing fruit that will last (ὁ καρπὸς ὑμῶν μένῃ) foremost of which is love for one another (15.12-17, see especially v. 16). As the narrative ends, it opens to a future in which the beloved disciple might possibly remain (μένειν) as a witness until Jesus comes.

We have been examining textual indications of the Gospel's themes. This largely entails an analysis of the narrative's surface level where plot, settings, characterization, dialogue and narrative comment combine to create the total discourse-act. Many of the speech-acts are explicit, carrying an overt illocutionary point or force, or performing specific perlocutions. Thus, the implied author explicitly delineates the δόξα of Jesus by his use of titles, images, scriptural quotations, confessional statements from characters, or direct narrative comment. Together these provide a number of assertives which contribute to the Fourth Gospel's summary assertive that Jesus is the Christ, the son of God. They are also the means by which the implied author fulfills the preparatory rule for assertives and honours the maxims of quantity and quality.

On the other hand, the speech-acts, either in their individual implicatures, or by a cumulative implicative effect, take the implied reader below the surface level to the deeper level of communication. Here the implied author implicitly sets up intertextual resonances with the Jewish scriptures, or cultural expectations and beliefs of the time.[70] Communication also occurs through the network of associations set up within the text. The implied author may approach a theme openly by

---

70. See, for example, J.L. Martyn, *History and Theology in the Fourth Gospel*, (Nashville: Abingdon Press, 2nd rev. edn, 1979), chapter 6, on the Gospel's argument that Jesus is the expected Moses-like Prophet/Messiah.

the use of theme-words (e.g. μαρτυρεῖν, μένειν, γινώσκειν[71]) or *leitmotifs*; or more by way of implicature in the way in which a word or phrase recurs, or through the delineation of character. A response may be openly invited from the reader, as in the narrator's comment at 20.30, 31 or 12.44-50 (see further below p. 106) or by implication, as the reader watches and weighs the response of a character, and associates or disassociates him/herself from the stance displayed in the narrative.

Themes: Structural Indications
The themes outlined in the previous section are so intertwined in the discourse that it is difficult to disentangle them. This is because, of course, they belong together. C.H. Dodd, writing about the Gospel's structure, has likened it to a musical fugue in which themes are successively introduced and interwoven to produce an 'intricate pattern' in 'an artistic and imaginative whole'.[72] Yet, to change the metaphor, there is an ebb and flow in the manner in which these themes appear. M.-F. Lacan, writing about the structure of the prologue, has described its movement as being like waves on a beach.[73] It is, in many ways, a helpful image for the structure of the narrative as a whole. A particular theme, or cluster of themes, may appear at one point, as it were surging up the beach. Then this theme, or theme-cluster, will recede while another takes its place. At the same time, there is often an overlap of themes, and traces of an earlier theme may later reappear. Thus, the structure of the discourse suggests that one must hold in tension two dynamics: one in which the themes follow successively, yet interweave one with another; the other in which they surge and recede, each dominating the narrative at some points and falling into the background at others.

Taken as a whole, the narrative displays two major thematic movements. Study of the Gospel has long revealed that the narrative falls into two blocks. One runs from 1.19–12.50; the other continues from ch. 13 until the end of ch. 21. The prologue should be set aside as an

71. To mention but three; others of importance in this study are λόγος, δόξα. . . cf. also here, Davies, *Rhetoric*, especially e.g. chapter 7; or Mussner, *Historical Jesus*, chapter 3.

72. C.H. Dodd, *About the Gospels* (Cambridge: Cambridge University Press, 1952), pp. 36-37.

73. M.-F. Lacan, 'L'Oeuvre du Verbe Incarné', *RSR* 45 (1957), p. 76.

3. *Speech-Act Theory and Meaning in the Fourth Gospel*   105

introduction to the Gospel as a whole for, as suggested above, all the major themes outlined above appear in embryo in these first eighteen verses.

In the first section of the narrative, 1.19–12.50, the implied author is particularly concerned with the theme of Jesus' identity and status. Here he presents the reader with a picture of Jesus as he was known by the first witnesses of his δόξα. This theme is played out in the public arena of Jesus' ministry in Judea and Galilee. Jesus' public acts, many of them performed at or near the time of a Jewish feast, are the catalyst for an ongoing debate about his identity. In this first section of the narrative, Jesus is on public trial amongst his own people.[74] It is an informal trial which proceeds to a formal, and more private, trial before Pilate in the second section. Ironically, the people are themselves also on trial (as are 'the world' and Pilate later): they are required to respond to Jesus, to weigh his words and works and decide on this basis whether he is from God or not (7.16, 17; 10.37, 38), and whether or not he is the Christ (10.24-30).

The issue of response to Jesus is also a dominant theme. What does it mean to respond positively to Jesus? What are the causes and the consequences of a negative response? The narrator presents the multitude of responses elicited during Jesus' ministry and charts the growing opposition on the part of the Jerusalem authorities and others who reject Jesus. These first chapters represent the day of salvation, the time of opportunity before the gathering gloom brings on the night of crisis (12.31 κρίσις) and judgment. The section ends with a significant episode in which some Greeks seek an audience with Jesus. It is the cue that 'the hour' has arrived (12.27). Now it is time for the judgment of this world to begin when Jesus will enter into his glory (or rather, when his true stature will finally be revealed) and which in turn will bring salvation to all peoples (12.32). The Greeks, who enter the narrative to make the request, 'Sir, we wish to see Jesus' (12.21), and are thereupon forgotten, are representatives of the wider world; they stand on the brink of a new era of salvation. Interestingly, however, the implied author has chosen to anticipate this broader realm of mission in the account of Jesus' meeting with the Samaritan woman, which opens onto a mission to the whole village. That scene closes

74. A.E. Harvey, *Jesus on Trial* (London: SPCK, 1976), specifically examines the Gospel under the trial motif. On the change of focus from 'public' to 'private' at Jn 13, see pp. 104-105.

with the Samaritans affirming that Jesus is the 'Saviour of the world' (ὁ σωτὴρ τοῦ κόσμου).[75]

It is important to note that the narrative includes a coda at this point (12.37-50); a conclusion to the first movement, as it were. The narrator reports that despite the many signs Jesus has performed, the Jews did not believe him. He then quotes from the second of the Servant Songs (Isa. 53.1) and from the passage where Isaiah receives his commission to preach (Isa. 6.9, 10)[76] by way of explaining the Jews' unbelief. Coming at this point in the narrative, after the failure of both John's testimony and Jesus' preaching to win the Jews, Isa. 6.9, 10 carries an added poignancy. Nevertheless, all is not entirely lost, for some do believe, even among the authorities, though secretly (being more concerned, says the narrator, about their honour among men than their standing with God; 12.43).[77]

There follows in 12.44-50 what Brown describes as a 'summary proclamation'. The reader notes that, according to the narrator, Jesus has already gone into hiding. This fact leads Brown to assert that the discourse is not in its original context, and to quickly summarize some proposals as to its displacement. Happily he allows that 'the redactor's judgment was a good one, for his discourse, which now comes at the end of the Book of Signs nicely summarizes Jesus' message'.[78] What Brown fails to note, because he misunderstands the nature of the speech-act here, is that the intended audience is the implied reader. By introducing these words of Jesus into the narrative at a point where there is no audience and no setting, and where the narrator's commentary has already effected a turn to the reader, the implied author directs these illocutions (and their perlocutions) at the implied reader. This is a summary proclamation intended not for the public of the story world but for the public of the discourse-act, that is, the readers to whom the story is narrated. (Perhaps, the Greeks are a textual evocation of the

75. Cf. chapter 7, pp. 241-43, on the reasons why Jn 4.1-42 is placed where it is.

76. These, especially the first, were favourite '*testimonia*' in the early church, and would resonate with 'subtext' for the first Christian readers.

77. It may well be, as the theses of Martyn, *History and Theology in the Fourth Gospel*, and Brown, *The Community of the Beloved Disciple*, would suggest, that the implied author is directing his narrative to 'crypto-Christians' within the local Jewish synagogue.

78. Brown, *John*, p. 490; cf. his title for this section on p. 489. In the context of this study for 'redactor' read 'implied author'!

implied readers.) In placing this kerygma of Jesus here (note the verb ἔκραξεν: this *is* indeed a proclamation), the implied author not only provides a summary of Jesus' message, but issues an invitation and a warning to the reader. It may be rendered something like this: 'You, too, have now "seen" (read of) Jesus' signs. If you believe, you may join those on whom the light shines, who may leave the realm of darkness and receive power to become a child of God (cf. 1.9-13). Refuse to believe and you will be judged by the logos (a pun on the Logos?) which Jesus has spoken.' The proclamation ends with a final reminder about the divine source of its authority.

I have noted that Jesus' δόξα and response to Jesus are major themes in this first section. Witness is also an important chord, but more in terms of the authentication of Jesus' status brought by the witness of the Baptist, the signs, the Father, the preaching of Jesus and so forth.[79] Now, as the second major movement of the narrative begins, the emphasis falls on the themes of witness (in terms of the testimony of the Spirit in the life of the believer, as well as the believer's own witness) and of 'remaining' in Jesus. Rather than draw the distinction too finely between these two movements (after all, they belong to the one narrative through which the themes run in major and minor key) it would be better to say that there is now a turn from outward public teaching to inner private teaching. Or, we may say, the focus shifts from the public arena of proclamation, where the foremost questions have to do with Jesus' identity and status and response to him, to the inner circle of the believer, where the issues are discipleship and bearing witness.[80] Under the issue of discipleship are included such matters as the character of the Christian community: the defining characteristic is ἀγάπη and the unity that flows from this (13. 34, 35; 15.12-17; 17.20-24[81]); and the footwashing episode (13.2-17) is the model of this love in action. It includes also the question of commitment, and faithfulness, and the believer's relationship with the world (15.18-21). Witness has to do with the role of the Holy Spirit, not only in maintaining the disciples' faith and continuing the teaching ministry

79. We should note that scripture also has an important testimonial function.

80. Note how this latter movement begins with an emphasis on Jesus' love for 'his own' (13.2). In other words, Jesus has withdrawn from public ministry among 'his own people' (12.36) and now concentrates on the encouragement and building up of those who are truly 'his own'.

81. Notice, too, how unity flows from a shared δόξα (17.22).

of Jesus, but also in equipping the disciples for witness by bringing to their minds all that they have learned from Jesus. The disciples' own witness in the world is also important here and, as we shall see in a moment, is brought to the fore as the story closes.

We have seen, then, that the implied author has structured his discourse so that the themes emerge in two major sections: the first with an outward, and the second with an inward looking focus. I have characterized these as waves, for the themes surge and recede in both sections, more dominant at certain points than at others, bringing different aspects to the fore at different times. Within these two major waves are a series of smaller waves. To put the matter more in terms of the discourse's literary structure: the implied author often presents his argument in a series of doublets, or repetitions. This doubling or repetitive effect allows the implied author to treat a theme or themes from a number of different angles; or, alternatively, to put the focus upon one theme before moving on to explore another.[82] It is this wavelike, doubling and repetitive effect which accounts for the narrative's double ending found in chs. 20 and 21.

We might note, before passing to these two endings, that it is this doubling or repetition which might account for one of the discourse's most puzzling aporias. This is the presence at 14.31 of the words, "Rise, let us go hence". This statement appears misplaced because the discourse (ending with Jesus' prayer for the disciples) continues for three more chapters and there is no indication of a move until 18.1. This feature has led scholars to conclude that the farewell discourse is a combination of two separate discourses (perhaps more?) and that the original discourse ended at 14.31. At the same time it has been noted that there are parallels and repetitions between the first and latter parts of the discourse. I suggest that what we have at 14.31 is a form of narrative caesura.[83] It brings the implied reader to a pause, and

82. The implied author's practice, at least in the central section of the narrative, to narrate a sign which serves as a 'visual aid' for the discourse to follow, is a strategy of reinforcement allied to this repetitive effect. There is, unfortunately, not the space to develop this point here.

83. 14.31 is a further instance of what can occur when there are apparent gaps in a narrative. The temporal linearity of the narrative leads the reader to expect a statement such as 'Rise, let us go hence' to be followed by an account of the leaving. When it does not, or when it is delayed as in this case, the reader then fills the gap with interpretive speculation. One such is the theory that the implied author wishes the implied reader to understand a departure occuring here and the continuation of the dis-

allows the implied author to begin apparently on a fresh line of thought, while bringing in matters which have already been raised, so that these are not only repeated but amplified and given emphasis. There is a certain contrastive parallel between 14.1-7 and 15.1-10 in that one speaks about a dwelling place with Jesus in the future while the other speaks about the disciples' present abiding in Jesus. However, in terms of the narrative structure, it is more likely that 15.1-17 (and perhaps even the whole of ch. 15) stands in parallel with the account of the footwashing and the departure of Judas which begins this latter major section. So often in this narrative, illustrative event is followed by elaborative discourse and vice versa,[84] that one suspects that the implied reader is meant to pick up resonances between 13.1-30 and 15.1-17. There are correspondences in the ideas: washing by Jesus, pruning by the Vinedresser; the departure of Judas into the night and the casting out of the fruitless branch; the need to be part of Jesus (by being washed) and the need to abide in the vine; the example of Jesus' humble, loving service and the command to love (15.12-17; cf. also 13.34, 35). Note that there is a correspondence of certain key words e.g. καθαρὸς, καθαροί (13.10, 11), καθαίρει (15.2), δοῦλος (13.16, 15.15), ἐξελεξάμην (13.18, 15.16), and cf. ἐντολὴν/ἐντολὴ, ἵνα ἀγαπᾶτε ἀλλήλους (13.34, 15.12).

Our discussion of the double ending of the narrative, that is 20.30, 31 which is followed by ch. 21, must begin with a defence of ch. 21 as an integral part of the narrative.[85] It is largely because 20.30, 31 carries with it such a strong sense of closure that readers consider the Gospel must originally have ended here. John 21 is regarded as an

course in another place. Thus, the references to the vine, and vinedressing, evokes an imagined scene whereby Jesus delivers this discourse while pointing out frescoes of vines on the Temple building, or as they pass through vineyards on the way to the garden (cf. Brown, *John*, p. 583; or Carson, *John*, p. 479). Alternatively, on another reading, the statement, 'Rise, let us go hence' might be an invitation to a spiritual readiness to engage the prince of this world (Dodd, *Interpretation*, pp. 407-409).

84. See, for instance, the feeding of the five thousand which is followed by the discourse on the bread of life. I suggest that the farewell discourses pick up on the footwashing episode (13.1-17) and, by reverse process, are picked up in the rehabilitation of Peter (21.15-22), see below p. 113.

85. On Jn 20 and 21 as a double ending, see B.R. Gaventa, 'The Archive of Excess: John 21 and the Problem of Narrative Closure', in R.A. Culpepper and C.C. Black (eds.), *Exploring the Gospel of John* (Louisville: Westminster John Knox Press, 1996), pp. 240-52.

appendix, which has been added at a later date, or is, more properly, the result of (and evidence for) redactional activity on the part of editors. But 20.30, 31 follows on immediately from the appearance to Thomas when Jesus, having heard Thomas' great affirmation of faith, commends those who believe without the benefit of having seen him. This is a statement directed at the implied reader and so it is an appropriate point for the implied author to underline the fact that the purpose of his narrative is precisely to elicit that belief from his readers. It is, arguably, this turn to the reader and the statement of the Gospel's purpose that evokes in the reader a sense of closure. However, it must be recognized that these verses are more important for their illocutionary force and perlocutionary effect than for their closural function. We shall see that they do provide a thematic closure but the narrative continues, and an analysis of resonances with earlier themes and an understanding of the structural flow of the discourse reveal that the verses which follow belong with the rest.

Certainly, on stylistic grounds there is no conclusive evidence that John 21 comes from another hand. Though the assessment of stylistic features inevitably turns somewhat on subjective judgment, on balance it would seem that the style of the chapter is sufficiently Johannine to warrant the conclusion that it is penned by the implied author of the previous twenty chapters. Many of the instances where significant differences in the vocabulary are noted, derive from the fact that the words used are appropriate to the circumstances of the event described. Some of the other less distinctively Johannine vocabulary is not so easy to account for, though the implied author's fondness for variety and the use of synonyms may account for some of the instances (e.g. οὐ μακρὰν for ἐγγύς, πρωΐας in place of πρωΐ, ἐπιστραφῆναι rather than στραφῆναι).[86] A more subtle artistry may be at work in some cases; e.g. the use of παιδία reflecting a new, intimate relationship (cf. 1.12, or 15.15).

On the whole, the style betrays many of the characteristic ways in which this implied author expresses himself. In his choice of vocabulary and phraseology, we might instance the use of the characteristically vague μετὰ ταῦτα to link this pericope with the previous section, or the use of ἐκεῖνος (21.7); ἀμὴν, ἀμὴν (21.18); σημαίνων (21.19

---

86. On the stylistic features of this pericope see the commentaries, especially Barrett, *John*, pp. 576-77; Brown, *John*, pp. 1079-80; Bultmann, *John*, pp. 700-701; or Carson, *John*, pp. 665-66.

cf. 12.33); ὀψάριον (21.9). Notable, also, is the way in which the writer reverts to the use of the historic present (see e.g. 21.13, 20 = βλέπει; and the present tense use of ἐστιν (21.4) and λέγειν (*passim*). The incident is recounted in a typically laconic manner, leaving the reader to fill in the details, or else to puzzle over the gaps in the story. For instance, when Peter learns that the stranger on the shore is Jesus, he throws himself into the sea. That he does this so that he can swim ashore to greet Jesus ahead of the others must be inferred from what follows. Jesus later asks Peter, 'Do you love me more than *these*?' but the implied author leaves the referents of the word 'these' unspecified. No explanation is given as to how Jesus is able to have some fish already cooking on the fire when the fish-laden boats come to shore.[87] The terse, simple construction of the sentences is such as we have come to expect from this author.

But it is the thematic unity of this chapter with what has gone before that is decisive in regarding John 21 as integral to the narrative. We have seen how the Gospel examines the themes of the identity and status of Jesus and response to, or belief in him, and those of witness to and remaining in Jesus; and how it does this in two great movements, or thematic 'waves'. The encounter with Thomas brings the first of these thematic waves to its climax. The narrative has presented its portrait of Jesus, it has put before the reader the signs selected by the implied author to convey his significance; and it has illustrated types of believing response to him and the rejection of his status by 'the Jews'. Now, this appearance of the risen Jesus elicits from Thomas the narrative's last and, in many ways, its greatest affirmation of faith: 'My Lord and my God!'. It is the only appropriate response, the implied author infers, to the Jesus portrayed in his story. Immediately he turns to the implied reader and invites a similar response. It is a fitting end to this aspect of the Gospel's message.

Next, the implied author moves to bring to a climax the second

---

87. If there is a significant subtext lying behind the details of the large catch of fish and the prepared breakfast, it is likely to have to do with the role of the disciples in continuing the mission of Jesus, equipped with resources that Jesus himself supplies (cf. 20.21, 22). More particularly, the large catch may illustrate the principle of the 'greater works' enunciated at 14.12; while the fact that this is achieved only when obedient to the command of Jesus (21.6) and is superfluous to his own work (represented by the fish already cooking) illustrates the fact that without Jesus they can do nothing (15.5).

great thematic wave; and to close the narrative as a whole. 21.1 begins
with a deliberate mention of three significant characters found in the
preceding story. First he mentions Simon Peter, who has lately denied
Jesus, and over whose discipleship a question hangs. It is his rehabilitation as a disciple, in a commissioning for service combined with a
renewed call to follow Jesus, which forms the centrepiece of this
account. In 21.18, 19 the implied reader will be reminded of this
fallible disciple's ultimately faithful witness to death. Next, the implied
author refers to Thomas, the disciple who has just been shown to move
from doubt to belief; and in whose mouth has been put the supreme
confession of faith which the implied author invites his reader to make
(or to re-affirm) for him/herself. Third, he speaks of Nathanael. In so
doing, he deftly provides an inclusio with the early scenes of the
Gospel, and reminds the reader of a disciple who, like Thomas, moved
rapidly from skepticism to belief and in whose mouth was also placed
a resounding affirmation of Jesus' status. Nathanael, the implied reader
recalls, was described by Jesus as a 'true Israelite': he is the paradigm
of those who are truly Jesus' 'own people'. The implied author proffers
the previously unmentioned detail that Nathanael was from Cana in
Galilee, the location of the first two events which were explicitly
designated as 'signs'. Thus, three disciples are named here who have a
significant role in the discourse-act. Nathanael and Thomas are para-
digmatic types of a true response to Jesus. The way they are characterized as moving from unbelief to belief represents in concentrated
form the journey every believer is called to make. Peter is a representative type of discipleship and belief in Jesus rounded out to present
these aspects in all their hues.[88]

It must be admitted that the mention of the sons of Zebedee which
comes next is a puzzle. It is possible that they are mentioned because
this is how the event was remembered, or, if the implied author is
elaborating upon a tradition shared with Luke (cf Lk. 5.1-11), it is
simply their presence in the received tradition which accounts for their
inclusion here. It is also possible, given their absence from the story
so far, that this is the closest that the implied author comes to revealing
his identity or the identity of the beloved disciple. Any reader familiar
with a Synoptic-type tradition will, perhaps, have already included the
sons of Zebedee in the narrative by inference. The disciple John may
have been identified as Peter's companion in the high priest's courtyard,

88. See further below pp. 135-37.

and at the tomb.[89] However, the reason for their inclusion here must, in the end, remain conjectural. It is possible that, at this distance from the original context of the narrative's production, the modern reader no longer shares with the first readers the common knowledge which would provide the key to unlock the mystery. The reasons for the presence of the two unnamed disciples here will be examined below (cf. pp. 131-33). As the internal evidence that the beloved disciple is to be identified with one of the sons of Zebedee is not strong, I contend that the implicit message of the narrative is that the beloved disciple must be one of these unnamed disciples (and *ipso facto* not the apostle John).

Having set the scene, the implied author turns to the matter in hand, which is to round out the themes of discipleship and witness. The result is a story rich in subtext and symbolism which cannot be examined in detail here. Suffice to say that the rehabilitation of Peter resonates with teaching found in the farewell discourse and elsewhere. First, the need to abide in Jesus' love and to express love for Jesus in the service of fellow believers and in obedience to Jesus' commands provides an intratextual subtext for the three-fold challenge and commission (21.15-17). Second, the fact that in Peter specifically (and in the disciples generally, for Peter is the representative disciple) the work of Christ continues: the Chief Shepherd commissions the under-shepherd to continue the care of the flock (cf. 17.18-21; cf. 10.16).[90] Third, as the reference to Peter's eventual death demonstrates, 'in the world [the disciple] will have tribulation' (16.33). Suffering, persecution, and possibly even death, are all to be expected if one follows Jesus (15.18–16.4). Each is called to a personal faithfulness, each needs to remain united to the vine, regardless of the fate of others (21.20-22). The ringing command, 'You follow me!' (21.22) serves as a fitting conclusion to this narrative, and as a pointed reminder to the believing implied

89. Arguments for identifying John, son of Zebedee, as the author of the gospel may be found in the major commentaries. Perhaps, the most significant intertextual clue for identifying John with the beloved disciple would be the central place that the two sons of Zebedee have with Peter in the Synoptic tradition. James, John's brother, is put out of contention as a candidate because of his early martyrdom (cf. Acts 12.1, 2).

90. If, as is possible, the event rests upon an historical base; and if, as I think likely, Peter had a part in writing (causing to have written!) the First Epistle of Peter, then 1 Pet. 5.1-5 may well derive in part from Peter's remembrance of his lakeside commissioning.

reader that this is what discipleship is all about.[91]

In the closing sentences of the narrative, the spotlight falls upon the story's putative implied author. It is his witness that stands behind this story; it is his witness that is true. It is his witness that continues for, even though he will die, his story will live on. In a very real sense his witness remains, living on in the narrator and his narration. Of all the books that could be written about Jesus (and there are many), this one achieves its purpose. The beloved disciple, who has lain close to the bosom of Jesus, has seen the Son and has made him known.

I began this discussion of the discourse-act by referring to the fact that the implied author's speech-acts are performed both at the surface level of individual speech-acts performed by the narrator and by the characters. I stated also that the Gospel as a whole is itself a discourse-act; it is the implied author's speech-act. By both explicit and implicit commentary, the implied author achieves his theological purpose and conveys his message. Irony, implicature, imagery, and symbolism, *leitwörter* and *leitmotif*, *topoi* and themes, all combine to provide a network of signification. And this network is achieved by the overall structure of the narrative, as part relates to part, as scene and summary, as dialogue and commentary, as characterization and plot-sequence all interweave to produce a total act of illocutionary stance and perlocutionary effect.

As is the case with any complex speech-act, especially a literary speech-act, implicature opens up areas of indeterminacy which invite interpretation. It is the nature of narrative, in its mediated aspect (which includes the selectivity of the material used) and its temporal linearity, to open up gaps and textual fissures which invite the reader's affective and interpretive response. It is because the implied author has put his theological message about Jesus into story form (rather than say as an apologetic argument, or theological discourse as found in a Pauline epistle, or even as a collection of sayings such as the Gospel of

91. If the following verse be taken to mean that the beloved disciple has died, then vv. 23-25 may well be the later addition of an 'editor', acting as spokesman for the beloved disciple's community, reminding the implied reader (members of the community?) that Jesus never said that the disciple would not die, and hence allaying misapprehensions or disappointments arising from his death. He also vouches for the reliability of the beloved disciple's witness (a speech-act which surely looks to readers beyond the community) and concludes with a 'conventional' closing statement which picks up once more the thought of 20.30.

Thomas) that it opens up such wide vistas of meaning and gives it interpretative depth. But how the story is told helps to determine what the story means. We proceed in the next two chapters to examine how the telling of the tale has helped to structure the meaning, and how point of view is conveyed through narrative mediacy.

Chapter 4

THE BELOVED DISCIPLE AS A REFLECTOR-CHARACTER

The Issues

The beloved disciple appears in John 13–21 as an anonymous and elusive figure. Yet there is a curious solidity to the characterization: he materializes in the narrative in a wholly substantial way. So much so that he is often referred to in Johannine scholarship as the Beloved Disciple (and very often now as the BD!). The figure of this unnamed disciple, then, exercises a fascination over the reader and has thrown up a host of questions and puzzles. Why does the beloved disciple emerge only in the latter part of the Gospel, and what is his place and function in the narrative? Why is he anonymous? How does he relate to the anonymous disciples mentioned at 1.35, 37 and 18.15, 16? Can he be identified with any of the named characters or with an historical person? What is his relationship to Peter? What is the beloved disciple's relationship to the discourse, that is to the telling of the story, or, to put the matter in more traditional terms, to the composition of the Gospel? We have already begun to consider these questions in Chapter 2, where I gave an outline sketch of the way in which a variable narrative situation modulates the narrator's relationship to the story world, and thus affects the reader's spatio-temporal orientation both to the story and to the implied author. In Chapter 3, we considered how speech-act theory might affect a reader's understanding of the nature of the speech-acts performed, especially where the implied author gives clues to illocutionary stance and perlocutionary intent.

In this chapter, I wish to extend the discussion of the narrative situation which emerges in John 13–21, as well as to look at some of the other narrative dynamics which determine the status and place of the beloved disciple within the narrative, and the function he serves. Insights drawn from speech-act theory, particularly relating to the expectations generated by the co-operative principle and the dynamics of implicature, combine with this analysis of narrative strategy to describe the way in which the status, place and function of the beloved disciple is implanted and secured as the narrative is read. These dynamics of narrative mediacy and communication have implications for the point of view adopted by the implied author and the reader's perception of this. Scarcely any of the exegetical points proposed or the conclusions drawn will be entirely new, though hopefully they will be freshly illuminated by a different approach. What is achieved here, I think, is that a methodological framework is provided to give names to the processes by which others have reached their conclusions. For example, many have argued the connection between the occasions when the beloved disciple appears in the narrative, and other occasions when an anonymous disciple (or disciples) have appeared, but have not always been able to articulate the narrative dynamics by which this linkage occurs. Many have noted the operation of implicature and described the signals by which it occurs (the words 'implied', 'very probably', 'almost certainly' and other such indications of implication occur frequently in scholarly discussion) without realizing the rule-governed structure which determines the outcome. The discussion here will lend support to some conclusions already established within scholarship and, by contrast, may render others less cogent.

It is impossible to survey all the many solutions proposed in answer to the questions raised by the beloved disciple's presence in the narrative. The questions themselves are interrelated and answers to one have implications for an understanding of the others. In broad outline, however, scholarly interest in the issues may be summarized under three headings: the identity of the beloved disciple, his function in the Gospel, and his relationship to the production of the Gospel. The issue of *identity* has largely been approached by asking whether the beloved disciple may be identified with an historical person known to tradition. Here, attention has quickly focused upon the ascription of the Gospel to 'John' and the traditional association of this ascription with the apostle John, the son of Zebedee. Other Johns, such as John Mark or John the Elder, have also been proposed. Identification of this sort cannot be decided on the basis of the text alone, but only by recourse to external evidence from tradition. This issue will thus be treated as a subsidiary question and set aside.[1] Not that the question is unimpor-

---

1. For discussion, in addition to the commentaries, see a useful survey in J.A. du Rand, *Johannine Perspectives* (Doornfontein: Orion, 1991), chapter 3 and, for

tant, and given that the Gospel may have circulated with the title KATA IΩANNHN from the outset, it has important implications for the status the narrative has traditionally enjoyed, and for matters relating to authorial 'contact' with intended and actual readers.[2] But the tradition leaves scholars in some doubt as to which John is meant, and, as we shall see, there is nothing in the narrative to provide a clear connection with any named figure, textual or historical. While it is recognized among scholars that the external evidence must be assessed separately from the internal, it is perhaps inevitable that, given the nature of the external evidence, the fact that the internal evidence tends to invite speculation, and the conventional or dogmatic interests of both readers and the Church, the two should often be confused.

On internal evidence, Lazarus has also been proposed as a figure, historical and/or literary, with whom the beloved disciple may be identified. For literary reasons, there is some justification for this and we shall have to return to the matter later. B.F. Westcott represents an early attempt (at least in English scholarship) to identify the implied author on the basis of internal evidence (i.e. questions of form, style, vocabulary, themes, implied cultural context and so forth). Inevitably, perhaps, in view of the weight of tradition, his examination leads him by careful stages to the apostle John.[3] By contrast, Margaret Davies begins her survey of the implied author by examining the external evidence (which, in her view, does not support authorship by the apostle John) and then concentrates on the textual indications by which an image of the author may be constructed.[4]

The question of the beloved disciple's *function* in the narrative

patristic evidence (and argument in favour of identification with John the Elder), R. Bauckham, 'Papias and Polycrates on the Origin of the Fourth Gospel', *JTS* 44.1 (1993), pp. 24-69.

2.   The addition of the word εὐαγγελίον to the title in some manuscripts is also important in terms of status and contact (for discussion of these terms, see above pp. 81-83). There is some doubt as to when the titles were attached to the Gospels, but it may have been about 125 CE. See Burridge, *What are the Gospels?*, p. 192; Carson, *John*, pp. 23, 24. On titles, see M. Hengel, *Studies in the Gospel of Mark* (London: SCM Press, 1985), pp. 64-84.

3.   B.F. Westcott, *The Gospel according to St John* (London: John Murray, 1882), pp. v-xxviii; the author was a Jew, a Jew of Palestine, an eyewitness, an apostle, St John. Cf. also L. Morris, *Studies in the Fourth Gospel* (Grand Rapids: Eerdmans, 1969), pp. 218-56, where he builds on and extends Westcott's arguments.

4.   Davies, *Rhetoric*, chapter 11.

turns, for the most part, on the issues of anonymity and his relationship to Peter, which has very often been seen as one of rivalry and competition. Many have regarded the characterization of the beloved disciple as an attempt on the part of the implied author to portray him as superior to Peter. Thus he represents a more faithful disciple, one who is more percipient than Peter and who perseveres to the end. The motivation for this relationship has been variously attributed to a desire to undercut a notion of Petrine supremacy, or to portray the adversarial relations existing between different branches of the early Church, e.g. Johannine versus apostolic,[5] Gentile in contrast to Jewish, or to represent differing concerns, e.g. spiritual versus ecclesiastical.

The perceived contrast with Peter, coupled with his anonymity, has led many scholars to consider that the beloved disciple functions as an 'ideal disciple', whether as an idealized historical figure or as a purely literary fiction. A number of more recent interpretations see the relationship less in terms of rivalry and contrast and more in terms of a type of complementarity or division of functions between the two.[6] Thus both characters represent unity in diversity and 'two faces of the church, the contemplative and the official'.[7] Alternatively, they take different but complementary roles: Peter that of a leader and a focus for unity; the beloved disciple as a faithful, abiding witness,[8] perhaps even a 'suprapersonal... "remaining" witness'.[9]

The third cluster of issues deals with the *relationship* of the beloved disciple *to the composition of the Gospel*. In traditional terms this is posed as a question of the relationship of the beloved disciple to the evangelist. Here we meet a veritable thicket of difficulty, both exegeti-

---

5.   K. Quast, *Peter and the Beloved Disciple* (JSNTSup, 32; Sheffield: Sheffield Academic Press, 1989), p. 13, points out that the relationship between Peter and the beloved disciple often forms the basis upon which are built reconstructions of the Johannine community.

6.   Quast, *Peter*, may serve as a recent example of this approach. See also, T.L Brodie, *The Gospel according to John* (Oxford: Oxford University Press, 1993), pp. 560-64, 580-86; R. Bauckham, 'The Beloved Disciple as Ideal Author' *JSNT* 49 (1993), pp. 34-39.

7.   Brodie, *John*, pp. 563-64.

8.   Quast, *Peter*, pp. 159-69; see here also S.C. Barton, *People of the Passion* (London: SPCK, 1994), pp. 81-82.

9.   F. Neirynck, 'John 21', in F. van Segbroeck (ed.), *Evangelica II: 1982-1991, Collected Essays by Frans Neirynck* (BETL, 99; Leuven: Leuven University Press, 1991), p. 614.

cal and literary, much of which is generated by the problematic assertions made in 21.23-25. Does, or does not 21.23 imply the death of
the beloved disciple? Is the assertion made at 21.24 that the beloved
disciple is the author correct? (This would to all intents and purposes
make him 'the evangelist'.) In any case, what exactly is being asserted
here: that he is the author or the author's authoritative source? How
many hands were involved in the composition of this Gospel? How
many, if any, were 'eyewitnesses' to the events it recounts?

The Status of the Beloved Disciple in the Narrative

The character of the beloved disciple, and hence his place and status
within the story, is defined by a number of narrative strategies. The
first of these is the device of anonymity.[10] This appears to be quite a
deliberate strategy on the part of the implied author and is recognized
as such even by scholars who would want to go on and identify the
beloved disciple with a particular individual in the tradition.[11]

Although he is not named, the beloved disciple is defined by a particular relationship to Jesus. Stephen Barton has aptly said that he is
not 'identified by means of a proper noun... [but] by means of verbs
which show his relationship to Jesus'.[12] As this manner of identification
exerts a powerful pressure upon the reader's understanding of the place
and function of the beloved disciple in the story world, it is as well to
consider what is contained within the description. When the beloved
disciple first appears in the narrative as an identifiable character, he
is introduced as εἷς ἐκ τῶν μαθητῶν αὐτου... ὃν ἠγάπα ὁ Ἰησοῦς

10. Hengel, *The Johannine Question*, pp. 74-76 and Bauckham, 'Papias and
Polycrates', p. 65, argue on the basis of the title which they assert belonged to the
Gospel from the beginning, that the Fourth Gospel's author never was anonymous.
Neither clearly establishes the case for accepting the title as part of the Gospel as
originally published. But, in any case, this question relates to the identity of the real
author and does not bear directly upon the status of the beloved disciple within the
story. His relationship with the author is problematic anyway.

11. See e.g. Hengel, *The Johannine Question*, p. 128: 'The editors—like the
author—want the riddle [of the beloved disciple's identity] to remain unsolved, the
issue left open.' Cf. B. Lindars, *John* (NTG; Sheffield: Sheffield Academic Press,
1990), p. 21. See also J.H. Charlesworth, *The Beloved Disciple*, pp. xix, xxii;
Charlesworth believes that the author has left clues as to the identity of the beloved
disciple, which the perceptive reader is able to decipher, but a complete revelation is
not given.

12. Barton, *People of the Passion*, p. 71.

(13.23). Jesus and his disciples are at table, and this disciple is also described as 'lying close to the breast of Jesus' (RSV). It is a significant detail of the description, as we shall see.

Thus, the beloved disciple is identified as one of Jesus' disciples. It is important to recognize that he is defined first in his role as a disciple of Jesus, although it is a role which is further defined as being a disciple 'whom Jesus loved'. Despite the fact that elsewhere he is called 'another' or 'the other disciple' (e.g. 18.15, 16 where the same disciple is meant, as I shall seek to show), it is because the relative clause, 'whom Jesus loved', is most often used to identify him on those occasions when he appears in the narrative, that he is known as 'the beloved disciple'.[13] The repeated stress upon Jesus' love for him has led readers to understand that he enjoys a special or exclusive love. It is true that the implied author wishes to stress the fact that the disciple receives Jesus' love and that he occupies a privileged position within the band of disciples, and more particularly, in relation to the events unfolding. But the motivation for this arises from his special role as witness and not because the implied author wishes to show that Jesus' love for him is of a special quality or of an exclusive nature in comparison with his love for other disciples. Other characters enjoy Jesus' love, notably Lazarus (11.3, 36) and his sisters (11.5). Moreover, it is a strong theme in the farewell discourses, which occupy much of this part of the narrative, that discipleship should be characterized by a 'oneness' that arises out of 'love for one another' (13.34, 35; 15.12, 17) and is founded upon the prior love of Jesus and the Father for the chosen ones (15.13, 16; 17.23). It would surely undercut this theme of the nature of mutually shared love amongst believers if the portrayal of one particular disciple was designed to show him as loved more than other disciples.

Indeed, the implied author has guarded against the reader attributing exclusive love to the beloved disciple not only by specifying others whom Jesus loved, but by introducing this disciple into the narrative in the latter section where he may function anonymously as a representative disciple who is, *ipso facto*, loved by Jesus. We noted in the last

---

13. There are six narrative events in which he appears (1.35, 37; 13.21-30; 18.15, 16; 19.25-27, 31-35 [taken as one occasion]; 20.1-10; 21). In four of these, some form of reference to him as 'beloved' is found. In two of these instances (1.35; 18.15, 16) it is disputed whether the beloved disciple is meant. The reference at 19.35 is also disputed; and perhaps this should be taken as a separate (and seventh) event.

chapter that there is a turn, in John 13–21, from the public sphere of
Jesus' proclamation by sign and word among his own people, to the
private world of teaching among and focus upon those who are truly
his own. This movement is introduced by a statement at 13.1 that Jesus
'having loved his own who were in the world, loved them to the end'.
It is in this context that references to the beloved disciple are to be
found: he represents one whom Jesus loved to the end (and it may be
this which accounts for the repeated reminders that he is loved).[14] What
better epithet might the implied author choose for a disciple, whom he
wishes to remain anonymous, yet to particularize as a disciple, and one
who will be revealed as the 'eyewitness' source for the narrative, than
'the disciple whom Jesus loved'? While the reverse is never explicitly
said of this disciple, that he loved Jesus, the narrative implies this
quality of love in its depiction of the beloved disciple as one who
follows Jesus faithfully to the cross, and beyond. Thus he may embody
the qualities of reciprocal love which also characterize discipleship
(14.21, 23; 17.23, 26).

Now we must meet an objection which might be raised here. Far
from intending the beloved disciple to remain anonymous, the argument might go, the very fact that the implied author specifies him as the
disciple whom Jesus loved, shows that he intends the reader to identify
him with Lazarus. This is a thesis supported by Stibbe and, in terms of
the dynamics of narrative mediacy, there is, *prima facie*, some strength
to it. On clues supplied by the narrator, Lazarus is the one named
character with whom the beloved disciple might reasonably be associated. This is because, as Stibbe shows in his first and strongest point in
favour, Lazarus is referred to at 11.3 as 'the one whom you love' (ὃν
φιλεῖ cf. 20.2 τὸν ἄλλον μαθητὴν ὃν ἐφίλει ὁ Ἰησοῦς), which love is
emphasized twice more in the narrative (11.5, 36). It is after Lazarus
has been introduced into the story that, within a relatively short space

14. The phrase might be translated, 'the disciple (one [understood]), whom Jesus
loved'. Obviously, there is latitude here for readers to put a different stress upon the
significance of the concentration of references to being loved upon this particular
disciple. In the end, the narrative provides inferences which can be accumulated in
favour of a reading going in either direction. The above suggestion may seem to
understress the relationship of love enjoyed by the disciple. It does so, I feel, no
more than does the tendency to particularize and heighten the loved status of the disciple by capitalizing the B and the D. For this reason I prefer to retain lower case
letters when referring to this character.

of discourse time, the disciple whom Jesus loved appears. There are other narrative clues, such as the fact that both Lazarus and the beloved disciple recline at table with Jesus, and (a possible clue only) that Lazarus is a resident of Bethany, hence a Judean and living near Jerusalem where much of the Gospel's action takes place.[15]

However, it seems to me that on balance, Lazarus cannot be identified with the beloved disciple. There are two reasons for this. First, it is true that Lazarus is described as 'the one whom you love' but not in an exclusive manner. Stibbe's point that because no name is found at 11.3 the Gospel's first readers would have recognized that a community code-name for Lazarus is being used, is undercut by the fact that Lazarus has already been referred to by name as an introduction to this story (11.1). Therefore, the first readers would have understood the statement at 11.3 as referring back to the sick man Lazarus, and not necessarily as establishing a code-name. Also, the narrator almost immediately goes on to stress that Jesus loved (this time the verb ἀγαπαν is used) Martha, her sister and Lazarus. The narrative which follows illustrates this love for the two sisters as much as it does Jesus' love for Lazarus.

Second, and more importantly, the implied author makes every effort to subvert attempts the reader might make to identify the beloved disciple with any of the named characters. Throughout the narrative the implied author has deliberately left a textual indeterminacy in the form of gaps into which the figure of the beloved disciple may slip. He consistently refuses to make an opportunity to reveal the identity of the beloved disciple. Had he intended to identify Lazarus as the beloved disciple, then any of the many references to either Lazarus or the beloved disciple might have offered a good opportunity to have made the connection explicit. Twice the narrator reminds the reader that Lazarus is the one Jesus raised from the dead (12.1, 17) and once that the beloved disciple leaned on Jesus' breast at supper (21.20). Had these two been the same person the next logical step would have been to have brought these two identifying statements together in some way.

Especially in ch. 21 does the implied author turn away such opportunity. For example, 21.2 begins this pericope with a careful naming of the fishing party where, almost gratuitously, even the sons of

---

15. See Stibbe, *John as Storyteller*, p. 78. Most of Stibbe's other points (ref. pp. 79-80) rest on a combination of inferences drawn from intrinsic factors supported by extrinsic considerations, e.g. reference to details in the Synoptics.

Zebedee are mentioned but which then inexplicably tails off with a vague reference to two unnamed disciples. If Lazarus was present, why not name him too, especially if he is the all-important beloved disciple, and especially if 21.23 is meant to allay misapprehensions about Lazarus' longevity.[16]

Reflection on the strategy of the implied author reveals that at 21.2 he uses a rhetorical ploy previously employed at 1.35. That is, he creates a 'space' for an elusive, unnamed disciple. In both cases the space is created initially by mentioning two unnamed disciples, then partly filled with a particular disciple. But there is a subtle difference. In the first case, the place of one of the unnamed characters is taken by Andrew (1.40), hence by a named and unmistakably identifiable and identified character. He is Simon Peter's brother and features a number of times in the gospel (also at 6.8 and 12.22). However, in ch. 21, one space remains open (as is the case at 1.35-42) while the other is filled by none other than the beloved disciple who, the reader discovers at 21.7, is a member of the party.[17] By this time in the narrative he is a wholly substantial and personalized character, but still unnamed. And so he remains at the close of the story.

To the anonymity of the beloved disciple is joined (as has already been said) a certain elusiveness. The implied author makes the character fade from the scene only to reappear in the narrative at a later point. By contrast, in the case of his appearance in ch. 21 it is his

16. See Stibbe, *John as Storyteller*, p. 80.

17. Narrative theory has it that it is in the nature of textual gaps and indeterminacies (aporias) to invite interpretation and attempts by the reader to fill them. It seems to me that, just as it is impossible to identify the beloved disciple with a named character with any certainty, so any attempt to fill the places of these two unnamed characters mentioned at 21.1 (one of whom would inevitably have to be the beloved disciple, if he is not one of the sons of Zebedee!) is bound to be frustrated. On what basis does one make the selection: Andrew and Philip because one is Simon Peter's brother (and also a fisherman!; though a reader of the Fourth Gospel on its own is not to know this) and the other found Nathanael; and because the principle of inclusio might suggest that characters who are found in ch. 1, are thereby to be imaginatively included by the reader at the narrative's end? These two also feature together at 6.5-10 and 12.20 and are both from Bethsaida, hence on location as it were! There are plenty of narrative clues to suggest their inclusion in ch. 21. However, one might, if inventive enough, even find plausible reasons for selecting Nicodemus and Joseph of Arimathaea. In fact, almost any disciple might do. What is certain is that a suppression of names is a deliberate act by the implied author, and should be accepted by the implied readers as a given narrative fact.

presence in the scene which is not reported straight away. At one point, where a reader might be induced to assume that the beloved disciple has departed (19.27), a direct intervention into the narrative by the narrator shortly after (19.35) suggests that the reader must revise this understanding. Thus, this anonymous disciple is made to disappear and reappear at will. We shall see shortly how the implied author creates a link between the beloved disciple's appearances and other instances where an unnamed disciple appears. For the moment, we may note that the combination of anonymity and elusiveness endow him with qualities of fascination for the reader and, thereby, identify him as a character who may be imaginatively on hand whenever an unnamed witness-disciple appears. It is part of the implied author's strategy in building to the revelation of the beloved disciple's special role as witness to the narrative events.

But if anonymity and elusiveness are hallmarks of this disciple's characterization, it is equally the case that he is identified as a disciple. This fact, noted briefly above, must be enlarged upon for it has an important bearing on the precise way in which the disciple's status and place in the narrative is to be understood. Indeed, an argument might be mounted that he is primarily '*the* disciple', a description to which an identifying adjective (ἄλλος) or a relative clause (ὃν ἠγάπα ὁ Ἰησοῦς, or something similar) is attached. Five times he is identified as the disciple whom Jesus loved (13.23; 19.26; 20.2; 21.7, 20). At 21.7 the intensifying demonstrative pronoun ἐκεῖνος is found, as if the implied author wants the reader to be in no doubt as to whom is meant. He says, in effect, 'the disciple, that one whom I have already mentioned as the one whom Jesus loved'. Otherwise this disciple is most often referred to as 'another' or 'the other disciple' (18.15, 16; 20.2, 3, 4, 8) and in three instances the use of the adjective ἄλλος is almost pleonastic.[18] The repeated use of ἄλλος, especially in ch. 20 and where it is redundant, suggests that the disciple is also to be defined in relation to Peter, either in contrast or in complementarity. That is, he is not only the disciple whom Jesus loved, he is also the *other* disciple, in

---

18. Ref. 18.16; 20.2, 8. With this note cf. n. 13 above: it is true that there is a concentration of the use of ἄλλος on one occasion, namely 20.1-10. We might say that of the eighteen times that reference is made to him, the most constant reference is ὁ μαθητής, usually with some other identifier attached. Cf. 1.35; 13.23, 25; 18.15 (twice), 16; 19.26, 27, 35; 20.2, 3, 4, 8; 21.2, 7, 20, 23, 24: this list includes the two instances (1.35; 21.2) where he is mentioned as one of a pair.

addition to, or together with, Peter. Certainly in almost every instance where the beloved disciple appears, and when he is specifically designated as the beloved disciple, he appears in company with Peter. This, as we have seen, raises the question of his function and whether he is intended to represent a figure in competition with Peter or as a deliberate contrast, perhaps an exemplar of ideal discipleship against fallible Peter's feeble efforts.

It is as well to recognize that by identifying this figure as a disciple, one who enjoys a close relationship with Jesus and who is identified with Peter, we have a character who is a member of the inner band. This does not necessarily mean that he is a member of 'the twelve' (it is a concept by which the implied author puts very little store),[19] but that he is a disciple, who, as such, is included in what the story tells us of the disciples' experience. He sees the signs, he receives the teaching, and, above all, shares in the love. However, this raises a tension in the narrative between the role of the beloved disciple as an 'ideal' disciple and witness and one who, like the others, is limited in knowledge and is as fallible a follower. In the discourse there is a curious disjunction between the privileged position which the beloved disciple occupies as a participant in a number of the narrative events and statements made by the narrator which subtly undermines this position. This is a rhetorical device that has implications for the traffic of meaning between implied author and implied reader. It is also suggestive of the implied author's perspective on the historical events to which the narrative refers, and is part of the Gospel's theological rhetoric.

The beloved disciple, then, is given a privileged position in the narrative, suggesting to the reader that he has a close knowledge of and insight into the significance of the events to which he is a witness. But at the same time the implied author includes narrative statements which subvert this perception. We have already seen how the beloved disciple, on his first introduction into the story, is placed in a position of special knowledge regarding the identity of the betrayer.[20] We noted that 13.28, 29 place the reader in a dilemma. Should the beloved disciple be excluded from this (seemingly all-inclusive) assertion or

---

19. 'The twelve' are mentioned in the Fourth Gospel, at 6.67, 71, in a manner which suggests that the implied reader knows who they are (cf. also 21.24). He may have been a Judean disciple, which may account for a close knowledge of Judaea and the predominance of Judean settings in this Gospel.

20. See above pp. 65-66.

not? This might seem to be simply a piece of confused narration, but for the fact that the narrator does it twice more. At 20.8 he states that the beloved disciple, having reached the tomb first, having looked in and seen the state of the burial winding sheets (20.4, 5), then follows Peter into the tomb, sees and believes. (It is possible to overread the narrative, but it would seem that the beloved disciple, reaching the tomb first, gets a general impression and then, upon entering the tomb, sees what Peter is described as noticing—namely that the head cloth is lying by itself—and *thereupon* believes). The very next statement is to the effect that 'they did not as yet know the scripture, that he must rise from the dead' (20.9). The statement is made contrastively: the implication must be that without the benefit of scriptural understanding or a sighting of the risen Jesus, the beloved disciple believes that Jesus has risen from the dead. But what does the beloved disciple believe precisely and how much does he understand? The way the story is told sets the reader a conundrum and the questions it raises may be found in the commentaries. Why, for instance, if the beloved disciple believes in the resurrection, does he not share his insight with the others, especially Mary Magdalene (or Peter for that matter)?[21] Why are no traces of this faith (or even the beloved disciple himself) found in the resurrection appearances recounted in the rest of the chapter?[22] Finally, in ch. 21, it is the beloved disciple who first recognizes Jesus on the shore (21.7). Yet, over breakfast, he apparently shares in the other disciples' double-minded certainty about who Jesus is (again the statement is all-inclusive; 21.12). This time, however, they are all in the same situation; they are all sure (yet not decidedly sure) that it is the Lord!

It is the beloved disciple's privileged position and presence in close proximity to Jesus at so many crucial points that leads many commentators to speak of the beloved disciple as an 'idealized' disciple. Yet there is a tension between the ideal and what is conceived to have been the actual situation of an historical disciple. As an ideal disciple, did he ever truly exist?[23] I suggest that this tension between the ideal and

21. See here Brown, *John*, p. 987; also, Charlesworth, *The Beloved Disciple*, pp. 89-90.

22. If the beloved disciple was present at the appearance recounted in vv. 19-23, we must assume he shared the other disciples' fear and new found joy on that evening.

23. His elusiveness and ability to disappear from and appear again in the narrative at will no doubt increases this sense of his ideal, but unreal status.

the actual is one which exists within the implied author's portrayal of the beloved disciple. It is, as it were, a tension built into the character.[24] The motivation for this derives, I suggest, from the dual perspective of the narrative as a retrospectively told story and an eyewitness account. It reflects both the lack of understanding, and gradual dawning awareness of the significance of Jesus by the first disciples. It combines the confusion and incomprehension of the first eyewitnesses (a 'darkness' illuminated by flashes of insight and the glimmer of half-formed hopes) with the subsequent settled understanding and certainty formed by post-resurrection experience, retrospective remembrance and reflection on scripture.

Further support for this position will be given as we consider the nature of the implied author's speech-acts and the implications of these for the truth-telling status of the discourse. For the moment, we note that the nature of the discourse, as retrospectively told story and vivid eyewitness account, is fruitfully illuminated by analyzing the way the story is told under the methodology of Stanzel's typological circle. A narrative mediated largely from an authorial narrative situation displays features which suggest the gradual removal of the narrator to a figural stance. With a final flourish the narrator reveals the character who has emerged as the beloved disciple to be none other than the authoritative source for this story.

---

24. It might be that this tension arises through a deliberate ploy on the part of the implied author who sets an ironic distance between the beloved disciple's narrative persona and his 'real life' self. If the identity of the beloved disciple is known to the intended readers, or to the implied author's community, then there may here be a shared joke which is lost to subsequent generations. These readers know the beloved disciple, in his 'ideal' persona (and as a respected and trustworthy witness), and also his personal history as 'one of the disciples' whose path to faith was as marked by misunderstandings and failures as the rest.

If we accept that we are being given a somewhat ironic picture of the beloved disciple, then Peter's question about him at 21.21 takes on a new and ironic note: 'Lord, what about him?' A chastened and wounded Peter has now been rehabilitated under Jesus' threefold questioning and commissioning. He has been challenged to follow. He turns and sees this 'other disciple'. The narrator reminds the reader that he is the one who asked the question about the betrayer. The reader now knows the identity of the betrayer, but the atmosphere is charged with questions of commitment and faithfulness. Indeed, what about this one?

The Status of the Beloved Disciple Secured by Narrative Strategy
and Implicature

The implied author presents the beloved disciple at 21.24 as the reliable
witness to and purveyor of the tradition contained in the Gospel. Before
the reader reaches this point, the beloved disciple has already been
accorded this status because of the implied author's narrative strategy.
This strategy secures the beloved disciple's place as a member of the
inner band by the repeated mention of his identity as a μαθητής and
by the link made between him and Peter. He is thus in an ideal position
to act as an authoritative witness.

This strategy is undergirded by the privileged position he is accorded
through being described as 'the beloved disciple'. The love which Jesus
bears for this disciple is not intended to be understood as an exclusive
love, although it certainly suggests a specialness of relationship which
borders on exclusiveness in the minds of many readers. Rather, this
status of love identifies the beloved disciple as most certainly to be
counted amongst Jesus' 'own' and, as such, in a similar relationship to
Jesus as the Son is to the Father. This is further emphasized by the fact
that when first seen in his role as 'the beloved disciple', he is described
as being ἐν τῷ κόλπῳ τοῦ Ἰησοῦ (13.23), which is similar to the way
in which 1.18 describes the position of the Son in relation to the Father.
Indeed, moving into a position of greater intimacy, the beloved disciple
apparently becomes privy to privileged information about the identity
of the betrayer (13.25-26).

On his next appearance, the beloved disciple is seen to have privileged
access to the high priest's house, to which he also effects the entry of
Peter. This privilege of access combines with a certain elusiveness so
that the reader is no longer, for the present, aware of the beloved
disciple's whereabouts. The situation of Peter and of Jesus is, however,
precisely given. Peter stands warming himself with others by a fire in
the courtyard, Jesus stands before the 'high priest' (actually his father-
in-law, Annas). The narrative spotlight moves from Peter to Jesus and
back to Peter. When it fades to leave Peter in textual obscurity, he is
found to have fulfilled both Jesus' prophecies of 13.36-38. He denies
Jesus before cock crow and proves unable now to follow Jesus to death.
Perhaps the absence of the beloved disciple means that he cannot
follow either.

However, his next appearance (when he is specifically identified for the second time as 'the beloved disciple', 19.25-27) finds him standing near the cross, where he receives a new status as Jesus' mother's son (hence Jesus' brother) and a commission to care for Jesus' mother, who becomes a member of his household (τὰ ἴδια). Thus, the reader perceives the beloved disciple to be well placed to act as a witness to all that has transpired thus far: by implication he has continued to follow Jesus throughout the proceedings.

The place and status of the beloved disciple as the reliable witness to the events recounted in 13–21 (whether he is described as 'the beloved disciple' or simply as 'another/the other disciple') is effected by the operations of the co-operative principle and the implicatures which arise from this. Thus the link between the beloved disciple and the unnamed disciple at 18.15, 16 arises because no other individual unnamed disciple has been mentioned in the intervening narrative. All other individual disciples are named (13.36; 14.5, 8, 22; 18.2, 10, 15) and only when the disciples are mentioned as a group is there no specification of names (16.17, 29). Hence, under the assumption that the implied author supplies all the information necessary to the exchange so that communication may proceed felicitously, the implied reader deduces that the unnamed disciple here is the beloved disciple, the only one not to have been named as yet. The fact that he appears again with Peter lends support to this association. We should note that at 18.16 the disciple is no longer just another disciple but specifically the disciple defined to be in partnership with Peter (ὁ ἄλλος).

Certainly the identification between the beloved disciple and this disciple is not yet an absolutely necessary one. However, the probabilities are strong, though the response of real readers shows that absolute unanimity is not assured.[25] However, at 20.2 the assumption that 'the other disciple' and 'the disciple whom Jesus loved' are to be identified as the same person is made virtually certain when the phrase τὸν ἄλλον μαθητὴν is used in conjunction with the relative clause ὃν

25. See F. Neirynck, 'The "Other Disciple" in Jn 18.15-16', in F. van Segbroeck (ed.), *Evangelica: Gospel Studies, Collected Essays by Frans Neirynck* (BETL, 60; Leuven: Leuven University Press, 1982), pp. 335-63; and commentaries. The article and commentary notes well illustrate how easily extraneous considerations intrude. The presence of the article at 18.16 and 20.2, 3, 4, 8 apparently exerted a strong pressure upon scribes to include it at 18.15 as well (cf. R. Schnackenburg, *John*, III, p. 235; Brown, *John*, p. 822). Might not this point to an assumption which would 'naturally' occur on the basis of the co-operative principle?

ἐφίλει ὁ Ἰησοῦς. The use of the article with the adjective 'other' means that this phrase cannot but refer back to the disciple who has already, at 18.16, been described as the companion of Peter. The very specificity of the reference makes it certain on the grounds of maintaining the co-operative principle. If another, as yet unmentioned, disciple is meant, then the speech-act is infelicitous because misleading; if another disciple is understood, the reading is surely counter-intuitive. We might note that, as the implied author obviously wanted to refer to the beloved disciple, the ἄλλον is to that extent redundant, unless he also wants to make a connection with the Peter's companion of 18.15, 16.[26] The variation in the manner of referring to this disciple's status as beloved (ἐφίλει instead of ἠγάπα) is immaterial. The verbs φιλεῖν and ἀγαπᾶν are used interchangeably in the narrative.[27] Thus the beloved disciple is here referred to *also as the other disciple* making the link with 18.15, 16. The implied reader notes that this is his third appearance with Peter. He is now defined by the two characteristics which give his distinct narrative identity, namely, (a) by 'otherness' in complementarity to Peter and (b) as one loved by Jesus.

Finally, the implied author links the beloved disciple with the unnamed disciple at 1.35, 37 by the fact that he appears again as one

26. Schnackenburg's second objection (*John*, III, p. 235) against identification of the anarthrous reference to 'another disciple' at 18.15 being referred to the beloved disciple surely applies equally strongly here. There is no reason why the beloved disciple, already introduced simply as 'the disciple, whom Jesus loved' should not be so described here!

27. Cf. Barrett, *John*, p. 562. If a significance is to be sought, might it be that the use of φιλεῖν here provides a narrative echo effect with Peter's (and Jesus') use of it at 21.15-18? Also, ἀγαπᾶν is used in contexts where the beloved disciple's relationship *with* Jesus is directly in view; that is, Jesus is on the scene and the beloved disciple is defined in some sort of connection with him (leaning on his breast, 13.23; standing by his cross and hearing his commission, 19.26; recognizing him, 21.7; and following him [and Peter!], 21.20). Here Jesus is not present, the beloved disciple is simply in company with Peter. And at 18.15, 16, by the way, the focus is upon Peter and the beloved disciple (Jesus is temporarily in the background)—a fact which might meet Schnackenburg's objection that if the implied author wished to indicate that this disciple was the beloved disciple he would have said so. Rather, he simply does not need, or wish, to draw attention to this aspect of the characterization. If anything, the use of φιλεῖν here has the effect of equating the beloved disciple's status as one loved by Jesus with that enjoyed by others (cf. 11.3).

There is no textual evidence that the variation indicates redaction. That is an unnecessary hypothesis, as I trust the present argument shows.

of two unnamed disciples at 21.2.[28] The reader, of course, is not aware
of the beloved disciple's presence in ch. 21 until 21.7. That he is one
of those two previously unnamed disciples is implied by two narrative
echo effects. In the first place, there is the use of the word ἄλλοι. Here,
then, we have 'two *other* disciples', so that each may be understood as
another disciple in addition to those already named. 'Otherness' is a
feature of the elusive, anonymous, beloved disciple. Second, there is
the similarity of wording between 1.35 and 21.2; in both cases the
partitive use of ἐκ (common enough in the Fourth Gospel) introduces
the same genitival phrase:

> 1.35:   ἐκ τῶν μαθητῶν αὐτοῦ δύο
> 21.2   [ἄλλοι] ἐκ τῶν μαθητῶν αὐτοῦ δύο[29]

This helps to create an inclusio. The two unnamed disciples of 1.35 who
detached themselves from John to follow Jesus at the beginning of the
story, now reappear (the reader may surmise) amongst the band of
Jesus' disciples who make up the fishing party. But this time, by a neat
reversal, the identity of one of them is revealed as being the beloved
disciple while the other remains unnamed. Earlier, one is revealed
as being Andrew, while the other remains a mystery. This reversal
strengthens the possibility that the implied author intends the implied
reader to assume that the beloved disciple is to be identified as the
figure who remains unnamed at 1.35, 37. There is also a continuity in
the roles played by Andrew at 1.41, 42 and the beloved disciple at
21.7. On Peter's first encounter with Jesus, it is his brother Andrew
who tells him that the Messiah has been 'found' and takes Peter to
him. On Peter's last encounter with Jesus, it is the beloved disciple
who makes him known to Peter ('It is the *Lord!*'). The commissioning
of Peter, witnessed by the beloved disciple, itself forms an inclusio
with his naming in 1.42. It marks the end of the process of 'becoming'
initiated in the naming.

As one of the disciples, that is *another* though unnamed disciple, the

28. Of course, it is not impossible that the beloved disciple is to be identified as
one of the sons of Zebedee. The reference is to οἱ τοῦ Ζεβεδαίου, making them virtually anonymous. But the hint, if there be one, is very slight. And, on balance, the
implicature set up by the rest of the narrative seems to tell against it, see also above
pp. 112-13. Stephen Barton has made the attractive suggestion to me that the implied
author introduces the sons of Zebedee thus so as not to detract from his focus on Peter.

29. See here F. Neirynck, 'The Anonymous Disciple in John 1', in F. van
Segbroeck (ed.), *Evangelica II*, pp. 646-47.

beloved disciple has been present when Jesus gives his farewell discourse (John 14–16). Thus he too is included in Jesus' words at 15.27:
he too has been with Jesus from the beginning. The implied author
confirms this by his narrative strategy as the implied reader now retrospectively associates him with the unnamed disciple at 1.35. Having
simply 'appeared' in the story at 13.23 as εἷς ἐκ τῶν μαθητῶν, he has
implicitly been a member of the band of disciples all along. 1.35
offers the reader the only narrative moment when he conceivably
made his first appearance.

The implied author's narrative strategy and the operations of implicature have secured for the beloved disciple a central place in the
narrative as a participant in the events and as a witness who has been
there from the beginning. Now the implied author underwrites this
status with a direct assertion at 21.24. '*This* is the disciple who is
bearing witness to these things...' (RSV) 'These things' may be a
reference to the events which have transpired after the beloved disciple's entry into the story i.e. the events contained in John 13–21. But
since the beloved disciple may be taken as one who has witnessed everything from the beginning, the phrase includes everything in the story.
This supposition is strengthened by the addition of the words, καὶ
γράψας ταῦτα, for the natural assumption under the co-operative principle is that this refers to the entire written narrative, not simply a part
of it. Other readings are possible, but must unnecessarily assume a
breach or suspension of the co-operative principle, especially that
requiring perspicuity.[30]

The use of the present participle, ὁ μαρτυρῶν, suggests that the
beloved disciple is still living at the time of the discourse. However, it
may simply point to the 'narrative present', that is, the continuing life
of this witness in the narrative. At any rate, without direct access to
the beloved disciple, the implied, intended and actual reader *has* to take
this statement in a 'metaphorical' sense. At the heart of the locution is
an irresolvable aporia over the precise relationship of the beloved
disciple to the discourse. We shall return to the implications of this
later; the discourse here implies that the beloved disciple is the author
of the narrative.

We must now consider another locution every bit as difficult. John

30. As 21.25 returns to the mention of other things which Jesus did which have
not be recorded here (in implicit reference to 20.30), taking 'these things' in 21.24 to
refer merely to the verses immediately preceding makes the speech-act incongruous.

19.35 is a parenthetical remark in which the narrator vouches for the authenticity of the account of the flow of blood and water from Jesus' pierced side. 'The one who saw it has borne witness, and his testimony is true, and he knows that he speaks the truth, that you may believe.' The beloved disciple is, by implication, the most likely referent for the perfect participle, ὁ ἑωρακώς. He is the only male witness whom the reader can identify as having been at the scene.

The speech-act has the force of a first person statement in third person form vouching for the authenticity of the account and the reliability of the witness. As such it is self-involving and amounts to a first person belief statement. The form of the locution is strange, given that it is ostensibly a third person reference to someone else's affirmation. What is said is not, 'I know (or we know) that he speaks the truth', but '*he* knows that he speaks the truth'. This is either an indirect first person statement, that is, the witness, to whom the ἐκεῖνος most naturally refers, is speaking about himself, or it is the report by the narrator of a third person's affirmation. If the latter is the case, then the assertion is infelicitous unless the one making it has good grounds for maintaining that he can affirm this on another's behalf. A third person report about someone else's assertion 'can only be intelligible if another first person present tense utterance is antecedently understood'.[31] Thus we must understand that implicit within the assertion is the formulation, 'I (the speaker/narrator) am telling you that he said, "I am speaking the truth"'. Furthermore, as Bauckham points out, 'second person address to readers/hearers [such as we find in the clause ἵνα καὶ ὑμεῖς πιστεύητε] draws attention to the writer who addresses them, in a way that third person narrative does not'.[32] Thus, if the implied author is not the witness, he is at least giving his personal backing to the witness and is indicating that he has grounds for believing him. The form of the assertion suggests that these grounds rest upon a personal relationship of some sort with the witness. If the statement, 'he knows he speaks the truth', is to be taken as an oblique self-reference, the motivation behind adopting this form may be in order to avoid the charge of witnessing to his own legitimacy. This is a charge which a

31. D.M. High, *Language, Persons and Belief* (New York: Oxford University Press, 1967), p. 158; on this see also generally pp. 157-63.

32. Bauckham, 'Ideal Author', p. 39. Cf. Lindars, *John*, p. 589: 'As it then goes on to second person address. . . it is inevitable that we should take *he* to mean the author of the gospel, using the third person for a veiled self-reference.'

skeptical reader might well formulate on the basis of the implied author's own discourse (see 5.31, 32)!

The Beloved Disciple's Relationship with Peter

The narrative presents Peter as a representative disciple. He alone is not *the* representative disciple, for others, such as Nathanael and Thomas, also function as representative of discipleship. But, in contrast to these two and, indeed, to other named followers and friends of Jesus, Peter's role as a representative disciple is foregrounded and filled out by a number of narrative strategies. In the first place, when Peter is brought to Jesus he is given a new name (1.42). This signals that Peter embarks upon a process of becoming a new person (he *is* Simon, he *will be* called Cephas).[33] He is named by Jesus and hence 'chosen': he is one of those sheep who are named by the Good Shepherd, and who follow him (10.3). In John 13.1-11 he has his feet washed by Jesus, thus confirming that he has a 'part in' Jesus. He is pronounced clean. He is among those who are truly Jesus' 'own'. Second, at 6.68, 69, Peter acts as the spokesman for 'the twelve' in affirming loyalty to and belief in Jesus. Third, he is shown as both faithful and fallible. In his commitment to Jesus, he is committed though imperfect and mistaken. When Jesus wishes to wash his feet, he fails to understand the significance or the necessity of this (13.7): first he refuses to allow Jesus to wash his feet (13.8), then he enthusiastically offers hands and head as well (13.9). He is unable to follow Jesus fully, though he offers to lay down his life for him (13.37). To be sure, he attempts a defence of Jesus (18.10), then follows Jesus to his trial (18.15), but there he denies him (18.17, 25-27). Over Peter's discipleship there hangs a question mark for the bulk of the narrative. Will he, indeed, lay down his life for Jesus (13.38a, cf. 15.13, 14)? It is of interest that so often the issues of fidelity and faithlessness, betrayal and belonging are in the air when Peter interacts with Jesus. Though the implied author always deflects identification of the betrayer away from the person of Peter (6.70, 71; 13.10, 11), and though Peter remains a part of the group after he has denied Jesus (20.2; 21.2), a suspicion hangs over him until he is finally reinstated in John 21.

Peter is only able to take up true discipleship after Easter, when

33. Is there an intertextual resonance here with Gen. 35.10 (LXX), as in 1.51 there is a resonance with Gen. 28.12?

Jesus renews a call to discipleship in a threefold challenge to love and a commissioning for service (21.15-19, note especially the concluding ἀκολούθει μοι).[34] Now Jesus asserts (so the narrator indicates, cf. v. 19a) that Peter will lay down his life for him. In a sense, he accepts Peter's earlier offer, though ironically he states that this will not be something that Peter will do of his own accord. Peter, then, represents the pre-Easter perspective of the disciples: he is one who can only understand later (13.7), who can only follow later (13.36). This 'later' is the time beyond the story time: the post-Easter era of scripturally-informed understanding and spirit-empowered commissioning (20.21, 22). As a representative of the pre-Easter disciples, Peter is both loyal and able to comprehend in part, but he is also flawed and suffers from misapprehension, lack of scripturally-informed understanding, and failure in discipleship.

The beloved disciple is placed not so much in competition with Peter as a foil to Peter's pre-resurrection perspective. The beloved disciple combines both pre-resurrection and post-resurrection perspectives. The post-resurrection point of view obtrudes into the pre-resurrection story time. Thus the beloved disciple is portrayed as one who resides close to the heart of Jesus where he enjoys access to privileged information. He displays a faithfulness which is in sharp contrast to the failure of Peter and, for that matter, the other disciples. He alone is to be found standing by the cross. Here his relationship with Jesus is defined in a new way and he is given a special commission. Proleptically, then, he enjoys the status of 'brother', that all the disciples enjoy after the resurrection (cf. 20.17: τοὺς ἀδελφούς μου). In John 20 he is the first male disciple to reach the empty tomb where, eventually, without the benefit of scripture (20.9) or sight of Jesus, he is the first to believe in the resurrection (20.8). In John 21 he is the first to recognize the risen Lord (21.7). All of this gives him the qualities of an 'ideal' disciple; qualities which are enhanced by the elusiveness of his being and the anonymity of his characterization. His ideal status (in which all disciples share) is summed up in the description: ὁ μαθητὴς ὃν ἠγάπα ὁ Ἰησοῦς.

Nevertheless, as we have already seen, there is a tension in the

34. This command (Ἀκολούθει μοι) echoes Jesus's words to Philip (1.43) thus forming a nice inclusio; cf. Stibbe, *John*, p. 207. Philip is another disciple put to the test by Jesus (6.5-7). Like Peter, he is slow to comprehend who Jesus truly is (14.8-11).

narrative as to how much the beloved disciple actually knows and understands, and a subtle undercutting of his privileged position. It is a tension which arises through the peculiar relation of the beloved disciple to story time as the one who has witnessed the events (some at least, 19.35) and the one who is witnessing at the time of discourse (21.24). The beloved disciple, through reminiscence, places himself back in pre-resurrection story time. At the same time, because he now engages in retrospective reflection, and because of the spatio-temporal distance which now exists between then and now, he can see the wider perspective and take a longer view. Thus he can adopt the stance of a privileged insider: one who both saw and believed *then* (20.8) even though that belief was not fully informed (20.9), and can now witness from the situation of a belief which is deeper and more comprehending in the light of subsequent reflection and insight.

The discourse further portrays a complementarity of function(s) between Peter and the beloved disciple, as well as mediating different perspectives on story time. Peter inherits and fulfills Jesus' role as shepherd, in the future beyond story time (21.15, 16, 17; cf. 10.11). In 10.9 Jesus describes himself as the provider of pasture, and in 21.15-17 Peter is given the task of feeding Jesus' sheep, as understudy, if you like, to the Good Shepherd. Also, Peter will follow Jesus in the death by which he will glorify God (21.19a cf. 12.33, 18.32 and also 12.23-26).

The beloved disciple takes on the role of witness. Whatever else the beloved disciple might symbolize for the reader, it is his role as witness which is stressed both in the descriptions at 19.35 (ὁ ἑωρακὼς) and 21.24 (ὁ μαρτυρῶν), where his reliability as a witness is directly affirmed, and in the way in which he functions as a character. In this he follows both John and Jesus. Hence, at the narrative's conclusion, his witness which remains and carries forward into the future beyond story time and time of discourse, forms an inclusio with John's witness which stands at the beginning of story and discourse time. That the beloved disciple assumes a role as witness similar to that undertaken by Jesus within story time is seen by the fact that he assumes Jesus' position of 'being in the bosom of. . . ' (13.23; cf. 1.18) and because he is loved by Jesus. Indeed, it is this relationship of love which authorizes the beloved disciple to act as witness, for it mirrors the love which the Father has for the Son. Like the Son, he is the recipient of privileged information (5.20; cf. 13.25, 26) and privileged responsibility (3.35; cf.

19.27). Just as Jesus can make known the Father (the verb, ἐξηγήσατο, which might bc translated as 'narrated' or 'recounted' is suggestive at the introduction of a *narrative* in which the witness Jesus gives is both lived as well as spoken) because he is εἰς τὸν κόλπον τοῦ πατρὸς (1.18), so the beloved disciple is well situated to make known the Son in his narrative, placed as he is ἐν τῷ κόλπῳ τοῦ Ἰησοῦ (13.23).[35]

The Relationship of the Narrator/Implied Author
with the Beloved Disciple

Thus far we have considered the status, place and function of the beloved disciple within the narrative. We have seen that his place is defined by anonymity and a certain elusiveness, but that he is clearly defined as a disciple of Jesus, one who has been with him from the beginning, who enjoys a place of special intimacy and insight. As such his role is to act as a foil to Peter, not so much in contrast as in complementarity, representing the fusion of two perspectives upon story time (that of story time itself and that of the time of the discourse). The subtlety of his characterization, particularly in his relationship with Peter, suggests to many readers an element of the 'ideal' in his discipleship.[36] Above all, it is his role as witness that is emphasized.

Now we must consider his relationship to the act of narration (represented by the narrator) and to the production of the discourse (represented by the implied author). We have seen that the narrator's comment at 21.24 specifically identifies the beloved disciple as the implied author. The comment at 19.35 implicitly supports this, especially as the narrator's turn to the reader ('that you may believe'), echoed in 20.31, brings to mind the author whose mouthpiece the narrator is, and creates a link between the act of witness whose reliability is vouched for and the written form in which that witness is handed down. But this creates a puzzle for the reader and seems to create a rift between narrator and implied author. It is one of the narrative's aporias over which even a narrative approach has difficulty, as is witnessed by

---

35. See here Barton, *People*, p. 80-81 and Bauckham, 'Ideal Author', pp. 33-39.

36. In a narrative where the traffic at the level of implicit commentary is heavy, it is impossible to determine all the nuances and foolhardy to close all options. On this, however, it must also be remembered that it is the portrayal of Peter's failures (which is part of *Peter's* characterization, not the beloved disciple's) which sets up the contrast every bit as much as the beloved disciple's 'ideal' characteristics.

the confusion between beloved disciple's function and implied author/
narrator functions referred to earlier.[37]

The problem is generated by the use of the third person references
and the first person plural reference, as well as the possible implication of 21.23 that, at the time when the discourse was completed, the
beloved disciple had already died. It is also created, I suggest, by the
fact that the discourse brings together the perspective of the beloved
disciple and the narrator in such a way that, on a number of occasions,
the narrator appears to share the same spatio-temporal location as the
beloved disciple. By the same token, the reader is invited to share the
spatio-temporal location of this merged character and thus is encouraged to accept the discourse as a reliable, eyewitness account of the
event related.

The relationship of the narrator with the beloved disciple is established by a narrative strategy in which the form of narrative situation
adopted in John 13–21 is largely that in which the teller-character
becomes a reflector-character. In other words, the narrator sees with
the eyes of the beloved disciple. Here I must assert again that in this
narrative there is no essential difference between the narrator and the
implied author. While it is true that not every narrator can be identified
with the implied author, for there are implied authors who, through the
use of irony, set themselves apart from their immature, self-deceived
or unreliable narrators, in the case of the Fourth Gospel the narrator
may safely be accepted as a reliable mouthpiece of the implied author.
The narrator's authorial stance, omniscient, omnipresent and informative, makes him reliable and associates him, in the reader's mind, with
the implied author. Not only this, but even where the narrator withdraws, or appears to merge with a character (Jesus, John the Baptist,
the beloved disciple) and to speak their words, or see events through
their eyes, he nevertheless conveys the sense that this is an authoritative
and trustworthy stance. Even though he may appear to 'victimize' the
reader (as in Staley) or tease him and gently suggest an ironic distance
between the beloved disciple's persona as 'ideal' and as 'actual' (as I
have suggested above), he never finally betrays the reader's confidence.
This narrator speaks for the implied author and, though the narrative
strategies employed may raise questions in a reader's mind about
faithfulness to matters of historical actuality (and we must consider

37. See pp. 49-50, 67-68. It is a problem which in traditional Johannine scholarship has spawned the creation of editors and redactors in addition to 'the evangelist'.

this more fully later), the narrative nevertheless gives no grounds for thinking that it is not true to itself or true on its own terms.

What are the dynamics by which the transition from teller to reflector takes place? What narrative strategies are employed to enable the discourse to convey the impression that the narrator sees with the eyes of the beloved disciple? A close link between the narrator and the beloved disciple is suggested to the reader when the latter is first introduced into the narrative (13.21-30). The way in which the beloved disciple is portrayed as leaning close to Jesus and being privy to what goes on between Jesus and Judas, means that the narration is focalized through his perception. The implication is that what is described is what the beloved disciple sees. Thus he shares the same spatio-temporal location as the narrator (who is doing the telling). The reader also shares this spatio-temporal location. As the perspectives of beloved disciple, narrator and reader converge, the narration of the narrator-cum-beloved disciple is given the aspect of a reliable, first-hand report.

We note that at every point where the beloved disciple appears (and this includes those narrative moments when he is not designated as 'the beloved disciple') the narrative includes items of close detail which suggest 'on the spot', eyewitness report. Thus, for instance, at 18.18 we have a description of the scene in the high priest's courtyard: it is cold, there is a charcoal fire around which the servants and soldiers, joined by Peter, are standing. At 19.34 the narrator describes how the soldier lances Jesus' side whereupon there is a flow of blood and water. This is immediately followed by the narrator's confirmation of the reliability of the report. The fishing party and the breakfast by the lake (John 21) is especially closely recounted. Among other things, the narrator tells the reader the time of day (21.4), that Peter is unclad (21.7), that when the catch of fish was made, the boat was not far from land, only about 200 cubits off shore (RSV; ὡς ἀπὸ πηχῶν διακοσίων; 21.8), a charcoal fire with fish on it was already lit (21.9) and that the catch amounted to 153 big fish (21.11).

This attention to detail is especially sharp and significant at 20.6-8 where the focalization is through Peter. Thus what is described is apparently what Peter saw upon entering the tomb (20.6, 7). But the reader is then told (20.8) that the beloved disciple also entered the tomb. It is at this point that the narrator chooses to give the reader an *inside view* of this disciple's reaction ('he saw and believed'). This has the effect of transferring the reader's spatio-temporal location to the beloved disciple so that what has been described can now be taken either as what the beloved disciple *also* saw, or as what the beloved disciple saw and reported, which is then imputed to Peter. The implication is that what the beloved disciple saw, Peter must surely also have seen. Thus, the discourse relates what amounts to a visual perception shared by both Peter and the beloved disciple.[38]

It is important to bear in mind in all this Genette's distinction between 'who sees' and 'who speaks'. What is described is what the beloved disciple sees, but what is recounted is what the narrator tells and knows. Thus, for instance, at 13.21-30 the beloved disciple sees Jesus share the morsel with Judas, and he sees Judas depart. But it is not clear that he *knows* why Judas is leaving or that he understands that it is because Satan has entered into Judas and he goes to set in motion his act of betrayal. Similarly, while he sees and believes on the evidence of the 'signs' in the tomb (for in this story this is surely what they are) it is not clear that he so fully understands the implications of this evidence that he, unlike the other disciples, will not skulk fearfully behind closed doors (20.19) or will immediately and unambiguously be able to identify the risen Christ (21.4, 12). The reader is left in some doubt as to how much the beloved disciple knows and understands, and when exactly full belief is realized.

It is precisely because the narrative situation adopted is that of a reflector-character that this tension arises, a tension between story time (where the events happen and are witnessed) and time of discourse (when they are recounted and interpreted from a retrospective point of view). But it is a *tension* between the times and not a divorce: which is why I suggest that Stanzel's more fluid schematization renders possible a more subtle reading of the discourse than one, such as Genette's, which tries to determine levels of narration (inside story time or outside story time). It is a tension which has implications for the deep level communication between implied author and implied reader, for it signals, as is now becoming clear, a merging of horizons and a modulation between the times, then and now. The mode of narrative mediacy is one which is both inside story time and outside it, and which entails a constant shifting between the two. It alerts the reader to the fact that the discourse is founded upon reminiscences of the pre-resurrection events which are now refracted into the time of discourse through the reordering and shaping which is enabled by distance in

38. See also p. 153 below on 'transfiguralization'.

time from the events, retrospectively considered in their overall significance and placed into perspective by a post-resurrection understanding.
Thus, to take but two instances from the material under consideration
here, references to a betrayer are understood as specifically adhering
to Judas, who, it is now known, was the disciple to have fulfilled this
role. The pattern of Peter's discipleship, on the other hand, is seen to
have led through misunderstanding and failure to his present revered
status as a well-known, leading figure, a 'shepherd' and martyr.[39]
Again, whatever else the implied author might have wished to convey
in his account of the *crurifragium* (19.31-36), he certainly wants the
reader to understand that what happened to Jesus meant the fulfillment
of certain scriptures (19.36).[40]

The narrative is mediated in such a way as to suggest a very close
correspondence between the beloved disciple and the narrator/beloved
disciple. As to the question whether the narrator/implied author and
the beloved disciple are to be identified as one and the same, this is left
open because, on the one hand, all the references to the beloved disciple
are in the third person, and the crucial references to the eyewitness
authority in 19.35 and 21.24 are also in the third person. Furthermore,
the verb used at 21.24 (γράψας) might well be construed as meaning
that this witness caused the narrative to be written rather than that he
wrote it himself.

In the end we are left with two possibilities, but, I believe only two.
First, the implied author/narrator and the beloved disciple are one and
the same person. We may take the statement made at 21.24 at its face
value. The beloved disciple is the implied author who is witnessing to
these things (hence the present participle in the Greek) and has written
about these things. I believe a strong case can be made for this possibility but a final judgment will have to be made after we have examined
more of the evidence.

The second possibility is that the implied author/narrator and the
beloved disciple are two distinct persons but that the implied author's

---

39. It is this retrospective narration which accounts for the fact that Peter is called
Simon Peter even before he meets Jesus, who thereupon gives him the sobriquet,
Peter. He is well known to the implied author and, by extension, the 'we' community to which he refers. It does not necessarily follow that he is well known to the
implied reader.

40. Which also had implications for the truth of the claims that Jesus was the
Messiah, and that undergirded the narrative's portrayal of him as the 'Lamb of God'.

authoritative source of information for his narrative is the beloved disciple. The implied author's relationship with the beloved disciple is very close. Either the implied author is the literary genius who has taken the beloved disciple's reminiscences of and testimony to Jesus and has creatively reworked them to produce his story;[41] or the implied author is the beloved disciple's *amanuensis*, working with him to put his reminiscences and testimony into narrative form.[42] Some of the features of this discourse, the use of the historic present for instance, suggest that the reminiscences are coming into the written narrative almost directly.

Here, then, is a secure inference that we can draw about the real author. He is one who has direct and immediate access to the events to which his narrative refers. To what extent he has imaginatively reworked the testimony he receives, his identity and relationship to the beloved disciple, are matters over which the discourse permits no final answers and, in the end, readers will need to form their own judgments. But that the implied author affirms that he has a trustworthy, authoritative source as the basis for his narrative, there is no doubt. That his relationship with this source is close and personal is, I think, certain; and we are given a clue to the status of this source if not a name. He is a disciple who was with Jesus, most probably from the earliest days of his ministry, whom the implied author chooses to describe as 'the disciple whom Jesus loved'.

Conclusion

As a conclusion to this chapter, we may return to the question of the anonymity of the beloved disciple. It may be, as Richard Bauckham suggests, that his identity was well known to the intended readers or,

41. It is possible that the implied author is working from a written source, e.g. a 'Signs Source' or a 'Bethany gospel' (as in Stibbe, *John as Storyteller*, pp. 81-83) but I do not think that this is likely. Any dependence upon written sources is far more likely to have been a dependence on one or more of the Synoptic Gospels; or, more likely yet, upon earlier written or oral tradition upon which both they and the Fourth Gospel depend. Sometimes, indeed, the Fourth Gospel reads as if it were the first commentary on the Synoptics, creatively reworking and, in the discourses, drawing out the inner significance, as the implied author sees it, of selected Synoptic stories.

42. Of course, this *'amanuensis'* may have been more than one person, members of a community in fact. There is some attractiveness in the early tradition that the apostle John was persuaded by the other apostles to write a Gospel with their help.

at least, to some of the first readers of the Gospel. Implicit within 21.24 is the understanding that he is known to the writer and the community of believers associated in the validation of this witness. But why is he '*portrayed* anonymously' in the narrative?[43] There are five possible reasons: the first and the last are ones I would put the least weight upon; the central three are to some extent interrelated and are, I think, at the heart of the implied author's motivation.

The first has to do with the status the implied author wishes to adhere to his narrative. The anonymity of the beloved disciple is possibly motivated by a sense that anonymous writings are more authoritative. Meir Sternberg states that 'anonymity in ancient narrative validates supernatural powers of narration'.[44] Kevin Quast, drawing upon an observation of Kurt Aland's, suggests that anonymity is an 'authenticating factor' of the earliest non-epistolary Christian writings. It confirms the author's status as one writing under the inspiration of the Holy Spirit,[45] which is surely an impression that the implied author would want to convey. Indeed, his discourse implicitly lays claim to divinely assisted authorship: the authority of the beloved disciple rests upon his relationship with Jesus, and as a disciple he shares in the promise of the Holy Spirit.

Second, the beloved disciple remains anonymous in order to emphasize his role as witness. The implied author's strong desire is not to detract from the narrative's central focus upon Jesus. He wishes to avoid a cult of personality adhering to the beloved disciple (as possibly happened to Peter). It would seem that some of the 'brethren' had already harboured misapprehensions about the beloved disciple's mortality. In the implied author's opinion, a named disciple may have attracted undue and unhealthy attention. He surely would not have reckoned with the powers of fascination an anonymous disciple would exert on future generations of readers! Like John, who simply wished to act as the bridegroom's friend (3.29, 30), the beloved disciple's identity must 'decrease' so that Jesus' might increase.

Third, the function of the beloved disciple is to act as the 'ideal author' in the sense to which Richard Bauckham has drawn attention; that is, as a disciple ideally situated to act as witness. His anonymity,

43. See Bauckham, 'Ideal Author', p. 43 (emphasis his).
44. M. Sternberg, *The Poetics of Biblical Narrative* (Bloomington: Indiana University Press, 1987), p. 33; cf. also pp. 65-66.
45. Quast, *Peter*, p. 19.

and, for that matter, the elusiveness that attaches to him, allows the implied author to suggest that he is present and 'on hand' as witness to the events throughout the narrative without requiring that he obtrude at every point. This is especially the case in the all-important Passion narrative. Constant reference to his name would fix his presence in the story to the locale of each reference; as an anonymous disciple he can reside in the background, his presence noted in varying degrees of specificity from 'one of two unnamed disciples' and 'another disciple' to 'the other disciple' or 'the disciple whom Jesus loved'. When the focus of the narrative moves from the public sphere of Jesus' ministry to the private world of his relationship with his own, where the issue of their role as witnesses will become important, the beloved disciple emerges with an ever increasing concreteness of characterization. Also, this is the time of Jesus' hour, to which the story has been building up, and where the issue of belonging is also focussed, so it is appropriate that the beloved disciple be in evidence. Anonymity allows the implied author some creative play with the characterization of the beloved disciple as a foil/complement to Peter, a perceptive witness, a faithful disciple, without allowing him to become completely 'idealized' (though for many readers the epithet, ὁ μαθητὴς ὅν ἠγάπα ὁ Ἰησοῦς, very nearly achieves that effect) or a one-dimensional representative figure such as a 'guileless Nathanael' or a 'doubting Thomas'.

This raises a fourth and related reason, and one to which Bauckham's comments also point.[46] We have seen that the form of narrative mediacy (a teller who becomes a reflector, an authorial narrative situation which moves into the figural) witnesses to the tension inherent within a retrospective point of view which combines with the 'presentness' of the time of discourse. 'Then' is to some extent gathered up into the longer, fuller perspective of 'now'. Reflection on the true significance or inner meaning of past events inevitably shapes and reshapes those events, but not to the extent that the discourse completely parts company with past event as it is remembered. If the present obtrudes into the past, so the past breaks through into the present in the reminiscences of the eyewitness source. It might be that a first-century writer had no other way to distinguish reporting self from the self who lived then, except by placing a nominal and pronominal distance between the two 'selfs'. Thus a character emerges: a 'he' who is the disciple whom

46. See Bauckham, 'Ideal Author', pp. 43, 44.

Jesus loved.[47] Whether the implied author creates, in the beloved
disciple, a character who represents himself or another person (his
authoritative eyewitness source), the narrative situation adopted enables
the implied author to keep in tension story time and time of discourse.
Paradoxically, it also creates the tension, as the narrator both stands
back from story time and moves into and within it. As narrator he
maintains an external, omniscient point of view but, in merging with
the figure of the beloved disciple, he is able to enter the story world,
and give an inside view as he participates in the events of the story.

Birger Olsson makes some brief comments on point of view which
touch upon the tension but, at the same time, he is unable to define its
dynamics clearly. Consequently, he makes some remarks which are both
perceptive and contradictory. For example, he states that 'the Johannine
presentation gives a good example of an external point of view', to
which external point of view, he indicates, 'the anonymous character
of the Gospel should be linked'.[48] But it is precisely this anonymous
character's presence in the narrative which makes it impossible to say
that the point of view is wholly external. This is borne out by another
of Olsson's statements. 'In the Johannine presentation the narrator
is standing at a distance from the events, *at the same time* he possesses
an insight and a knowledge which makes him a *constantly present,
although invisible, witness.*'[49] Again he draws attention to the anonymous witness and (in a footnote) cites several references where the
beloved disciple appears. But the beloved disciple is hardly invisible.
The effect, I suggest, is more adequately described by understanding
his function to be that of a reflector-character. The question which
arises here is what has *generated* this kind of narrative mediacy? Is the
implied author's motivation that of a writer of fiction, i.e. creating a
character purely for literary and theological purposes? Or does it arise
out of some sort of close relationship which he has with the material
of the story, either at first- or second-hand via the report of an eyewitness? While the contours of an answer to these questions are

47. Brown, *John*, p. 936, cites an instance where Josephus refers to himself in
the third person, using ἐκεῖνος (cf. Josephus, *War*, III.vii.16). Paul also employs a
similar device in 2 Cor. 12.2-5. See also, Staley, *First Kiss*, p. 40 on Xenophon,
and the tension between reference to self as agent and self as restricted narrator.

48. B. Olsson, *Structure and Meaning in the Fourth Gospel* (ET: J. Gray,
ConBNT, 6; Lund: Gleerup, 1974), p. 92, also n. 50.

49. Olsson, *Structure*, p. 94 (italics mine). See also his n. 57.

becoming clear, we shall return to a final judgment in the concluding chapter.

Finally, we may say that the beloved disciple's anonymity enables him to function as a character with whom the reader can identify and whom, perhaps, he or she can emulate. Peter, of course, as a representative disciple, illustrates within the boundaries of the story world, the progress of a disciple towards a more complete understanding and a fuller commitment. Peter can be an encouragement and a beacon of hope to believers who likewise struggle to understand and to follow. But he is an identifiable character, well known in the tradition, and as a named character, an unmistakeably distinct third party. The beloved disciple, by his very anonymity and by virtue of type of narrative mediacy adopted, provides the reader both with an entrée into, and a space within, the story world. The process of reflectorization affects the reader's spatio-temporal location so that he or she also sees things with the eyes of the beloved disciple. Not only does this encourage acceptance of the beloved disciple's witness as reliable but it invites the reader to see in the beloved disciple, a symbol of his/her own situation vis-à-vis both the story and the Jesus to whom the story testifies. In 20.8 the beloved disciple is represented as 'believing', not on the basis of having seen Jesus (in contrast to Mary and Thomas whose faith is awakened by an encounter with the Risen Christ) but on the basis of what he sees in the tomb. Similarly, in 20.30, 31, the implied reader (for whom the possibility of a physical encounter with Jesus does not exist, 20.29) is invited to believe on the evidence of the textually mediated 'signs', as well as on the basis of eyewitness report (something, again, that Thomas was unwilling to do). Furthermore, the disciple whom Jesus loved enjoys a status in which all who will believe in and love Jesus are invited to share (14.23; 15.9, 10). And if Thomas represents the challenge to believe, and Peter the challenge to serve and to follow, the beloved disciple represents the challenge to 'remain', not deflected by concern for the fate of others, as is Peter (21.21), and regardless of the direction of one's personal future (21.23).

Chapter 5

FROM TELLER-CHARACTER TO REFLECTOR-CHARACTER:
THE NARRATIVE DYNAMICS OF JOHN 3

The Issues

In this chapter we shall examine two problems of interpretation in the third chapter of the Fourth Gospel. These problems raise questions regarding the coherence of the narrative. They also have a bearing upon the perspective from which the implied author is understood to have viewed his subject matter, both here and in the Gospel as a whole. The first problem is that of distinguishing the 'voice' of the narrator from those of Jesus and John the Baptist. In simple terms, it relates to the question of whether the quotation marks denoting the conclusion of Jesus' speech should be placed at the end of 3.15 or 3.21. In the discussion between John and his disciples, which follows Jesus' discourse with Nicodemus, does John stop speaking at 3.30 or at 3.36? A second subsidiary, but related, question is that of the strange appearance of the first person plural pronoun, 'we', in 3.11. How is this 'we' to be understood? To whom should it be attributed: to Jesus himself, to Jesus and his disciples, to a later Johannine community, or to Jesus and the narrator?

On the first issue, the nature of the discourse and the indeterminacy of the question of who is speaking lead both Bultmann and Schnackenburg to propose a transposition of verses. Bultmann brings forward vv. 31-36 to follow vv.1-21, thus making these verses all part of the 'discourse of Jesus'. He sees the discourse as comprising material which the evangelist has taken from his 'revelation discourse' source, and 'historicized' by working them into 'his portrait of the life of Jesus'.[1] Schnackenburg proposes the following rearrangement: 1-12, 31-36, 13-21. Both the latter sets of verses (i.e. 31-36, 13-21)

---

1. Bultmann, *John*, p. 132.

form a 'kerygmatic discourse', vv. 31-36 preceding vv. 13-21 because they more naturally pick up on the 'from above'/'heavenly things' versus 'from below'/'earthly things' motif raised in the preceding dialogue with Nicodemus.[2] Schnackenburg asks whether these verses are meant to be a 'revelation discourse' of Jesus himself or a 'kerygmatic discourse of the evangelist'.[3] While he holds to the latter view, he acknowledges that the question is 'perhaps falsely put' because the revelation discourse of Jesus merges into the kerygmatic testimony of the evangelist.[4]

I do not propose to discuss the relative merits of these transpositions, but rather suggest that it is precisely to address the problem of 'who speaks?' that these proposals are put forward by Bultmann and Schnackenburg. It should also be noted that the proposals rest upon questions of source and redaction, so that compositional incoherence is assumed as opposed to narrative coherence. The question of 'who speaks?' also raises the issue of *Sitz-im-Leben*.[5] Most commentators, including Bultmann and Schnackenburg, agree in regarding the discourses (13-21, 31-36) as being reflections of the evangelist (though there is no agreement on where the reflections begin).[6]

On the second issue, a full discussion of the various ways in which the 'we' of 3.11 may be understood is undertaken by Schnackenburg.[7] For our purposes we may summarize them as follows. First, the 'we' refers to Jesus either as a 'royal we' (unlikely according to Schnackenburg, as the usual form is based upon the use of ἐγώ), or as a designation of himself as 'the heavenly revealer in an absolute and exclusive sense'. This, thinks Schnackenburg, 'fits the context well'. Second, 'we' refers to Jesus and the disciples. Schnackenburg favours this alternative and sees it as implying a time when 'the disciples makes [Jesus'] testimony their own, as part of the preaching'.[8] We may note here C.K. Barrett's observation that 'Jesus associates himself with his

2. Schnackenburg, *John*, I, pp. 360-62.
3. Schnackenburg, *John*, I, p. 380.
4. Schnackenburg, *John*, I, p. 381.
5. Cf. here Barrett, *John*, pp. 202, 204.
6. Bultmann, *John*, p. 132; Schnackenburg, *John*, I, p. 360, see n. 52. See also Morris, *John*, pp. 228, 243; but cf. Dodd's cautious remarks, *Interpretation*, p. 308 and Brown, *John*, p. 136.
7. Schnackenburg, *John*, I, pp. 375-76.
8. Schnackenburg, *John*, I, p. 376.

disciples who have seen, believed and known'.[9] Third, 'we' may be taken as a '*pluralis ecclesiasticus*, either in the sense that a certain group of preachers speak or that the community as such joins in'.[10] C.H. Dodd states that the 'we' betrays 'the fact that the testimony of Jesus is mediated corporately by the church':[11] while Bultmann says that 'the "we" goes back to the source, where the speaker was speaking as one of the group of messengers from God'.[12]

Finally, I note a collection of differing observations on the use and significance of the 'we'. Bultmann states that it gives the discourse an air of mystery.[13] Dodd observes that the verse 'represents a transitional process from dialogue to monologue' and is a 'kind of heading to the series of reflections which follow'.[14] Other viewpoints noted by Bultmann and Morris are that of Hirsch: the verse is an editorial gloss (Schnackenburg rules out an 'editorial we' as out of place here); Weiss and Zahn: the 'we' refers to Jesus and the Baptist; Hoskyns: the Baptist, Jesus and the Christian witness; Abbott: 'The Father and I'.[15] The wide range of readings indicated here highlights the puzzle which exegetes face in coming to grips with this change from first person singular to first person plural. Perhaps equally puzzling, if the discourse which follows is to be attributed to Jesus, is the move to the third person; and, in particular, the distancing effected by the self-reference, 'Son'/ 'Son of Man'.

The Problems in the Light of Stanzel's Theory of Narrative Situations

I suggest that a new perspective may be put on these problems if we approach them with the narrative technique as propounded by F.K. Stanzel in mind. Specifically, we may ask what insights are gained if we consider that the progress of the narrative in the Gospel's third chapter displays features which occur when a narrative moves from an authorial narrative situation to a figural narrative situation; and when the mode of the narration moves away from that of a teller-

9.   Barrett, *John*, p. 211; cf. also Morris, *John*, p. 221.
10. Schnackenburg, *John*, I, p. 376.
11. Dodd, *Interpretation*, p. 328 n. 3.
12. Bultmann, *John*, p. 146.
13. Bultmann, *John*, p. 146.
14. Dodd, *Interpretation*, p. 328 n. 3.
15. Bultmann, *John*, p. 146 n. 2, 4; Morris, *John*, p. 221 n. 41.

character towards that of a reflector-character (following Stanzel, I shall use the terms 'teller' and 'reflector' hereafter). In passing it should be noted that in the process of narration, according to Stanzel, the pendulum may swing back and forth constantly between the teller mode, where the emphasis is on narrating and giving information (cf. Wayne Booth's 'telling') and the mediacy of narration is evident, and the reflector mode, where the emphasis is on 'showing' which creates 'an illusion of immediacy in the reader'.[16] It is so in the Fourth Gospel, and in this chapter in particular. Thus, the transition from teller to reflector which occurs in 3.1-21, begins again at 3.22 when the narrative situation returns to that of a teller.

Several features of an 'immediate' presentation are observable in the narration which occurs in this chapter. To begin with, there is the withdrawal of the narrator which takes place in the introduction of a dialogue scene. Indeed, the verses immediately preceding 3.1 retain all the marks of narration by an omniscient narrator who is fully able to give the reader an inside view of Jesus. The narrator, for instance, explains that Jesus did not entrust himself to those who believed in him because he knew the nature of humankind (2.24, 25). There follows what Bultmann refers to as a 'realistically described scene'[17] which, he observes, is never brought to a conclusion for it issues onto the discourse.

Thus the narrator withdraws and presents the reader with a scene in which Jesus is engaged in discussion with Nicodemus, the 'Teacher of Israel'. This dialogue gives way to what appears to be a monologue by Jesus, though, as we have seen, many scholars hold that the evangelist (i.e. narrator) reappears again to offer a reflection on the significance for salvation of the Father's sending of the Son.

In this scene, that narrative process may best be described as 'the reflectorization of a teller-character'. In this process a teller assumes, or begins to assume, the particular attributes of a reflector. At one level it is 'making an authorial narrator think and speak as if he were one of the characters of the story'.[18] At another level it is extending the consciousness of an authorial medium over the consciousness of a figural medium.[19] Thus the effect is to assimilate the thought and speech

16. Stanzel, *Theory*, p. 141.
17. Bultmann, *John*, p. 132.
18. Stanzel, *Theory*, p. 172.
19. Stanzel, *Theory*, p. 177.

patterns of the narrator/teller to those of one of the characters (or even a group of characters). At the same time, when the narrative perspective cannot be attributed wholly to an external omniscient narrator, because of a certain subjectivity and proximity to the thoughts, attitudes and perspective of a character, then the reflector mode is being super imposed upon a teller.

When the process described as 'the reflectorization of a teller-character' is occurring, the narration begins to display characteristics more akin to the mode of a reflector than a teller. A number of features in this process have particular application to the narrative situation found in the Gospel's third chapter. One such feature is the fact that 'variation between third-person reference and first-person reference in the rendering of consciousness is unmarked'.[20] In other words, the use of first-person reference and third-person reference is virtually interchangeable. So, for instance, Jesus may apparently refer to himself as 'I' and as 'the Son' in the same dialogue. By the same token, the use of the 'we' may represent an assimilation of the voice of Jesus with the voice of the narrator. In this process, the 'we' may be taken as a self-referencing 'royal we' or as having a wider reference which includes the Father, or, more probably, the narrator (who is associated with the disciples and the church).

Allied with this phenomenon is the use of free indirect style, which again is one indication of a transition from an authorial medium to a figural medium, from a teller to a reflector. Free indirect style is a technique for the rendition of speech (or thought) which places the narration somewhere between direct and indirect speech (or, in the case of thought, between the direct reporting of thought and interior monologue—the dramatic monologue of an 'I' narrator—so that the interior perspective is nevertheless presented in a third-person voice). This technique has the effect of presenting the narration from a dual perspective, that of the narrator, and that of a fictional character.[21] The interpretation of the 'reflections' in this chapter may be helped if they are understood as a form of free indirect style.

A further indication of a transition from the stance of a teller to that of a reflector occurs when the spatio-temporal perspective changes from a 'there-then' mode to that of a 'here-now', and when an explicit narrative distance is removed by a scenic presentation of events. The

20. Stanzel, *Theory*, p. 170.
21. Stanzel, *Theory*, p. 191.

action is portrayed '*in actu*'. Thus the report of Jesus in Jerusalem gives way to a dialogue between Jesus and Nicodemus in which the reader is the silent participant. The report of the baptizing activity of Jesus and John the Baptist (3.22-24) is followed by a discussion where the reader is engaged 'immediately'.

In discussing two modern novels which display the characteristics of the reflectorization of a teller, James Joyce's *Ulysses* and Thomas Mann's *The Magic Mountain*, Stanzel makes two observations which bear fruit for a consideration of the Fourth Gospel. He raises the possibility of interpreting a novel such as *Ulysses*, based as it is upon phenomena such as the reflectorization of a teller-character, as a 'compositional monologue'. That is, it is 'the interior monologue of the author or of an authorial medium while his imagination is occupied with the composition of the story of 16 June 1904 in Dublin'.[22] He then relates this concept to Mann's work, at the same time referring to the intercommunion of characters, and perhaps the narrator, by the term 'transfiguralization'.[23]

> Transfiguralization means the participation of an individual consciousness in a more comprehensive, super individual consciousness or the removal of the boundaries separating one individual consciousness from another. In this context, the flowing of notions and motifs from the narratorial, that is, the authorial consciousness to the figural consciousness of a fictional character and vice versa is of special interest, because it offers a parallel to the process of reflectorization of the teller-character. Here, too, an authorial and a figural medium seem to share the content of their consciousness with one another.[24]

The significance of these observations for the Fourth Gospel lie in their suggestiveness for seeing the narration as a form of 'compositional monologue' arising out of the implied author's reflection upon the 'events' of the life of Jesus. Specific to ch. 3, the discourses may represent a type of transfiguralization of the reflector medium (or the implied author) with the characters of Jesus and John the Baptist. Be that as it may, we now pass from this theoretical discussion to a specific analysis of how the move from a teller to a reflector takes place in John 3. But first we must note the effect of reflectorization and the use of free indirect style upon the reader's perceptions of the

22. Stanzel, *Theory*, p. 178.
23. A term actually coined by F. Bulhof.
24. Stanzel, *Theory*, p. 178.

characters, and his or her understanding of the discourse.

First, the process has the effect of identifying the narrator with the attitudes, thoughts, and perspective of the character(s). As Stanzel shows, this identification (or assimilation of narrator with character) can lead either to a sense of discrepancy between the narrator's perspective and that of the reflector-character which produces irony, or it may evoke an even stronger rejection of the attitudes and opinions of a character, or characters, by the reader.[25] On the other hand, it may be a way of creating and reinforcing sympathy with the character(s) in the reader's mind. Thus it functions as a method of encouraging a link in the reader's mind between the perspective of a reliable narrator and the reflector-cum-actual character. It operates as a way of directing the reader's sympathies towards or away from the perspective of the character(s). Second, it provides a method by which the perspective of the narration is a dual perspective, that of narrator/reflector with fictional character. The narrator becomes camouflaged as a reflector who is then brought into proximity with the perspective of the character(s).

Analysis of the Reflectorization of the Teller-Character in John 3

The chapter begins with the narrator as teller firmly in place. The narrator sets the scene with a brief report giving details of time and place, and introducing the person of Nicodemus. Scene setting begins in 2.23 for Nicodemus is one of those who have seen the signs which Jesus performs. It is because these signs raise questions in his mind that he comes to Jesus. The first reference to Jesus, in 3.2, uses the third person pronoun (not the proper name 'Jesus' as in the RSV, and many English translations). This is another indication that the narrative unit begins at 2.23. There follows a brief dialogue which leads Nicodemus rapidly to incomprehension.

When Nicodemus, in complete bafflement, says, 'How can this be?' (v. 9), Jesus replies with a question which leads into the discourse. The solemn asseveration, ἀμὴν ἀμὴν λέγω σοι ὅτι ὃ οἴδαμεν λαλοῦμεν καὶ ὃ ἑωράκαμεν μαρτυροῦμεν carries the first suggestion of reflectorization as the narrator widens the self-reference of Jesus to suggest the inclusion of other unspecified parties. The inference that this is

---

25. Stanzel illustrates this process at work with regard to the Sheridans in Katherine Mansfield's *The Garden Party*, see *Theory*, pp. 171-72.

more than just a royal 'we' is encouraged by the juxtaposition of the first person plural verb endings with the first person singular usage λέγω. The reader is reminded of the previous occasion in which a 'we' reference has intruded. This is in the prologue, where there is an underlying freight of reference to those among whom Jesus has lived (ἐσκήνωσεν ἐν ἡμῖν, 1.14), and who have therefore seen (ἐθεασάμεθα, 1.14) and received (ἐλάβομεν, 1.16), have come to know Jesus (1.18) and, by inference, can now bear witness. By implication this, in particular, includes the narrator.

In 3.12 Jesus again uses the first person singular, but the next self-reference is a detached and 'distancing' third-person reference to the 'Son of Man'. The reader presumes that this is indeed a self-reference on the part of Jesus because the context suggests that Jesus is making his remarks in response to Nicodemus' implied question about Jesus' identity (3.2). In other words, the assumption that the co-operative principle is in force means the reader assumes that Jesus (despite a somewhat oblique approach which confuses Nicodemus) is discussing the relationship of his activity to the activity of God. Furthermore, John 1 has piled title upon title on Jesus, and has concluded with an exchange between Nathanael and Jesus where the titles 'Son of God' and 'Son of Man' have been used in conjunction with one another. There Jesus has said nothing to suggest that the title 'Son of God' has been misapplied by Nathanael, yet refers to himself as the 'Son of Man'. If the implied author's intended readers recognized 'Son of Man' as a messianic title, then there ought to have been no doubt in their minds by the time they had read as far as John 3 that the narrator intends the title 'Son of Man' (= Christ) to refer to Jesus. The term 'Son of Man' is regularly used by Jesus in the Synoptic gospels as a self-reference. Hence, many modern readers take its usage at 3.13,14 as a clue that this part of the discourse, at least, may be attributed to him.

The next self-reference, to 'the Son' (3.16), is typically 'Johannine'. It is, no doubt, on this account that many scholars consider this evidence that here the evangelist himself is speaking. That the voice of the narrator is now heard is further strengthened by the fact that the phrase τὸν υἱὸν τὸν μονογενῆ echoes the narrator's comment in the prologue about the Logos who is μονογενοῦς παρὰ πατρός (1.14) and especially the reference to μονογενὴς θεός (1.18), coming as it does after the introduction of the named Jesus Christ in 1.17. Throughout this discourse the reference to Jesus is as 'the Son', so that this together with the fact that the discourse picks up themes introduced in the prologue (light v. darkness, belief v. unbelief, acceptance v. rejection) lends further weight to the supposition that here it is the narrator who speaks.

Nevertheless, the discourse is also thematically coherent with the dialogue between Jesus and Nicodemus. Furthermore, as commentators point out, the narrator quite frequently puts speech which includes reference to 'the Son' on the lips of Jesus (cf. 5.19-29; 6.40, 53; 12.23; 14.13; 17.1).[26] We might note that in a number of these instances the self-reference employs the term 'Son of Man' rather than simply 'the Son' (e.g. 6.53; 12.23) and that sometimes references to the Son, the Son of God, and the Son of Man are used more or less interchangeably, and interspersed with first person references (as in 5.19-47). Brown maintains that there are no stylistic differences in vv. 12-21 where a division between the words of Jesus and the words of the evangelist/ narrator can be detected.[27]

Thus, taken overall, the reported speech of Jesus in the Gospel displays a tendency to slip easily from the first person to third person reference, employing either 'the Son' or 'the Son of Man'. In this discourse, the transition from the self-reference 'I' to the 'Son of Man' and finally to the simple 'the Son' is unmarked in that there are no indications within the structure of the dialogue to suggest that Jesus has stopped speaking. Only in view of the echoes which the discourse has with other parts of the narrative, such as the prologue, where it is certain that it is the narrator's voice which is heard, does the reader have grounds for assuming that the narrator's voice takes over from Jesus' voice. We have here a narrative effect which is illuminated by Stanzel's theory of the move from a teller to a reflector. The voice of the narrator comes together with the voice of Jesus. The boundary between first person and third person becomes indistinct. There is an apparent 'transfiguralization' of consciousness between the narrator and the character Jesus. The theological significance of this will be discussed below.

As the narrative moves on, a new scene is set in which the disciples

26. See Schnackenburg, *John*, I, p. 380: 'The style in which [the discourse] is couched does not rule out the possibility that the evangelist wishes the lapidary phrases to be understood as Jesus' own words, since affirmations in the third person occur at times when Christ is speaking elsewhere. . . '

27. Brown, *John*, p. 136.

of John engage their master in discussion over Jesus' baptismal activity. The transition to this dialogue is made in a few brief remarks by the narrator to the effect that Jesus and his disciples go to the Judean countryside where Jesus spends some time baptizing. John is also baptizing at a place called Aenon near Salim. The narrator does not make it entirely clear whether John and Jesus are situated near each other. On the one hand, John appears not to be aware of Jesus' presence until his disciples come to him and inform him of Jesus' activity. On the other, they say ἴδε οὗτος βαπτίζει καὶ πάντες ἔρχονται πρὸς αὐτον: the ἴδε ('Look', 'See') and the verb 'coming' suggest proximity and 'presentness' not only temporally but physically (reinforced by the contrast with the previous clause where Jesus is stated to have been with John across the Jordan). Indeed, the ἴδε is translated in the RSV as 'here' ('*here* he is, baptizing...') and in the REB as 'now' (*Now* he is baptizing...). Thus it suggests a here/now deixis which is characteristic of a figural narrative situation and the process of reflectorization.[28]

The discourse which follows this exchange between John and his disciples (i.e. vv. 31-36) continues the theme of John's remarks about the distinction between Jesus and himself, and the need for Jesus' reputation to increase while his must decrease. Nevertheless, the references to the above/below motif, the use of the words 'the Son' (3.25, 36) and the theme of believing in him unmistakably connect these verses with the earlier discourse of Jesus, and place them in the wider context of the narrator's discourse. Again the discourse is fruitfully illuminated by recognizing here the process of reflectorization and, in particular, the technique of 'transfiguralization'. The teller (narrator) merges his voice and perspective with that of the reflector (John).

The Narrative and Theological Significance of Reflectorization

The implied author of the Fourth Gospel produces a form of 'compositional monologue' wherein he assimilates the character of Jesus to his conception of him, so that the narrator as reflector and Jesus as character become merged. The character of Jesus *is* the reflectorized character and the teaching of the reflector-character is the teaching of Jesus. Thus a dual perspective becomes apparent: that of narrator and that of Jesus, but it is a perspective in which one is so assimilated to

28. See Stanzel, *Theory*, pp. 92, 170, 199.

the other that it is difficult to separate the two components. It is an extension of the principle that 'the Father and I are one' (10.30) and derives from an understanding that those who remain in Jesus as he remains in the Father become, in a sense, an extension of Jesus. Thus, just as the first disciples who have seen Jesus have seen the Father (14.9), so the reader who has 'seen' the Johannine Jesus knows Jesus for who he really is, the Son of the Father, the Christ. The theological justification for this perspective is found in the implied author's understanding that the Paraclete is the one who provides the bridge between the Jesus who spoke to and taught the first disciples, and the Jesus who speaks and teaches in his narrative.

The relationship between the Johannine Jesus and the historical Jesus must be taken up under another section. The question of whether or not the implied author intended to give an accurate portrayal of the historical Jesus must be held in suspension. I suggest that for the implied author the question does not arise. The closeness of the narrator with the subject of the narration means that they are, in his view, one and the same and readers can take it on trust that his portrayal is one that is true to the historical Jesus. This point of view is encapsulated in the person of the beloved disciple who leans on Jesus' breast and who is, thus, in the bosom of the Son as the Son is in the bosom of the Father. He is the reliable witness whose testimony forms the basis of the story. This testimony is reinforced by the implied author's theology of the Holy Spirit as the one who will bring to remembrance all that Jesus has taught (14.26). In narrative terms, it is the merging of the narrator with the character of Jesus through reflectorization that enables the reader to accept the narrator's teaching and perspective as that of the character Jesus, and conversely, to give to the narrator the aspect of a reliable transmitter of Jesus' words.

When it comes to the narrator's characterization of John, the reader discovers it as one in which his witness is 'Christianized'. This begins as early as the first chapter when, for example, John proclaims Jesus to be the Lamb of God who takes away the world's sin. By process of transfiguralization, the witness of John is gathered up into the witness of the Johannine narrator and hence the implied author and his community. John speaks with the voice of the narrator; the narrator speaks with the voice of John. Both echo the voice of Jesus. In the end, in narrative terms, the reflector-character assimilates all voices and perspectives to that of the teller-character.

*Mussner's Johannine 'Mode of Vision' and its Relationship
to Modes of Narrative Transmission*

The basis of Mussner's understanding of the Johannine 'mode of vision' lies in the hermeneutical significance for the author of the Fourth Gospel, of the lapse of time between the event of the historical Jesus and the rendering of that event in his narrative. This lapse of time did not exist as a vacuum; rather, it contained a developing tradition on which the author drew and in which he stood. Allied with his situation of distance from the time of the historical Jesus and the events of which he wrote, was the need to address certain christological questions which had arisen in the Church of his own time. Building upon Gadamer's theory of interpretation, Mussner sees the author's hermeneutical situation as characterized 'by a peculiar merging of the two horizons of present and past'.[29]

'The Johannine mode of vision is that of a believing and informed witness who, in remembrance, "sees" his subject, Jesus of Nazareth, in such a way that the latter's hidden mystery becomes "visible" and expressible for the Church in the Kerygma'.[30] This is an 'actualizing anamnesis' by which the historical Jesus, through remembrance and reflection aided by the Paraclete, is seen in his true significance as the glorified Christ. This actualizing process is not something achieved *de novo* by the fourth evangelist but arises out of his status as an eyewitness to the event of the historical Jesus; and by way of standing within and building upon the apostolic tradition. '[T]he words and work of the historical Jesus become present at all times for the Church by way of the apostolic traditions and their transmission by the πολλοί narratives' of the apostolic *paradosis*, for example, the pre-Lucan narratives and traditions upon which Luke drew. 'This is a process which in the New Testament culminated and concluded in the fourth gospel.'[31] In this Gospel the actualizing process goes so far that not only is it now the glorified Christ who emerges from its pages, but the evangelist 'lends him his tongue, so that Christ speaks. . . in Johannine language'.[32]

29. Mussner, *Historical Jesus*, p.15.
30. Mussner, *Historical Jesus*, p. 45.
31. Mussner, *Historical Jesus*, p. 53.
32. Mussner, *Historical Jesus*, p. 52.

Mussner takes pains to point out that in all of this 'actualizing anamnesis', this merging of horizons by which the 'original act of vision of the apostolic eyewitnesses is. . . carried over into the process of kerygmatic utterance', the reference to 'attested history' and to the historical Jesus is not abandoned.[33] The 'Johannine mode of vision. . . extends. . .to the eternal dimensions of the historical figure of Jesus'.[34] However, as 'this eternal, permanently valid element showed itself precisely in. . .the historical Jesus, what is attested remains always linked to *history* and so the unity of the kerygmatic Christ with the historical Jesus is maintained'.[35] One way in which this historical rootedness is shown is in the 'more than thirty concrete topographical references' which occur in the Gospel.

The work of the historical Jesus and that of the glorified Christ, expressed through the operations of the Paraclete in the post-Easter community, are two stages of a complete whole; they form a unity as they are 'projected into one another by the evangelist'.[36]

> Fundamentally, therefore, it is impossible to say that in John's gospel the 'historical' Jesus acts and speaks until the crucifixion, and after Easter the 'glorified' Christ acts and speaks; the glorified Christ already acts and speaks all the time in the words and work of the 'historical' (prepaschal) Jesus. The classical examples of this are perhaps Christ's discourses in chs. 3, 6 and 17. Both the prepaschal and the postpaschal Christ speak the same language, and it is Johannine.[37]

It is Johannine christology which permits the identity of the historical Jesus with the glorified Christ. This is because there is no fundamental ontological difference (according to the Gospel's teaching) between the Christ who both pre-existed the historical Jesus (as the Logos) and after his death returned to his glorified existence. Moreover, the glorified Christ continues to speak through the Paraclete, whose 'inspired mouthpiece' is the evangelist. It is this dynamic of the glorified Christ speaking in the Church, through the Paraclete-inspired evangelist, which permits us to say that 'in John's gospel Christ proclaims himself'.

33. Mussner, *Historical Jesus*, p. 85.
34. Mussner, *Historical Jesus*, p. 83.
35. Mussner, *Historical Jesus*, p. 85.
36. Mussner, *Historical Jesus*, p. 86. Mussner is here drawing upon W. Thüsing, *Die Erhöhung und Verherrlichung Jesu im Johannesevangelium* (Münster: Aschendorff, 1960).
37. Mussner, *Historical Jesus*, pp. 86-87.

However, this does not mean that the apostolic tradition about Jesus is made void; rather it is 'made truly actual and interpreted anew'.[38]

Mussner's description of the Johannine 'mode of vision' as an 'actualizing anamnesis' receives support, in narrative terms, in the transference from a teller mode to a reflector mode of narrative transmission. We have seen that through this process the voice of the narrator merges with the voice of a reflector. The perspective becomes a dual one. In the case of the discourses in John 3, the reflector speaks by the mouths of both Jesus and John. This is not simply a matter of 'putting words into the mouths' of these characters, but of realizing in the mediacy of narration the essential significance of the historical Jesus, and the witness of John as the implied author draws both on eyewitness recollection and tradition. At work here is the implied author's strategy in creating a narrator who is both an ethereal figural medium present within the work as an undefined 'I' at the centre of what may be described as a 'we'-circle (to borrow Mussner's term[39]), who also withdraws to a point outside the story world (authorial narrative situation) or behind the characters (figural narrative situation/ 'showing' mode), and who also becomes 'dramatized' in the final stages of the narrative as the beloved disciple. It is as the beloved disciple that the narrator/implied author lays claim to the status of eyewitness. As eyewitness and as the beloved disciple the narrator/implied author not only stands within the authoritative circle of bearers of the tradition about Jesus but also shares in the promise of the Paraclete. The narrative, by discourse (e.g. 14.25-26; 16.12-15) and by event (20.22) establishes the function of the Paraclete in enabling the actualizing anamnesis.

Reflectorization and the 'Truth-Telling' Status of the Narrator/Implied Author

'Should the Vita Jesu which the fourth evangelist presents not rather be termed (even if in an elevated sense) a novel about Jesus?'[40] So writes Franz Mussner of the problematic relationship of the Fourth Gospel's

---

38. Mussner, *Historical Jesus*, p. 87. Cf. here also G.M. Burge, *The Anointed Community* (Grand Rapids: Eerdmans, 1987), pp. 210-17, and S.M. Schneiders, *The Revelatory Text* (San Francisco: HarperCollins, 1991), pp. 72-73.

39. Cf. Mussner, *Historical Jesus*, p. 90.

40. Mussner, *Historical Jesus*, p. 7.

presentation of Jesus to the figure of the historical Jesus. The question is an acute one not only for the historian but for the critical application of narrative theory and criticism to the study of the Gospel. For if it is correct to state that a part of the implied author's art is to move from an authorial to a figural narrative situation so that the voice of the narrator merges with those of Jesus and John, and that these characters speak Johannine language, is it not the case that the implied author presents us with characters of his own making? If he is representing his own perspective and understanding of Jesus as that of Jesus himself, or John's understanding of Jesus, is he not presenting the reader with a 'fictional' Jesus or John? If the Gospel story is an 'actualizing anamnesis' in which memories of the historical Jesus combine with a concern for a christological portrait addressed to issues in the contemporary church, what precisely is the relationship between portrait and historical person?

Part of the answer may lie in a discussion of the 'truth-telling' status of the implied author/narrator. In particular, we must direct attention to what the implied author's narrative strategy is intended to achieve. Here the implied author's strategy in adopting a variable narrative situation and in creating a multi-faceted narrator (who may be both teller and reflector) arguably has the effect of invoking 'belief' or confessional language in the discourse. A function of the variable narrative situation is to provide flexibility in the narrator's point of view. At one moment in the narrative the narrator may be omniscient, the perspective external, the narration explicit: and at another, the narrator withdraws, becoming a figural medium, or merging in voice and point of view with one of the characters, while the mode of narration is scenic and internal to the story. In this manner, the implied author creates in the implied reader the impression of a chain of connection between the narrator and characters such as Jesus or John, or later, the beloved disciple. These characters thus take on the aspect of reflectors or figural mediums. At the same time, this is a chain of connection which rests upon claims to eyewitness status, and an association on the part of the narrator/implied author with the events narrated. It is because the implied author stands within a Paraclete-inspired chain of connection, and an eyewitness tradition, that he feels able to adopt this strategy.

This means that the discourse, even though it may use third-person pronouns and other third person references (e.g. 'the Son'), takes on a logical valency of first-personal 'belief-talk'.[41] Thus in Jesus' dialogue-discourse with Nicodemus, the interchangeability of the first and third person references, and the use of 'we' (as in 3.11) become instances of what D.M. High calls acts of self-involvement.[42] Put one way, the narrator stands 'back of' the words of Jesus. Put another, in this discourse the words of Jesus convey the confessional stance of the implied author. Through 'an act of self-involvement' the narrator merges with (the character) Jesus so that the dialogue with Nicodemus is also a statement of the implied author's confessional stance vis-à-vis the narrative material and the tradition with which he works.

When Jesus says, 'we speak of what we know and bear witness to what we have seen' (3.11), this has meaning not only at the level of the story world but on the level of the discourse as well. For the implied author's perspective is based upon the reminiscences of an eyewitness and post-Easter believing reflection upon the significance of the events recounted. It is a view 'from above': a view which sees things whole from the distance of a later time. Retrospection informed by scriptural reflection provides a perspective in which event *then* may merge with and be informed by discourse *now*. Indeed, the concerns and circumstances of this later time also shape the telling of the story. Hence the οἴδαμεν of 3.11 stands against the οἴδαμεν of 3.2. Jesus and Nicodemus are representative spokesmen of two groups and two perspectives upon the meaning of the historical Jesus. One is the confessing, believing, 'knowing' community of disciples, the other, those who do not receive the testimony or who yet remain to be convinced.

We must set the dialogue-discourses of this chapter within the overall intentions of the Gospel. At 20.31 the narrator makes this statement: 'these are written that you may believe that Jesus is the Christ, the Son of God, and that believing you may have life in his name'. Leaving aside the critical issue of whether the verb should be read as a present subjunctive or as an aorist, and the related question of the belief situation of the intended reader (already Christian or yet to be persuaded non-Christian),[43] we focus attention upon the implied author's personal commitment to the material of the story implicit in this statement. It may be recast as 'I have written of these signs in order that you may believe...' The rhetoric of persuasion suggests that the implied author

41. Cf. High's discussion of 'belief-talk' in *Language*, pp. 159-63.
42. High, *Language*, p. 167.
43. See discussion above pp. 90-91.

desires the reader to adopt an understanding of the person of Jesus to which he is already committed. The statement thus falls within the category of 'first-person believing' and 'first-person-believing-in-first person' statements.[44] That is, it is committed, confessional discourse, belief-talk in which the speaker is self-involved.[45] The logic of the statement, then, is as follows. First, it has the effect of transforming what has in many respects appeared as an '*Er-Text*' ('third person pro- nominal reference to a reflector-character', or an omniscient, detached mode of narration) to an '*Ich-Du-Text*' ('the narratorial "I" addressing the "you" of the reader').[46] Second, it gives the statement, and the narrative to which it refers, the status of an assertion. 'This narrative is about Jesus, who is the Christ, the Son of God. I desire you, the reader, to accept this assertion (on the basis of the evidence here presented) and to place your trust (or, to believe) in him.' Of course, given the type of narrative the Gospel is, it remains for the reader to determine whether the assertion has the illocutionary force of a factual assertion or a fictive 'pretended' assertion. As Searle has pointed out, 'there is no textual property, syntactical or semantic, that will identify a text as a work of fiction', so it comes down to a question of the illocutionary stance that the implied author takes towards it.[47]

In respect of the implied author of the Fourth Gospel, the outcome of this question depends to some extent upon a determination of the complex relationship between his narrative and the events to which they refer, and to the historical figure of Jesus in particular. Thus the reader must determine whether or not the implied author is invoking the 'set of horizontal conventions' which suspend 'the normal operation of rules relating to illocutionary acts and the world'.[48] Or, in other words, does the implied author pretend to perform illocutionary acts in the manner permitted to a writer of fiction by the suspension of normal rules applying to assertions, or do, in fact, the rules such as those outlined by Searle apply?[49]

The narrative strategy is such that, on the face of it, this assertion

44. See High, *Language*, p. 163.
45. See also below p. 223-24.
46. See Stanzel, *Theory*, p. 142.
47. Searle, *Expression*, pp. 65-66.
48. Searle, *Expression*, pp. 66-67.
49. See Searle, *Expression*, p. 62. The rules applying to assertions are given above, pp. 73-74.

(20.31) is one in which the implied author fulfills the rules set down by Searle. Implied in the invitation to belief on the part of the reader is the fact that the implied author both 'commits himself to the truth of the expressed proposition' (the 'essential rule') and is already 'committed to a belief in the truth of the expressed proposition' (the 'sincerity rule'). The narrative situation adopted in ch. 3 has a part in undergirding these commitments, as does the 'we' statement of 3.11. The narrative (discourse and story) is intended to provide the evidence for the truth of the expressed proposition. The discourses, for their part, provide a theological exposition of the proposition: they fill in and give substance to the claim that Jesus is the Christ, the Son of God. They develop what it means to say this. The implied author's mode of narration, which brings the narrator into proximity (a proximity admittedly sometimes difficult to define) with the story and story time, places the author in a position necessary to the provision of such evidence as is required to fulfill the 'preparatory rule'. The fact that these things are written to persuade the reader to accept the implied author's assertions suggests that Searle's third rule that the expressed proposition must not be obviously true to both the hearer and the speaker in the context of utterance is also fulfilled.

Despite difficulties raised by the use of the third person pronoun at 19.35 (to whom does the narrator refer, himself or some one else, for example, the beloved disciple?), I think that the same logic may be applied to this statement. The phrase 'that you may also believe' gives the statement the function of creating an '*Ich-Du-Text*', suggesting in the mind of the reader the narrator's first-hand relationship to the event (either as an eyewitness, or as having received his material from a reliable informant). Thus it may be fairly inferred that the implied author's confessional stance is one of commitment to the truth of his portrayal of and propositions about Jesus. The argument I have developed here is that the narrator/implied author is, by a process of reflectorization, present also in the encounter between Jesus and Nicodemus, and between John and his disciples. His status as eyewitness, confirmed both at 19.35 and at the close of the story, enables the reader to accept him as a reliable witness to the Jesus his story presents.

The narrative written *that* the reader may know that Jesus is the Christ (20.31) also portrays the Jesus *in whom* the reader is to believe. There is no Jesus available to the reader of this story other than the Jesus of the narrative, the Jesus who speaks to Nicodemus in Johannine

language. The witness of John, likewise, is refracted through the interpretation of the implied author. To the testimony of Jesus and John is
added the testimony of the implied author and the believing community
he represents. We might even say that the Gospel is an extended definition, or delineation in story form of the early Christian confession
that Jesus is the Christ, the Son of God.[50] The function of this narrative is to persuade the reader so to appropriate this confession that the
life-giving effects of this 'act of self-involvement' may be fully
realized (cf. 3.15, 2.36a).

Conclusion

By understanding the narrative dynamics of this part of the Gospel
story as one in which the narrative situation moves from that of teller
to reflector, we remove the need for a re-arrangement of the text.
Furthermore, a fresh perspective is provided on the relationship of
the discourses (3.13-21; 31-36)[51] to the characters of Jesus and John,
and their place within the structure of the chapter. Now we may note
how each subtly picks up and develops the dialogue with which it is
introduced. The reflector-character in the first discourse develops both
the reasons why a 'birth from above' is necessary for understanding to
occur and what is the basis and outcome of that birth. The cue for the
first line of argument is Nicodemus's reference to the signs which show
that Jesus is from God. Not signs but spiritually informed sight ('vision
born from above') will bring true understanding of Jesus as the one
who brings the kingdom. The cue for the second is Nicodemus' puzzlement over this new birth: this new birth is Spirit-birth, available only
to those who come to the Light.

In the second discourse, the reflector-character develops John's statements about the relative status of the Christ and of himself. The discussion about the one from above and the one of the earth arises just as
naturally out of John's words as Jesus' words (contra Schnackenburg).
Jesus, the Christ, who comes from above must increase. John, who is
of the earth, must decrease. Yet John's testimony is not discounted.

---

50. For a discussion of the Johannine confession (*homologia*), see V.H. Neufeld,
The Earliest Christian Confessions (Leiden: Brill, 1963), pp. 69-107.

51. These divisions are somewhat arbitrary: the first discourse could easily begin
at 3.11; the discourse attached to the Baptist dialogue, at 3.29. The narrative theory
outlined in this chapter allows flexibility on this matter.

Indeed, his witness is correlated with that of Jesus and the believing community of which the narrator-cum-reflector is a part. V. 32 echoes 3.11, and thus refers not merely to the witness of Jesus but to that of John also. In this discourse, much of what is said of Jesus may be said of John as well. He too bears witness to what he has seen and heard (cf. 1.32-34), he too is one who has been sent from God (3.34, cf. 1.6), he too has received his commission from heaven (3.27).[52] Indeed, it is not by measure that God gives the Spirit, and the likely implication here is that John too shares in the Spirit which he saw descend upon Jesus (1.32) and which the disciples will later receive (20.22).

However, as we have seen, the merging of the voice of the narrator-cum-reflector with the voices of Jesus and John raises sharp questions in the historical-critical arena and for an understanding of the relationship of the Gospel to ostensive historical referents. It is to an examination of this relationship, and to the question of the precise nature of this narrative as a story of Jesus, that we now turn.

52. It is interesting that Jesus later both affirms John's testimony and sets up the same sort of tension between his status and that of John as is developed here (cf. 5.31-38).

Part II

HISTORY AND THEOLOGICAL DISPLAY

Chapter 6

THE FOURTH GOSPEL AS A DISPLAY TEXT

The Issues

On a number of occasions in this study I have spoken of events happening at the level of the 'story world'. Jesus, John, the beloved disciple and the narrator are all characters in this story world (as, of course, are Peter, Nicodemus and all other named and unnamed inhabitants of the world of this discourse). In the last two chapters we saw that the narrator can be both a teller-character and a reflector-character. The beloved disciple, Jesus and John may at times be described as 'figural mediums' or reflectors with whom the narrator becomes associated so that, on the one hand, they speak with a 'Johannine' voice, or, on the other, the narrator perceives events and other characters through their eyes or from their point of view.[1] All this raises questions about the nature of the narrative with which we are dealing. What is the relationship, for instance, between the 'story world' and the real, or historical world? How does the characterization of the people who inhabit this story world relate to what the real, historical figures said and did? (Indeed, are all the characters necessarily to be identified as having had an existence in the real, historical world?) If this Gospel is a story, how is it (or is it) also 'true'? If it is in some sense a historical narrative, is it appropriate or adequate to apply to it critical methods and techniques used in the study of modern fiction?

This chapter will address three issues in particular. First, can a reader distinguish historical narrative from fictional narrative at the level of the discourse? If so, how? We shall see that while there are certain features of fictional discourse which *tend to suggest* that the

---

1. In Genette's terms, they are the 'focalizers' of the action, see e.g. 13.23-30 where, arguably, Judas's departure is 'focalized' through the eyes of the beloved disciple.

world being presented is an imagined one, in the final analysis there
are no formal characteristics which assuredly demarcate fictional discourse from 'ordinary', non-fictional or historical discourse. This
being the case, by what criteria may a reader determine whether a
narrative is fictional or historical? We shall see that readers determine
a narrative's status as fiction or non-fiction by a complex process
which includes determining the function a narrative serves, whether it
purports to refer to the real world or an imagined one, what are perceived to be the author's intentions as conveyed by the literary speech-
acts, and the narrative's relationship with other types of narrative, in
other words, the particular genre with which it belongs or to which it
approximates. Where there is doubt, a narrative may be understood
either as fictional or nonfictional according to a decision made by the
reader; that is, it is simply 'taken to be' a given type of discourse and
read under that prejudgment.[2] Lastly, we shall consider how the criteria
discussed may be applied to the Fourth Gospel to provide a description of, and enable the reader to determine, the type of narrative it is.

Underlying the examination of these issues is the question of how
the Fourth Gospel is to be read. To put it in stark terms, as is sometimes the case in introductions to the Gospel, is it fact or fiction?[3]
Putting the matter in more nuanced terms, how does the discourse
relate to the historical Jesus whose story it purports to tell? How much
is it interpretation of the historical Jesus? How much can we rely on it
to help us discover 'what really happened'? This, of course, is an issue
which has been of particular concern to interpreters since the rise of
biblical criticism in the modern age. But it is perhaps implicit in the
ancient observation of Clement of Alexandria that the Gospel is in a
special sense a 'spiritual gospel'. As an issue it has been addressed in
very different ways. Here we may cite two modern assessments as
instances of the spectrum of opinion to be found. On the one hand,
A.T. Hanson states that 'John's presentation of Jesus has only a very
dubious connection with actual history':[4] on the other hand, S.S.
Smalley says, 'Since history is indispensible to his witness, John would
be less ready to corrupt than to preserve its historical basis.'[5]

2.   On this see further below pp. 196-200, 265.
3.   See e.g. Lindars, *John* (NTG), p. 25.
4.   Hanson, *The Prophetic Gospel*, p. 2.
5.   S.S. Smalley, *John: Evangelist and Interpreter* (Exeter: Paternoster Press,
1978), p. 172.

In his book, *The Eclipse of Biblical Narrative*, Hans Frei argues that the essential nature of biblical narrative literature as 'realistic' or 'history-like' became confused and forgotten in the rise of the Enlightenment and subsequent historical-critical interpretation of the Bible. At its simplest, what happened was that the distinctive quality of its 'realistic, history-like narrative' was not 'examined for the bearing it had in its own right on meaning and interpretation'. Rather the issue became one of the degree to which realistic narrative was actually historical: 'history-like' came to be confused with actual ostensive reference to historical reality.[6]

As the question became one of the truth of biblical narrative in its relation to ostensive historical reality, so difficulties arose. Biblical narrative was examined, and attacked or defended, on the basis of its failure or otherwise to accurately portray what was taken to be historical reality. Beyond this, biblical criticism moved toward new ways and means to sift the material in an attempt to establish what might be the historical substratum beneath the overlay, in the case of the gospels at least, of the early church's apologetic, kerygmatic, confessional or liturgical shaping of the narrative. In the application of the historical-critical method this usually meant reconstructing, by a process of extraction, historical reality from the stuff of the narrative. Alternatively, the critical approach sought the 'theological' meaning conveyed in the narrative form. In other words, meaning is located not so much in any reference to historical events but in the theological and symbolic purpose for which the narratives presented their version of events. A logical extension of this was the 'Bultmannian' disjunction between the Jesus of history and the Christ of faith.

Frei is primarily concerned with tracing, through the eighteenth and nineteenth centuries, the history of the 'simple transposition and logical confusion between two categories', namely, realistic narrative and historical account. He provides in bare outline a description of what he means by the realistic 'history-like' elements of biblical narrative, which he places in careful contradistinction to historical elements.[7]

6.   H. Frei, *The Eclipse of Biblical Narrative* (New Haven: Yale University Press, 1974), chapter 1; especially pp. 5, 10, 11, 16.

7.   See Frei, *Eclipse*, pp. 10-16. Briefly, these elements are: (1) that in realistic narrative, the narrative rendering is an indispensable part of the meaning of the narrative. (2) Realistic narrative sets characters, or individual persons, in the context of setting and incident (each being dependent on the other) so that their inner life and

Though he argues cogently for a return to a proper understanding of the significance of the biblical narratives as 'realistic' in the interpretation of their meaning, he gives no sustained or developed account of what it would mean to read a biblical text as realistic or 'history-like' narrative.[8]

Moreover, one senses that the application of the term 'realistic narrative' to the biblical narratives leaves open the whole question of the correlation of characters and events depicted in them to actual historical persons and events. It is as if Frei gets as far as saying that 'a realistic narrative is like an historical account'[9] but is not of the same sort. Such a position appears simply to accept the conventional polarization of 'realistic narrative' and historical account. This is a position which I believe is not tenable, especially in the light of some of the recent discussion about the relationship of historical to literary narrative, let alone an analysis of actual instances of the narrative form.[10] Furthermore, in his sketch of the characteristics of realisitic narrative, Frei provides a delineation which is certainly appropriate as a description of recognizably, that is self-evidently and 'self-confessedly', fictional discourse, such as modern novels, but becomes problematic when applied unreservedly to biblical narrative.[11]

The issue of the distinction between historical narrative which has overt, ostensive reference to real events in the real world, and that which is 'history-like', realistic narrative is a question which applies to the Fourth Gospel with consequent and sharp problems for exegesis and hermeneutics, theology and faith. In *John as Storyteller*, Mark

'their capacity as doers and sufferers of actions or events' are both illuminated and fitly render their external circumstances. (3) 'Believable individuals and their credible destinies are rendered in ordinary language and through concatenation of ordinary events' to become 'recognizable realistic "types"' of the human condition, set against the backdrop of powerful historical circumstances and forces.

8.   But see H. Frei, *The Identity of Jesus Christ* (Philadelphia: Fortress Press, 1975), especially Part Four, for a theological-exegetical application of the category 'history-like' to the gospel accounts of Jesus. This work, to my mind, is too theologically analytical (and hence better seen as a work of narrative theology) to provide a helpful model of an analysis of the gospel narratives as 'realistic' narrative.

9.   See Frei, *Eclipse*, p. 14.

10.   See below pp. 201-207. Frei refers to aspects of this debate in a footnote to chapter 1 (n. 5. p. 325) but does not elaborate on the issue.

11.   The sense in which a fictional discourse is 'self-confessedly' so is explored below (pp. 198-99).

Stibbe faults Culpepper for treating the Gospel as an a-historical novel, an approach taken under the influence, Stibbe claims, of Frank Kermode's *Genesis of Secrecy*. But Frei's approach, to whom Culpepper also refers, would yield this assessment of the Gospel narrative as well. Stibbe seeks to redress this deficiency. His description of John's story is that it is 'poetic history'.[12] This is a suggestive and attractive description, but hardly precise. What sort of history are we reading when we read 'poetic history'? Stibbe also refers to the Gospel as 'charismatic history', which is the history of Jesus redescribed christologically under the inspiration of the Holy Spirit.[13] How does this form of history relate to what might be thought of as a more conventional (i.e. scientific) type of history? The aim of this volume is, in part, to attempt to provide a description of the nature and character of the Fourth Gospel which will help in understanding what speaking of the Gospel as 'poetic history', 'charismatic history' or 'realistic narrative' ought to mean.

The debate over the essential character of the Gospels, and their relationship to history, is paralleled in literary theory by a discussion concerning the nature of fictional as opposed to nonfictional discourse. It is my intention in this chapter to examine aspects of this theoretical debate in an attempt both to examine the status of fictional discourse in its relation to 'reality'[14] and to illuminate the nature and status of the Fourth Gospel's discourse. In particular, I shall draw on the application of speech-act theory to literary discourse offered by M.L. Pratt in *Toward a Speech-Act Theory of Literary Discourse*. Here she provides a definition of literary discourse as 'display text' which is especially fruitful in giving a description, with certain reservations, of the Fourth Gospel.

Narrative is a broad generic field within which the gospels, and specifically the Fourth Gospel, may be placed. But narrative encompasses a spectrum of genres which run from historical narrative through to fictional or imaginative narrative, both that sort which may be broadly described as 'realistic' (and many modern novels are

---

12.   See Stibbe, *John as Storyteller*, pp. 89, 196. For his comments on Culpepper, see pp. 9-11, 73.

13.   Stibbe, *John as Storyteller*, p. 190; and cf. his *John*, p. 18.

14.   'Reality' being a shorthand reference to the world consisting of its 'elements (material and spiritual) of reality: things and states of affairs. . . "The sum total of reality is the world" [Wittgenstein]'; quoted from Hamburger, *Logic*, p. 52.

realistic and history-like in the sense that Frei intends) and that which
is plainly fantastic. Thus, in parallel with the description of the nature
of fictional discourse, I include an examination of the literary conventions shared by fictional and historical narrative. Finally, the construction of a model of narrative forms will enable us to discuss the
place of the Fourth Gospel's narrative within the broad spectrum of
narrative types.

The Logical Status of Fictional Discourse

In The *Logic of Literature*,[15] Käte Hamburger seeks to establish a
distinction between non creative (non poetic/non literary) and creative
discourse on the basis of a theory of language.[16] She contends that all
language is based on a subject-object structure; that is all sentences are
'statements of a statement-subject about a statement-object'. This is the
case regardless of the actual form of the sentence, whether it be a
declarative statement, a question, a wish, command or exclamation.[17]
The statement-subject is the real person, the one from whose 'here-
and-now' existence, the statement emanates. Hamburger's alternative
term is the 'I-Origo', the self situated in time and space from whose
perspective a statement is made and whose particular spatio-temporal
situation determines how the language used is oriented in time. Thus a
real I-Origo must always narrate events which happened in the past in
a manner which preserves the pastness of their occurrence. The relationship of a real statement-subject (I-Origo) to the object spoken about
never violates the subject-object relationship, so that, for instance,
narration about a third person always retains an objective, external
perspective. Hamburger calls this subject-object relationship the statement-structure of language and argues that all 'statement' (conceived
of as the statement of *someone* about *something/someone else*) is reality
statement. In her own words, 'that which is stated is the statement-
subject's field of experience, which is merely another way of expressing
the fact that there exists a polar reference, a relation between the

15.   K. Hamburger, *The Logic of Literature* (ET: M.J. Rose; Bloomington:
Indiana University Press, 2nd rev. edn, 1973).
16.   Debate about the ontological status of fiction is broadranging and complex.
It cannot be entered into in full here. See also Pratt, *Toward*, chapter 1; and Martin,
Recent Theories, pp. 181-87.
17.   Hamburger, *Logic*, pp. 31-39.

statement-subject and the statement-object'.[18]

In fictional narration, the 'I-Origo' of a real statement-subject disappears and is replaced by the 'I-Origo' of the fictive character (or the 'I-Origines' of fictive characters). The real spatio-temporal system of the real statement-subject is displaced by that of a fictive person, or persons. In terms of the logic of language structure, what occurs is that 'between the narrating and the narrated there exists not a subject-object relation i.e. a statement-structure, but rather a functional correspondence'. 'That is, the narrative poet is not a statement-subject. He does not narrate about persons and things, [rather] the persons in a novel are narrated persons, just as the figures of a painting are painted figures. [T]he act of narration is a *function*, through which the narrated persons, things, events etc. are created.'[19] 'The absence of the real I-Origo and the functional character of fictional narration are one and the same phenomenon.'[20] In summary, what this means is that the fictive world is a created one in which there is no real space and no real time. The fictive narrator is a function of the writer's narrative art. A narrative situation is created in which the objective relationship between the one who speaks and the ones spoken about (and their world) no longer exists.

This condition creates certain possibilities which themselves, somewhat paradoxically, are both 'symptoms' of a non-real fictive world, and help to create that world. These linguistic possibilities may be described as 'the grammar of [fictional] narration'.[21] The features of this 'grammar' are as follows.

The 'Grammar' of Fictional Narration

In the first place, the past (preterite) tense no longer functions as an indicator of pastness. The 'epic preterite', as Hamburger calls it, loses its past reference because the temporal function of tense is suspended.

---

18.   Hamburger, *Logic*, p. 51. An I-Origo may, of course, also make statements about himself or herself, but the same subject-object relationship must exist for it to be a reality statement. For example, narration about past events must retain past reference.

19.   Hamburger, *Logic*, p. 136 (italics mine). In quoting Hamburger, I have rearranged the order of the statements slightly.

20.   Hamburger, *Logic*, p. 137.

21.   Martin, *Recent Theories*, p. 136-42. That I have had to add the word 'fictional' to the description is an indication that Martin, like many other literary critics, writes in a context where 'narrative' is taken simply to mean fictional narrative.

This is because the past, present, or future denotation of tense is no longer tied to the temporal situation of the one making the statement (in the case of fictional narrative, the implied author/narrator). To illustrate, the statement, 'Mr Smith was on a trip and tomorrow he was to return home' is understood in a novel as 'Mr Smith is on a trip. . . ' As Roy Pascal says, 'the author has obliterated his separate identity, and we experience the statement as being neither in the past nor in the present'. Hence '[t]he epic preterite creates a fiction; and fiction is something that exists out of time and place'.[22] By the same token, the historic present, much used in ancient literature, has 'the function of presentifying past events'.[23] It may be used in historical narrative but when it is it has the effect of 'fictionalizing' the account and rendering it as a 'dramatic visualization' of the event(s) recorded.[24] There has been a good deal of discussion both over the origins of the historic present (e.g. whether or not it derives from oral narration) and its function or effects.[25] By and large its effect is to render past events in a vivid manner, and it functions as a 'signal of the narrator's mood, or his subjective attitude towards the experience he is relating imaginatively or as eyewitness'.[26] It may have the effect either of transporting the reader into the past, or bringing the past alive in the reader's present. Its ancient rhetorical purpose was especially to create 'a sense of eyewitness authority'.[27]

The historic present is used a great deal in the Fourth Gospel. The third person singular present indicative form of the verb λέγειν is used constantly throughout (amounting to about 42 per cent of all instances of the verb's use).[28] Some of the more striking examples of the historic present (including some instances where λέγει appears) are found in 1.29, 38, 43, 45; 4.5, 7; 13.4-6, 24-26; 20.2, 5, 6; all of

22.   R. Pascal, 'Tense and Novel', *The Modern Language Review* 57.1 (1962), p. 3. Cf. Hamburger, *Logic*, pp. 68-71, 98. Note that in a reality statement, the past tense cannot be used with the adverb 'tomorrow'.

23.   Hamburger, *Logic*, p. 99.

24.   Hamburger, *Logic*, p. 102.

25.   Cf. on this Hamburger, *Logic*, pp. 98-110; C. Casparis, *Tense without Time* (Swiss Studies in English, 84; Bern: Francke Verlag, 1975), pp. 15-23; Pascal, 'Tense', pp. 8-11.

26.   Casparis, *Tense*, p. 23.

27.   Casparis, *Tense*, p. 50.

28.   Cf. J.J. O'Rourke, 'The Historic Present in the Gospel of John', *JBL* 93 (1974), pp. 586, 589.

which help to give the narrative the air of an eyewitness report. Whether the aorist verbs, which often inhabit the same sentence or are found within the textual vicinity (cf. e.g. 1.43, or 20.2-5), thereby take on the aspect of the 'epic preterite' may depend somewhat upon the proclivities of the reader, and decisions taken outside of the reading experience regarding the relationship of the implied author to the material. Pascal notes the 'traditional distaste [on the part of English readers] for the use of the historic present', so that there is an inherent bias against rendering the Greek historic present in the same tense in English.[29] If this observation is correct, then cultural factors intrude on the matter from the outset. Nevertheless, I suggest that the continual shift between past tense and (historic) present tense inevitably tends to colour the whole narrative with a 'presentified' aspect. The reader is drawn into the narrative and, particularly when the narrative is in scenic mode or where dialogue-scene is concerned, reads it as an 'on the spot' silent observer. To this extent, and in the degree to which it may be said that the implied author's I-Origo disappears, as, for example, in the story of the Wedding at Cana or the woman of Samaria, the reader loses a sense of the pastness of the action. Dialogue-scene and conversational pieces are features which, in their own right, tend to give a narrative a fictional aspect, at least for the modern reader. The reflectorization of a teller-character, where the boundaries between narrator and character are blurred, also induce a fictional aspect in the narrative.

Another feature of the 'grammar' of fictional narrative is the way in which deictics (adverbs of time and place such as 'here', 'there', 'now', 'then', 'today', and so forth; or demonstratives such as 'this' or 'that') are used with verbs of past tense so that the sense of pastness disappears or is blurred. This phenomenon is especially striking when deictics which place the action in the temporal-spatial sphere of the here-and-now are associated with verbs of past tense. For example, a Hemingway story begins, 'It was *now* lunchtime and they were all sitting under the double green fly of the tent pretending that nothing had happened.'[30] Additional examples given by Hamburger are:

29. Pascal, 'Tense', p. 8.
30. Quoted by Martin, *Recent Theories*, p. 137. Martin uses this to illustrate the tense shift which this feature induces in past tense verbs: 'they were all sitting' takes on the sense of the present tense, while time past is now designated by the past perfect tense, as in 'had happened'.

... and, of course, he was coming to her party *tonight*.
Virginia Woolf, *Mrs. Dalloway*.

But in the morning she had to trim the tree. *Tomorrow* was Christmas.
Alice Berend, *The Bridegrooms of Babette Bomberling*[31]

Normally the meaning of these deictics is governed by the speaker's location in space and time. 'By eliminating all self-reference', says Wallace Martin, 'a narrator cuts deictics loose from their normal connection to an identifiable speaker: thus they are free to gravitate toward the here-and-now of the characters.' The use of such deictics means that '[t]he whole tense system is shifted forward in time'.[32]

By and large, the Fourth Gospel's use of deictics conforms to that of a retrospective point of view. The use of the aorist tense with there/then deictics (e.g. ἐκεῖ) ensures that the spatio-temporal orientation of the reader remains at a distance from the time of the story (cf. 2.1, 6; 5.5 note the juxtaposition of the narrator's comment about the location of the pool: instances of other temporal orientation with past tense are, e.g., 1.35, τῇ ἐπαύριον with the pluperfect εἱστήκει, and 2.13). On the other hand, the use of the historic present brings the spatio-temporal location of the reader closer to story time and, consequently, lends deictics and temporal indications the colouring of a 'here/now' deixis. At 1.29, for instance, the use of the (historic) present tense in the phrase τῇ ἐπαύριον βλέπει τὸν Ἰησοῦν ἐρχόμενον πρὸς αὐτόν gives the narrative the air of immediacy. This is, perhaps, increased by the fact that it follows a comment by the narrator using aorist verbs, which suggests an aside injecting a retrospective glance into a dramatically presented narrative. Dialogue, as has been noted already, tends to add to the present aspect of a narrative and thus 'here/now' deictics found in direct speech tend to add to the vividness of the presentation (cf. 2.16, 3.26).[33]

In addition to this, in its use of connective particles and demonstrative pronouns, the narrative displays some striking qualities. The way the particle οὖν is used has long been recognized as a peculiarity of this Gospel.[34] E. Ruckstuhl gives the various uses of οὖν as instances

31.   Hamburger, *Logic*, p. 72.
32.   Martin, *Recent Theories*, p. 137.
33.   ἴδε (1.29) though not strictly a deictic (but cf. REB 'There') nevertheless when used, as it is in the Gospel, in direct speech takes on the aspect of a 'here/now' deictic.
34.   Cf. Barrett, *John*, p. 7; E. Ruckstuhl, *Die literarische Einheit des Johannes-*

of what he calls the 'οὖν *historicum*'; though he differentiates between the use of οὖν where a strong consequential force is intended, or where it is causally linked with what precedes it (= οὖν *consecutivum*) and where the οὖν is used (more or less) simply as a narrative link (οὖν *historicum*/οὖν *connexivum*). These latter instances he says might better be called a 'narrative οὖν' (οὖν *narrativa*).[35] For our purposes, what is especially striking is the frequency of the use of οὖν, so that in places (e.g. 20.2-10; 21.5-11) the narrative takes on something of the almost breathless energy of a first-hand or anecdotal report.

Τότε οὖν, 'a striking pleonasm which sounds something like "then after that"',[36] is used four times in the Gospel (11.14; 19.1,16; 20.8) and in each case at a point where the action takes a dramatic move forward, or the implied author wishes to stress a point, e.g. when at last Jesus speaks plainly about Lazarus' death (11.14); when Pilate attempts to placate the Jews by having Jesus whipped (19.1), then finally capitulates (19.16); when the beloved disciple steps into the tomb, sees and believes (20.8). Thus we might imagine the narrator placing a stress on the connective, 'so *then*', in order to make an impact on the implied reader. All in all, the repeated use of οὖν adds to the dramatic, and eyewitness character of the narrative.

Is it possible to regard μετὰ τοῦτο/ταῦτα ('after this/these things') as an instance of the use of a present adverbial with past tense verbs (cf. 2.12; 3.22)? Perhaps these are used simply as a vague narrative

evangeliums (NTOA, 5; Göttingen: Vandenhoeck & Ruprecht, 1987), pp. 193-94, 197, 292-93.

35.   See especially Ruckstuhl, *Einheit*, pp. 292-93; cf. Barrett, *John*, p. 7. Ruckstuhl's careful distinctions are worth bearing in mind, though the distinction between an οὖν *consecutivum* and an οὖν *connexivum* is, I think, in some instances difficult to maintain. For example, why cannot these instances be taken as being οὖν *consecutivum*: 4.33, 40; 5.10; 11.14?

36.   E. Ruckstuhl, "Johannine Language and Style", in M. de Jonge (ed.), *L'Evangile de Jean* (BETL, 44: Leuven: Leuven University Press, 1977), p. 134; cf. *BDF*, p. 240 n. 459(2):'Jn uses τότε οὖν with a fuller sense = "now" (in contrast to the preceding time).' Ruckstuhl's inconsistency shows here, for though he describes τότε οὖν as a case quite different from the οὖν *historicum* (*Einheit*, pp. 193-94: 'und zwar als vom οὖν historicum allein verschiedene'), he includes it under the different categories of this overall type: once as an οὖν *consecutivum* (19.16), once as a 'simple' οὖν *historicum* (20.8) and twice as οὖν *connexivum* (11.14, 19.1); ref. *Einheit*, pp. 292-93. His article, "Johannine Language and Style", p. 134, states the case better: '[It] is not only a special case of the οὖν historicum. . . but a distinctive stylistic fact in its own right.'

link.[37] Yet, inasmuch as their use lends an asyndetic quality to the narrative,[38] they contribute to the distinctive Johannine style which gives the story a dramatic vibrancy. Finally, the Johannine fondness for οὗτος and ἐκεῖνος is striking. Of course, it may often be weakened simply to 'he/she' and to enable the narrator to refer back to a previously mentioned character. At 2.21, for example, the demonstrative pronoun refers back to Jesus, for the referent ('Ιησοῦς, 2.19) has been placed at a diegetic distance by the intermediary reference to the Jews in v. 20. Nevertheless, the use of these strong demonstratives evokes a narrative act on the part of the narrator of 'pointing out' the character. It is a use of the Johannine 'index finger' which has the effect of closing the gap between story time and time of discourse. The use of ἐκεῖνος is especially interesting in this regard in that it both sets a distance between the narrator and the one spoken about ('that one') and yet, by the very act of specifying, brings the object of such specification closer to the reader's spatio-temporal orientation.

It would be hazardous to claim a deictic function for every case where these occur. It would be even more difficult to argue that these necessarily fulfill a function such as that which obtains where here-and-now deictics are employed in a modern novel (as shown above). However, when *taken together with* such features of Johannine style as the use of the historic present, and asyndeton, the manner in which these 'deictics' are used does tend to colour the narrative with what might be taken as the aspect of either a fictional or a first-hand account.

Two further symptoms of fiction must be mentioned. One is that verbs of inner action (to believe, intend, think, reflect, feel, etc.) can be employed of third persons *qua* third persons, so that their inner life, the subjective 'I-originarity' of their inner mental processes, can be portrayed. Used as a distinguishing mark of fiction, this pheno-

37. Cf. Brown, *John*, p. 112 and Barrett, *John*, p. 194, on the use of these phrases and their relative specificity. Commentators generally discuss the function of these as indicators of temporal sequence, and the relative length of time between the events thus connected. I suggest they should rather be seen as devices for connecting segments of narrative. They function as a resumptive device whereby the narrator, as it were, picks up the tale again or indicates that he is moving on to a fresh narrative event. If there is any distinction between μετὰ τοῦτο and μετὰ ταῦτα (and it is likely to be slight), then it relates to the narrator's perspective on his narration and whether he is thinking specifically of the event (or even statement, cf. 11.11) just related or more generally of the events as a series of more or less discrete happenings.

38. Cf. *BDF*, p. 240 n. 459(3).

menon must be analyzed with caution. For, of course, it is perfectly possible in the real world to predicate the inner intention of a third person based on intuition or the percipient observation of external indicators of mood, physical expression and so forth.[39] But this will always be, and will be understood to be, an external view of an inner state. Without doubt, the access to characters' inner lives found in fictional discourse substantiates the truth that, as Hamburger states it, 'fiction is the sole epistemological instance where the I-originarity (or subjectivity) of a third-person *qua* third-person can be portrayed'.[40] The following are instances of verbs of inner action to be found in the Fourth Gospel: 2.24, 25; 4.1; 6.15? (using forms of γνῶναι); 6.61; 13.1; 18.4 (εἰδέναι); 19.8 (μᾶλλον ἐφοβήθη); 20.8 (ἐπίστευσεν). Some of these cases might be put down to retrospective consideration of what 'must have been the case', perception on the part of the implied author (e.g. 2.24, 25; 4.1; 19.8), genuine foresight on the part of Jesus (e.g. 18.4) or eyewitness reminiscence (20.8). But there is also no doubt that the implied author explicitly presents 'inside views' of some of the characters and events. For example, at 6.61 the narrator states that Jesus 'knew in himself' (εἰδὼς... ἐν ἑαυτῷ) that some of his disciples were unhappy with his teaching; and elsewhere he is portrayed as knowing what is to happen to him, who his betrayer is (13.21-27) and that Peter will deny him (13.36-38).

Allied with this feature is the use, widespread in modern fiction, of discourse which represents a character's inner thoughts by the process of 'interior monologue'. This phenomenon has been given a variety of names and descriptions. One of the most suggestive is that of the Russian critic, Bakhtin, who describes it as 'dual voiced discourse'... 'a mixture or merging of narrator and characters'.[41] On the model of

    39.   On this point, against Hamburger, *Logic*, p. 82, see Martin, *Recent Theories*, p. 146. On omniscience in a narrative, Martin writes: ' A narrator may "see with" one or more characters, presenting what they see, as if looking over their shoulders. Even if the narrator seems to have crossed the line between inner and outer worlds, using such phrases as "she noticed" or "he was surprised to see", we have no firm evidence that this has happened, because we all draw such conclusions about what others think, having noted their reactions, without claiming access to their minds.'

    40.   Hamburger, *Logic*, p. 83.

    41.   Martin, *Recent Theories*, p. 138. It is termed 'style indirect libre' by the French, 'erlebte Rede' ('experienced speech') by the Germans. 'Other (English) names are "represented discourse" (Dolezel), "represented speech and thought" (Banfield), "substitutionary narration" (Hernadi), and, as applied only to thought, "narrated

Stanzel's typological circle of narrative situations, the phenomenon emerges most clearly as a narrative approaches the 'ideal' of the figural situation. Though it does not always take the same form, Martin states that it appears to be a universal phenomenon.

We may ask whether it is also a feature of ancient literature. I have argued in the previous chapter that parts of John ch. 3, 16-21, 31-36 in particular, may be understood as a merging of the narrator's voice with those of the characters. Thus, the Fourth Gospel is one ancient work, at least, where this phenomenon appears to be found. Chariton's *Chaereas and Callirhoe* is a first-century Greek romance.[42] Here Chariton certainly gives the reader inside views of the characters, and in many cases the vivid narrative style produces the impression of a narrator who is 'close up' to his characters (cf., for example, I.7.1, 2; I.9.3, 6; II.7.1; III.2.6-9; IV.3.11; IV.4.1; VI.1.6-8; VI.9.4, 5, 7).[43] Yet, for the most part, the narrative situation never moves entirely into the figural. The narration remains authorial in that the reader is aware that it is the narrator who is speaking and the portrayal of a character's inner thoughts is generally done in the form of soliloquy.

Of the instances cited here, three may be taken as coming close to the narrative situation wherein a teller becomes a reflector. The first, at I.9.3, occurs when the use of asyndeton makes the transition from narrator comment to character's speech very sudden if not almost imperceptible.

> When they began to use crowbars and hammer heavily to open the vault, Callirhoe was gripped by a variety of emotions—fear, joy, grief, surprize, hope, disbelief. Where is this noise coming from? Is some divinity coming for me—poor creature—as always happens when people are dying. . . [44]

---

monologue" (Cohn)'. It is a phenomenon that has generated much discussion and a vast literature.

42. For further details see p. 213 below.

43. See G. Molinié (ed.), *Chariton, Le Roman de Chairéas et Callirhoé* [B = Budé], or B.P. Reardon (ed.), *The Collected Ancient Novels* (Berkeley: University of California Press, 1989 = R): I.7.1, 2 (B., p. 60; R., pp. 29-30); I.9.3 (B., pp. 62, 63; R., p. 31); I.9.6 (B., p. 63; R., p. 31); II.7.1 (B., p. 84; R., p. 45); III.2.6-9 (B., pp. 94, 95; R., p. 51); IV.3.11 (B., p. 123; R., p. 69); IV.4.1 (B., p. 127; R., p. 69); VI.1.6-8 (B., p. 152; R., pp. 89, 90); VI.9.4, 5, 7 (B., p. 167; R., p. 100).

44. Reardon, *Collected*, p. 31. (In view of the fact that an ancient text would have been without the benefit of quotation marks signalling the beginning of direct speech, I have omitted them from this extract.) Cf. Budé, p. 63: . . . τὴν Καλλιρρόην

At VI.9.4, direct comment by the narrator ('In fact, I rather think. . . ') serves to combine the narrator's judgment with a character's (Artaxates') opinions and feelings. Indeed, it is difficult for the reader to know what represents Artaxates' perspective and what the narrator's. Arguably, the narrative segment may all be attributed to Artaxates as reflected through the narrator.

> Artaxates too kept his peace: his excuse was that now that his master was in a dangerous situation he did not dare to remind him of an amorous dalliance, but the truth was that he was glad to be rid of her, as he would be of a wild beast. In fact, I rather think he was actually grateful to the war, for having broken this passionate attachment on the King's part—it was feeding on lack of occupation.[45]

Shortly after this segment comes a piece of narrative (VI.9.7) where the inner psychology of a character is skilfully and delightfully realized, both by narrator description and by direct speech. Each is brought into artful contiguity, through asyndeton, so that the King's dilemma (cf. VI.9.5) is vividly portrayed. He has by no means forgotten Callirhoe, but is embarrassed to admit his infatuation.

> After much preliminary talk, and first giving instructions for the disposition of everything, he ended up by mentioning Callirhoe with a well-counterfeited expression meant to convey it did not matter to him. 'Oh' he said, 'that foreign girl whose case I undertook to judge—she can come along with the other women.'[46]

These instances suggest that narrative situations which approximate to the figural were by no means impossible in ancient literature. We

κατελάμβανεν ὁμοῦ πάντα, φόβος, χαρά, λύπη, θαυμασμός, ἐλπίς, ἀπιστία. Πόθεν ὁ ψόφος; Ἀρά τις δαίμων κατὰ νόμον κοινὸν τῶν ἀποθνῃσκόντων ἐπ᾽ ἐμὲ παραγίνεται τὴν ἀθλίαν. (In giving the Greek, I have abbreviated the quotation, but I have supplied the text which, I trust, illustrates the point.)

45. Reardon, *Collected*, p. 100; Budé, p. 167: ἀλλὰ καὶ Ἀρταξάτης κατεσιώπησεν, ὡς δῆτα μὴ θαρρῶν ἐν κινδύνῳ τοῦ δεσπότου καθεστηκότος παιδιᾶς ἐρωτικῆς μνημονεύειν, τὸ δὲ ἀληθὲς ἄσμενος ἀπηλλαγμένος καθάπερ ἀγρίου θηρίου· ἐδόκει δ᾽ <ἂν> μοι καὶ χάριν ἔχειν τῷ πολέμῳ διακόψαντι τὴν βασιλέως ἐπιθυμίαν ὑπὸ ἀργίας τρεφομένην.

46. Reardon, *Collected*, p. 100; Budé, p. 167:. . . ὁ βασιλεύς, πολλὰ πρῶτον εἰπὼν καὶ τὰ ἄλλα διατάξας ὡς ἕκαστον ἔδει γενέσθαι, τελευταίας ἐμνημόνευσε Καλλιρρόης ἀξιοπίστῳ τῷ προσώπῳ, ὡς οὐδὲν αὐτῷ μέλον· Κἀκεῖνό φησι τὸ γύναιον τὸ ξένον, περὶ οὗ τὴν κρίσιν ἀνεδεξάμην, σὺν ταῖς ἄλλαις γυναιξὶν ἀκολουθείτω.

recall, too, that dialogue-scene (a feature of much Hebrew narrative[47]) also has the effect of moving the narrative toward a figural narrative situation, and hence giving it a fictional aspect. In some respects, I suggest, what we find in the Fourth Gospel is a refinement, and a carrying to a further stage (see especially chapter three) of what appears elsewhere. However, as I shall argue below, the motivation for the Fourth Gospel's narrative art springs from quite different circumstances and origins than that of, say, Chariton's romance.

We have seen, in looking at the 'grammar' of fictional narration, that an analysis of the Fourth Gospel's narrative style shows that it displays a number of characteristics which Hamburger identifies as 'symptoms' of (epic) fiction. Features such as the use of the historic present, or the 'epic preterite', the combination of 'here-and-now' deictics with past tense verbs, the use of verbs of inner action, reflectorization and 'dual-voiced' discourse, are all taken as indicative of a narrative's fictional status. Thus, the presence, or the perceived presence of such features in the discourse may well affect the way in which modern readers experience and react to the Fourth Gospel. Such features become determinants in the interpretative process by which readers today understand the discourse, and take it as more or less fictional. Proving whether this is the case, or how far it is the case, would require much more time and space than can be given here. And, of course, individual readers' responses will always range widely on this issue, and a single individual reader may well find his or her own response ambiguous and variable. Even a cursory survey of commentaries and monographs suggests that a sense of the 'fictiveness' of the Gospel is a common modern reaction to the discourse. It is important to bear in mind, as Frei's book shows, that the conventions of fictional discourse, and the culturally shared expectations of readers of fiction, have developed at precisely the same period as Enlightenment thinking brought into being the modern understanding of the nature of historical discourse, and, in the field of biblical studies, the historical-critical method.[48] Thus scholars such as D.F. Strauss and A. Schweitzer,

---

47. See Alter, *The Art of Biblical Narrative*, chapter 4, especially pp. 67-70; cf. pp. 182-83.

48. See Frei, *Eclipse*, chapter 7, especially pp. 135-54. But Frei does not consider the possibility that this also contributed to a false epistemological divide between how reality should be known and described, on the one hand, and how 'realistic narrative' (which was parasitic on reality but fundamentally not historical)

in their concern to differentiate the 'historical' from the 'mythical' in the gospel accounts, often had in mind categories of description drawn from the modern (developing) concept of fiction.[49]

It may be the case, then, that the symptoms of fiction we have been discussing have become conventional markers of fiction through the cumulative experience of reading modern fictional discourse. This perspective cannot but affect a modern reading of ancient texts even when they are read in the original language, and the cultural distance is kept in mind. But, we must ask whether these features, derived as they are from modern fiction, are applicable to an ancient work such as the Fourth Gospel? Can we know whether first-century readers would have received these features in the same way? Unfortunately, providing an adequate answer to these questions would take us well beyond the bounds of this present study. Here I would simply offer the following brief observation. The distinctions between what we would now call fiction and nonfiction were not as finely drawn in the ancient world, though ancient literary critics debated the issues of 'truthfulness' and 'falsehood' in literary discourse.[50] They also devised broad generic categories of discourse, based on concepts of the representation of reality and its imitation (*mimesis*).[51] But, when it comes to narrative discourse, the conception of 'plasmatic' narrative (i.e. 'realistic narrative') was still tied to its roots in *historia* and to events in the real world. It is as we move into the second century CE and beyond that the romance (as indeed the gospel form) becomes more fantastic.[52] 'Mimetic' fiction, in the modern sense of the portrayal of a story world *completely made up* out of the author's imagination, was as yet unknown, or in its infancy.

I would argue that a sharp differentiation between 'fact' and 'fiction', history and non-history, is to some extent misconceived. The question ought not to be put in those terms to the Fourth Gospel. For, even as

could be identified on the other.

49.   See here D. Norton, *A History of the Bible as Literature* (Cambridge: Cambridge University Press, 1993), II, pp. 349-57. The section is suggestively titled 'Schweitzer, Strauss and the discovery of fiction'.

50.   On this see the discussion in W. Nelson, *Fact and Fiction* (Cambridge, MA: Harvard University Press, 1973), pp. 2-6; B.E. Perry, *The Ancient Romances* (Berkeley: University of California Press, 1967), chapters 1 and 2.

51.   See Appendix, below p. 273.

52.   See discussion in Perry, *The Ancient Romances*, esp. pp. 28-30, 41, 146-48; also Reardon, *Collected*, p. 8.

regards our present discussion, it is not categorically the case that the features which Hamburger sees as defining characteristics of fiction, are necessarily always confined to fictional narrative. W.J. Bronzwaer has shown, in *Tense and the Novel*, that the tense shift effected by the use of here-and-now deictics, and the use of the epic preterite, are not confined to literature which is fictional. They may also be used in historical or journalistic writing when an 'empathetic or subjective identification of the writer and the objects of writing' comes into play.[53] M.L. Pratt asserts that two of the 'syntactic features' which Hamburger takes as unique to 'epic fictional discourse', that is, verbs of inner action, and present tense adverbials (deictics) with past tense verbs, also occur in natural narratives.[54] Natural narratives (anecdotes drawn from everyday experience) have to do with the real world rather than with a fictional world.

The Status of First Person Fictional Discourse
We must also take account of a further aspect of Hamburger's thesis which has relevance to the Fourth Gospel. She draws a sharp distinction between third-person fictional discourse, which she places firmly in the category of fiction, and first-person discourse, which is not fiction, at least not in the same sense. Third person narrative originates from a speaking 'I' created by, though distinct from, the 'narrative poet'. This 'I' is not a statement-subject *per se*, but the creation of a real statement-subject. As we have seen, when the created 'I' (the fictive narrator) is speaking, the statements have no real subject-object relationship with reality. They have only a functional narrative character: they are vehicles of an I-Origo, a real statement-subject, who has disappeared and has been replaced by a fictive I-Origo.

On the other hand, a narrative in the first person, according to Hamburger, always maintains the subject-object relationship and hence the structure of a reality statement. Even when 'the first-person narrator is himself a fictive person who is talking about other fictive persons', he will not step across 'that limit set by the first-person perspective, i.e. by the law of statement'.[55] Thus a first-person fictional narrative is described by Hamburger as a 'feigned reality statement'.

53. W.J.M. Bronzwaer, *Tense and the Novel* (Groningen: Wolters-Noordhoff, 1970), p. 69; cf also pp. 65-66, 47-48; and Martin, *Recent Theories*, p. 141.
54. Pratt, *Toward*, p. 67 n. 4.
55. Hamburger, *Logic*, p. 332.

It is 'feigned', rather than 'fictive', because in our experience of reading a first-person narrative the past tense retains the function of designating the past. Thus, in its feigned form it is a 'quasi-past' rather than a past that has been 'presentified'. It is a 'quasi-past' because, of course, the world referred to is an imagined one. It is feigned rather than fictive because it is capable of gradations of being feigned; more or less invented, more or less approximating to a reality statement.[56]

Despite the subtlety of Hamburger's argument, it is difficult to see how these features necessarily set first-person fictional discourse off from fictional discourse in the third person. At a commonsense level, we may feel that all realistic narrative fiction is 'feigned reality statement'. Indeed, put this way, it approximates to the description of fictional discourse as 'pretended speech-acts' which, as we shall see later, is the way in which speech-act theorists would define literary or fictional discourse. In any case, a number of the conventions that characterize fiction according to Hamburger's criteria are also to be found in first-person narratives.[57]

Now the Fourth Gospel, by the rhetorical stance and the narrative situation it adopts, makes a fair claim to being a first-person narrative. It may be said to originate from a statement-subject who maintains a subject-object relationship to the world presented. To this extent, it may be better to describe it as a feigned reality statement at those points where the reader feels that a degree of invention is present. Because it shares, or may be seen to share, some of the characteristics which Hamburger describes as being native to fiction, the Fourth Gospel's discourse may give the *appearance* of being fictional. However, because of the ambiguity in her theory over the status of third-person fictional discourse against first-person discourse which is merely feigned, in the final analysis it really does not help us in determining the Gospel's relationship to reality. Also, as we have seen, the characteristics she describes as indicative of fiction do not hold up on analysis of narrative generally, for nonfictional narrative may on occasion display 'fictional symptoms' as well. If in the end, her argument 'is intended to hold true only for pure fiction'[58] and applies only where the fictional

56.   Hamburger, *Logic*, pp. 333-36.

57.   Martin, *Recent Theories*, p. 142. Cf. natural narratives told in the first person, and see Pratt, *Toward*, p. 67 n. 4.

58.   Genette, *Narrative Discourse Revisited*, p. 81. '[A]nd fiction is rarely pure, more rarely, no doubt, than her thesis assumes.'

world is 'simply posited',[59] beyond the reach of questions of reliability or truthfulness to history, how are we to apply it in the case of discourse which claims to have some relationship to events in the real world?

Speech-Act Theory and Fictional Discourse

The description of literary discourse which derives from the application of speech-act theory, in contradistinction to the claims of Hamburger, and the Formalist school generally, starts from the premise that the language of literature is not of a radically different nature from that of ordinary, everyday language and discourse. M.L. Pratt argues that there is not a 'poetic' language which is formally and ontologically distinct from ordinary language.[60] Indeed, at the commonsense level, how could there be? If literary language was so distinct from ordinary language, how then would literary discourse be ordinarily understood? If the words and sentences in a fictional narrative did not semantically refer in the same way that they do in ordinary language, readers would have to learn a new 'language' before being able to understand it.[61] Neither in terms of the use of language, nor in terms of grammatical and textual properties, may a 'poetic' language be distinguished from 'non-poetic'.[62]

The Fourth Gospel as 'Natural Narrative'
Having set the premise that the distinction between poetic and non-poetic language is a fallacy, Pratt then shows that formally and functionally literary narrative is very much like 'natural narrative' or a story of personal and actual experience: it is an anecdote or an orally told story which relates some incident, such as an adventure or a narrow escape, or simply some occurrence or circumstance considered of interest to the hearer and drawn directly from the teller's own

59. Martin, *Recent Theories*, p. 141.
60. Pratt, *Toward*, chapter 1.
61. C. Hutchison, 'The Act of Narration: A Critical Survey of Some Speech-Act Theories of Narrative Discourse', *Journal of Literary Semantics* 13 (1984), p. 5. Cf. Searle, *Expression*, p. 64, where the argument is in terms of the types of illocutionary acts posited for literary as against non-literary discourse.
62. The arguments over the nature of 'poetic language' are detailed and complex; they cannot be engaged with in any depth here. See Pratt, *Toward*, Introduction and chapter 1; and Hutchison, 'The Act of Narration', p. 3.

experience.[63] Drawing upon the linguistic researches of William Labov, she describes how the structure of natural narrative is shared by many fictional narratives.[64]

A complete narrative, natural or literary, will be comprised of the following components.

1. The abstract: a summary which encapsulates the point of the story. Generally, though not always, this comes at or near the beginning of a story. In a novel, the abstract might be provided by the title.

2. Orientation: which provides the setting and circumstances of the characters, giving a context for the action which follows. Again, orientation usually comes at the beginning of a natural or literary narrative, though where a story begins *in medias res*, the orientation may be delayed or interwoven with the complicating action.

3. The complicating action, along with the resolution: the core of the narrative. It is the action which leads to the climax.

4. Evaluation: provided by devices used by the narrator to indicate the point of the story, its *raison d'être*, why it was told and what the narrator was getting at. In natural narratives this is often concentrated in a section immediately preceding the resolution. But evaluative devices may be scattered throughout the entire narrative. Evaluative devices or commentary are used to control the reader's attitude to the story and point of view.[65]

5. The result or resolution: the climax to which the narrative has been building. The resolution 'usually ends with the last (narrative) clause in the speech act'.[66]

6. The coda: functions to 'close off the sequence of complicating action and to indicate that none of the events that followed were important to the narrative'.[67] In many fairy tales a typical coda is 'and they lived happily ever after'. A novel's coda may be brief (e.g. 'The End') but often it is elaborate and explains, recapitulates and evaluates

---

63. Pratt, *Toward*, pp. 40-44. Cf. W. Labov and J. Waletzsky, 'Narrative Analysis: Oral Versions of Personal Experience', in J. Helm (ed.), *Essays on the Verbal and Visual Arts* (Seattle: University of Washington Press, 1967), pp. 12-44, on which Pratt draws for her two examples. One is a 'fight story', the other an anecdote about a hunter's clever retriever.

64. Pratt, *Toward*, chapter 2.

65. Pratt, *Toward*, p. 63.

66. Pratt, *Toward*, p. 45.

67. Pratt, *Toward*, p. 46.

the story's outcome, providing additional information and extending the story into the future so as to 'bring the narrator and [reader] back to the point at which they entered the narrative, and generally to 'leave the [reader] with a feeling of satisfaction and completedness that matters have been rounded off and accounted for'.[68]

Not only do novels of the modern period bear resemblances to natural narrative, but so, it can be argued, do the gospels. Indeed, they might well be described as a form of natural narrative, deriving as they do from the oral proclamation of the early church. This is because much of this oral proclamation will have originated in the testimony of the first disciples. The correspondence may be illustrated with reference to some of the components of natural narrative outlined above. In the Gospels, as in novels, abstract and orientation may often be mingled and difficult to distinguish one from the other. However, it seems clear, for instance, that as far as Mark's Gospel is concerned, 1.1 may be taken as abstract while the reference to Isaiah's prophecy and the account of John the Baptist serve as orientation.

In the case of the Fourth Gospel, the situation is not so clear. One might see the entire prologue as a form of abstract, while the remainder of the first chapter provides orientation. This is the case especially if one takes the prologue to be a type of theological *prolegomenon* to the narrative which follows. On the other hand, in so far as the narrative begins in the prologue itself, orientation is found even here. The beginning of many of the pericopes which make up the Gospel also contain orientation. In fact, each new phase of the action, or each fresh incident the narrator chooses to relate, is introduced with some form of orientation which sets the scene, introduces the characters and prepares the reader for what is to follow (see e.g. 2.1-3; 2.23–3.1; 4.1-6, 5.2-5).

Evaluative commentary runs throughout the Gospel. Jn 12.36a-50 provides a significant example, being placed just prior to the resolution, the glorification of Jesus in his death and resurrection. Other instances of evaluative commentary are 2.11 which indicates the point of the miracle just related as an indication of Jesus' δόξα, and as evoking the disciples' belief in him. 2.21-22 draws out the significance of Jesus' Temple act and the saying (cf. also 4.34-38; 5.16-18; 9.39-41). In a sense, Jesus' discourses may be taken as a form of evaluative

---

68. Pratt, *Toward*, pp. 56-57. I have substituted 'reader' where Pratt, speaking of oral natural narratives, has 'listener'.

commentary on the signs; or, in the case of 3.16-21, on the themes raised in Jesus' dialogue with Nicodemus.

John 20.30, 31 is a further instance of evaluative commentary. At the same time, it functions as a coda, closing off the first of the book's thematic climaxes and returning the reader to the themes of the prologue. Ch. 21 might also be regarded as an extended coda which has the function of legitimating the source of authority for the gospel *and*, I think, affirming the unbroken continuing witness to Jesus. 21.25 is the clearest instance of a narrative coda amongst the four gospels.

Individual units of narrative within the Gospel may also be analyzed as having the form of a natural narrative. A clear example of this is 4.1-43. Admittedly, the 'abstract' is not clearly present in that the point of the story is not encapsulated in a brief summary statement at the beginning of the unit. In the context of the first four chapters, however, 4.44 represents a form of delayed abstract (as well as evaluative commentary) in that the response of the Samaritans is set in contrast to the ambiguous, misplaced honour and the misunderstanding of Jesus by his own (cf. Nicodemus, 2.23-24; 4.48). The story's orientation is found in 4.1-6 which provides the motivation for the journey, the setting of the encounter, and a motivation for Jesus' request for water (tiredness implying thirst as well). The complicating action lies in the dialogue with the woman (4.7-29), that leads to the climax or resolution, which is both the woman's testimony (4.29) and the city's believing response to Jesus (4.39-42). Evaluative commentary is found in 4.31-38, while 4.43 provides a coda.[69] In a self-contained story which is also part of a larger narrative, of course, the coda never completely closes the action, but also provides a transition to the next segment of narrative.[70]

Pratt's purpose in discussing natural narrative in relation to literary narrative is to demonstrate the structural similarities between the two, and to show that the dynamics of literary narration do not exist in a sphere of their own requiring the use of a special 'poetic' language. Thus, we might say that natural narratives and literary narratives exist

---

69. Cf. also Jn 11 which may be analyzed as follows: 11.1-6 = abstract and orientation; 11.7-42 = complicating action; 11.43-44 = resolution; 11.45-53 = evaluative commentary (and 11.47-53 = coda); 11.54 = coda for this incident.

70. Jn 2.1 (abstract) and 2.12 (coda); or 20.1 (abstract/orientation), 20.10 (coda) provide two further examples of stories which show features of natural narrative.

not in disjunction to one another but along a narrative continuum. This insight will be important when discussing the nature of the narrative genus, and when we delineate the varied narrative genres in order to place the Gospel within the overall schema.

Here we must also note that the affinities the Fourth Gospel has with natural narrative, and especially the fact that some of the 'self-contained' stories within the Gospel have the structure of a natural narrative, provide further evidence of an eyewitness source lying behind it. It might also mean that, at least in part, the proximity of this eyewitness (and oral) source is very close to the time of the discourse. Given that natural and literary narratives may both share much of the same general structure, this point cannot be pressed too far; but taken together with some of the features noted above, especially, for instance, the use of the historic present, the affinities are at least suggestive. R.A. Culpepper, in a footnote on the use of the historic present, cites Casparis's comment that '[t]he accumulated occurence of these formulae [viz. historic present cases of *verba dicendi*, especially the verb "to say"] is notably restricted to colloquial or vulgar oral narrative situations'.[71] Culpepper has failed to see the significance of this for the status of the narrative as eyewitness report (or natural narrative).

The Fourth Gospel as a Display Text
Pratt also analyzes natural and literary narratives as 'utterances of the same type' in so far as they adhere to the appropriateness conditions required for assertive speech-acts. Her particular concern is with those conditions or rules which determine the relevance of an assertion. An assertion is concerned with 'getting the addressee(s) to believe or know or think something'.[72] More precisely, an assertion is an attempt to get the addressee(s) to recognize that the speaker believes, knows, or thinks something about a certain proposition, from which recognition the addressee(s) will be invited to believe, know and think the same thing. In order for an assertion to be appropriate or felicitous it must, as we have seen, fulfill certain conditions. It must be (a) true; that is, the one making the assertion must believe that it is true, and must be able to produce the evidence to support such a belief and (b) not be obviously true; that is, it should not pertain to something that

71. Culpepper, *Anatomy*, p. 31 n. 38.
72. Pratt, *Toward*, p. 133.

speaker and addressee already know to be true, or something for
which there is no possibility of its being false.[73] Fulfillment of this
condition is necessary for the assertion to be relevant. It is often called
the Assertability or Nonobviousness Condition.

Pratt expands this condition to include a further degree of relevance—that the assertion must have a real or supposed relation to the
interests and state of knowledge of the hearer. Types of relevance to
the interests of the hearer would be, for example, that the assertion
answers a question, or provides information which allays fears or
addresses anxieties about some matter. Relevant assertions fulfill the
co-operative principle by resulting in a 'maximally effective exchange
of information'.

There are certain types of assertion which seem to run beyond what
is required for a maximally effective exchange of information. They
impart more information than is necessary, or their relevance to the
needs, interests or knowledge of the hearer is not immediately obvious.
These types of assertion establish their relevance by being 'tellable',
says Pratt; that is, they set forth an unusual or problematic state of
affairs. They are relevant because of their inherent interest and newsworthiness. They seek to 'display' some event or state of affairs. Pratt
calls this type of relevance, the tellability condition.

This provides her with a definition of the types of speech-acts that
characterize literary speech-acts. They are 'an important subclass of
assertive or representative speech-acts that includes natural narrative,
an enormous proportion of conversation, and many, if not all, literary
works' whose relevance is of a display-producing, world-describing
sort that she refers to as tellability.[74]

> Assertions whose relevance is tellability must represent states of affairs
> that are held to be unusual, contrary to expectations, or otherwise prob-
> lematic. . . In making an assertion whose relevance is tellability, a
> speaker is not only reporting but also verbally *displaying* a state of affairs,
> inviting his addressee(s) to join him in contemplating it, evaluating it, and
> responding to it. His point is to produce in his hearers not only belief but
> also imaginative and affective involvement in the state of affairs he is
> representing and an evaluative stance toward it. He intends them to share

73. Pratt, *Toward*, p. 134. Pratt gives as an example the remark, 'Sister Martha
is wearing her habit today', which, if Sister Martha has never been known to wear
anything but her habit, would be an obvious and, hence inappropriate, assertion.

74. Pratt, *Toward*, p. 136.

his wonder, amusement, terror or admiration of the event. Ultimately, it would seem, what he is after is an *interpretation* of the problematic event, an assignment of meaning and value supported by the consensus of himself and his hearers.[75]

Texts whose primary relevance is tellability and whose representative speech-acts belong to a 'world-describing, thought-producing' class of speech-acts Pratt calls 'display texts'. The world to which a display text refers may be the real world, or 'a fictive or hypothetical one that will overlap (or rather claim to overlap) to varying degrees with the real world'.[76]

We should note two further features of display texts. First, they are susceptible to elaboration. In the interests of 'display' and of increasing newsworthiness, or of inducing the desired affective response in the hearer, a display text may provide material well beyond what is necessary for the simple imparting of information. Pratt states that in terms of the internal dynamics of a text 'the literary speech-act situation admits of enormous elaboration, accumulation of detail, and even pure repetition... Indeed, one might say that what literary works chiefly do is elaborate on the states of affairs they posit.'[77] Second, display texts are detachable from the immediate context of their production. The detachability of a conversational display text, that is a natural narrative, means that it can be introduced into conversation without any necessary or logical connection with prior discourse, and need not relate to 'the concrete, momentary concerns of the addressee'.[78] Literary, or written display texts are by their very nature 'detachable', physically available as they are between covers and able to be picked up and read by anyone, anywhere.

> These facts about display texts cannot surprise us in the least, given the communicative purpose they are designed to serve, a purpose I have described as that of verbally representing states of affairs and experiences which are held to be unusual or problematic in such a way that the addressee will respond affectively in the intended way, adopt the intended evaluation and interpretation, take pleasure in doing so, and generally find the whole undertaking worth it.[79]

75. Pratt, *Toward*, p. 136 (italics hers).
76. Pratt, *Toward*, p. 143.
77. Pratt, *Toward*, p. 148.
78. Pratt, *Toward*, pp. 144-45.
79. Pratt, *Toward*, p. 148.

I have quoted from Pratt's discussion of display texts somewhat extensively because I think it offers some fruitful insights into a way of categorizing the Fourth Gospel. It seems clear that it is at least part of the implied author's intention to represent a 'state of affairs' in elaboration of the thesis that Jesus is the Christ, the son of God (20.30, 31). The intention of the discourse as a whole is that, by means of 'signs' and a 'display' of the significance of Jesus, through representation of what he said and did, the implied reader is invited to share in the interpretation of, and concur with the meaning and value assigned to these events by the implied author. Furthermore, it may well be that it is in elaboration on the thesis that Jesus is the Christ, the son of God, that much of the discourse, and especially the discourses of Jesus, have their genesis. The essential detachability of the Fourth Gospel is well illustrated by the fact that, whatever the specific circumstances of its original production, it was eventually felt to be of sufficient general relevance and significance to have been included in the canon.[80]

However, there is one important respect in which discussion of the Fourth Gospel as a 'display text' would need to go beyond Pratt's analysis. Her argument is made in application to literary works that are fictional. She sees the primary relevance of a display text to be that of tellability, and carrying its appeal very largely in its capacity to provide pleasure by the verbal 'display'. Thus an aesthetic intention takes precedence over any didactic, or world-changing, action-inducing force. In a literary display text such world-changing, action-inducing aim as there may be is largely indirect and subordinate to its primary representational aim.[81]

Is it the case that the primary intention of the Fourth Gospel is to display a state of affairs with no intention that this should have an impact on the reader which is world-changing, or action-inducing? What is the implied author's commitment to the story over and above that it is tellable? Indeed, to what degree is the very 'tellability' of this story derivative of its rootedness in the historical fact of an historical figure's life and death? Is not the problematic nature of the state of

---

80. Detachability, and even elaboration, are not, of course, criteria that attach only to display texts. Any text is, in a sense, detachable from the immediate circumstances of its production. But tellability means that display texts are, perhaps, more likely to be relevant in a new context than other texts whose motivation is more specific to the circumstances of their production.

81. Pratt, *Toward*, p. 143, see especially n. 13.

affairs represented in this discourse precisely because the implied author claims, and the readers understand, that it has a relation to events and effects in the real world? We are brought up, once again, at the question of the relation of 'history' and 'fiction'.

It is also a question of the illocutionary and perlocutionary force of the speech-acts contained within the Fourth Gospel. By and large, speech-act theory, when it attends to the illocutionary force of fictional speech-acts, resolves the question by describing fictional illocutions as 'pretended'. In other words, in fictional discourse the writer presents his readers with a series of speech-acts whose illocutionary forces, that is the rules by which appropriateness or felicity is determined, are 'suspended'.[82] They are suspended because the context of the discourse within which they occur is 'abstracted, or detached, from the circumstances and conditions which make illocutionary acts possible'.[83] To put the matter somewhat baldly, the speech-acts in fictional discourse are 'pretended' speech-acts because the context of their utterance, the 'world' within which they occur, is also 'pretended'. It is an imagined world in which imagined speech-acts occur. Ohmann puts it thus: 'A literary work is a discourse whose sentences lack the illocutionary forces that would normally attach to them. Its illocutionary force is mimetic. By "mimetic", I mean purportedly imitative. Specifically, a literary work *purportedly imitates* (or reports) a series of speech acts, which in fact have no other existence.'[84]

This situation comes about in a complex of factors involving the 'illocutionary stance' of the author in writing the discourse and the attitude the readers take to the discourse based on their understanding of the author's intentions.[85] Put another way, the fictional discourse is the result of a compact between writer and reader to treat a particular discourse as one where the normal illocutionary forces of statements

---

82. R. Ohmann, 'Literature as Act', in S. Chatman (ed.), *Approaches to Poetics* (New York: Columbia University Press, 1973), p. 97.

83. R. Ohmann, 'Speech-Acts and the Definition of Literature', *Philosophy and Rhetoric* 4 (1971), p. 13.

84. Ohmann, 'Speech-Acts', p. 14. Cf. Searle, *Expression*, p. 65: '[T]he author of a work of fiction pretends to perform a series of illocutionary acts, normally of the assertive type.'

85. See Searle, *Expression*, pp. 65-66; and R.L. Brown and M. Steinmann, 'Native Readers of Fiction', in P. Hernadi (ed.), *What is Literature?* (Bloomington: Indiana University Press, 1978), pp. 148-50.

made do not obtain because the context in which they are made is taken to be an imagined one.

In a useful discussion, R.L. Brown and M. Steinmann define the distinction between nonfictional and fictional discourse as that between *situated* and nonsituated discourse. Nonfictional discourse is situated in that the writer is an 'I' addressing a 'you', the reader.[86] The words of the discourse are inextricably linked to the context of that 'I' addressing the discourse to that 'you'.

> Fictional discourse, on the other hand, is neither intended nor—by native readers of it—taken as situated. If there is an 'I', it refers not to the actual speaker or writer, but rather to a fictive speaker or writer. And so with the *you*: it refers not to the actual reader. . . or to the hearer. . . but to a fictive hearer or reader. What the speaker or writer of a piece of fictional discourse pretends to do is to perform the utterance-propositional-illocutionary act of *reporting* the speech acts of a fictive speaker or writer to a fictive hearer or reader. What the actual hearer or reader does is to *overhear* these reported speech acts. . . Simply stated, situated discourse is always spoken *in propria persona*: fictional discourse never is.[87]

The foregoing discussion puts the matter in a very compressed form, and conceals within it a wide-ranging and complex discussion about what it means to 'pretend' to make assertions, or how adequate it is to describe literary discourse as that in which the usual illocutionary force of speech-acts is suspended.[88] It should be noted that the fact that the illocutionary force of speech-acts is suspended in fictional discourse does not mean that it is not of the same kind as those in nonfictional discourse. Rather, as Brown and Steinmann point out, *'once the reader has accepted the pretence and entered into the fictional world of the discourse*, the propositional-act and illocutionary-act rules obtain. If they did not, the reader could not recognize unreliable

---

86.   Both these entities can be plural.

87.   Brown and Steinmann, 'Native Readers', pp. 150-51 (italics theirs). The discussion bears some resemblance to Hamburger's distinction between a statement-system which is predicated on a subject-object relation (as in nonfictional discourse) and one that is not.

88.   For further discussion of these issues, in addition to the works cited here, see Hutchison, 'The Act of Narration', pp. 3-34; and T.G. Pavel, 'Ontological Issues in Poetics: Speech-Acts and Fictional Worlds', *Journal of Aesthetics and Art Criticism* 40 (1981), pp. 167-78. The latter makes an important point that in certain circumstances a pretence can become as effective as the genuine act (cf. pp. 171-72).

narrators and characters who lie, make insincere promises, and other-wise violate these rules.'[89]

Having said this, we may adopt as a general rule of thumb the view that in a fictional discourse, as far as the real author and the real reader are concerned, and we may include here the implied author and the implied reader, the illocutionary force of an assertion is governed by the pretence entered into. The appropriateness rules follow upon a prior understanding that the assertion exists within the pretended and imagined world of the discourse and is not to be taken as applying to the real world. Thus Lewis Carroll is not held to the essential rule in respect of tardy white rabbits who wear gloves. Nor, to take a less fantastical, and widely used example, need Jane Austen defend the truth of the statement: 'It is a truth universally acknowledged that a single man in possession of a good fortune, must be in want of a wife.'[90]

The question we must put with respect to the Fourth Gospel is this: What is the status of the speech-acts contained therein? Does the implied author intend the illocutionary force suggested by a given assertion, or does the context of the discourse suggest that a prior 'pretence' condition must be understood? In short, does the discourse correlate to fictional or nonfictional discourse? It should be noted that the decision as to whether a piece of discourse is to be read as fiction or nonfiction is often taken prior to the reading of the discourse itself. The status of a given discourse is determined in many respects by factors which are external to the discourse, or which are what we might call minimally textual.[91] The genre to which a narrative is assigned will, to a large extent, determine whether it is read as fiction or nonfiction, with consequent entailment for the status of the speech-acts in it. The work which proclaims itself to be a novel, a romance, a history or an autobiography predetermines to a significant degree the manner in which the reader will attend to its speech-acts. Often, of

89. Brown and Steinmann, 'Native Readers', p. 152 (italics mine).

90. Jane Austen, *Pride and Prejudice*. Note that this is potentially a genuine assertion, but in the context of the novel, it does not stand or fall on whether it can be proved to be true. Cf. Ohmann, 'Speech-Acts', pp. 5-6; Hutchison, 'The Act of Narration', p. 6; Searle, *Expression*, p. 74.

91. The title of a book, the author's name and credentials, the publisher, the 'blurb' on the dustjacket are all features which are 'minimally textual' and external to the discourse as such. But they are factors which influence the decision as to a text's genre.

course, there is little or no evidence to guide the reader, who is left to infer or postulate the genre, and the status of the speech-acts thereby entailed, during the reading process. Sometimes, an author might deliberately set out to confuse, or to make playfully ambiguous, how the discourse and its speech-acts are to be received. For example, a novel may pose as a true account, or an autobiographer may present his or her material in such a way as to make the reader wonder how much and at which points the edges of factuality are being blurred.

That decisions are taken by readers to determine the genre of a work prior to the act of reading on the basis of features that are external and minimally textual, or that these decisions are inferentially derived from features within the discourse itself, are facts that have been explicitly noted by speech-act theorists such as Brown and Steinmann, S.S. Lanser and J.R. Searle.[92] Many literary critics, no doubt, have implicitly recognized the importance of these features, though they have often chosen to ignore or to overlook them.[93] Biblical critics have had an intuitive, if not theoretical, grasp of this issue, made evident in the continuing discussions over determining the genre of the gospels. It is important, however, to recognize the explicit connection between genre and the status of a given discourse's speech-acts.

In order to determine whether the Gospel is to be taken as fictional or nonfictional in character, it will be well to attempt to arrive at an understanding of where on the spectrum of narrative types it is to be set. Of all the genres which come within the broad genus we call 'narrative', to which does this gospel most approximate? As the argument being presented here is a cumulative one, I shall briefly summarize what has gone before, and indicate the course ahead. Under the rubric of a 'grammar of fictional discourse' certain features of the Fourth Gospel may wear the aspect of fiction. Nonetheless, there are no definitive linguistic indicators of fiction (that is, none such as may not also appear in nonfiction) which will settle the matter completely. In the end, the fundamental determining factor is whether the implied author intends to create a fictional world in which the appropriateness rules governing assertions may be suspended. The category 'display text' is a useful one in that it allows for a form of discourse where the assertions run beyond the mere imparting of information to that of

---

92.   See Brown and Steinmann, 'Native Readers', pp. 149-50; Lanser, *Narrative Act*, pp. 122-31 (on the 'extrafictional voice'); Searle, *Expression*, p. 59.

93.   See Lanser, *Narrative Act*, p. 129.

seeking to elaborate a state of affairs and elicit an affective response from the reader.

We shall see that historical discourse shares certain conventions with fictional discourse. Furthermore, when it comes to determining the 'historical' or 'fictional' status of a given type of narrative, it is better to see it as occupying a point along a continuum of types which run from those which aim at (historical) report to those which aim at invention. I shall propose a typological model based on a circular arrangement of types which attempts to modulate the distinction between the 'poles' and will seek to place the Gospel on this model. In pursuit of this, I shall place it in comparison with another form of ancient display text—the Greek novel.

Narrative Conventions in History and Fiction

We shall approach the question of the narrative genre to which the Fourth Gospel may be said to belong via a discussion of the narrative conventions which characterize historical and fictional narratives, particularly those conventions where the two types may be seen to converge. Of course, the conventions under which writers write and readers read a work of history must be different from those which govern a work of fiction. In so far as the 'pretence' hypothesis outlined above is a convention of fictional discourse, it sets such discourse apart from that which is historical.[94] This is, perhaps, something of a truism. Other distinguishing features, such as the objective, impersonal third-person style of much modern historical discourse, are alluded to in the discussion which follows.

On the other hand, inasmuch as historical discourse falls within the broad field of narrative discourse, it adheres to a number of conventions shared by its fictional relative. Three of these are pertinent to our discussion. They are:

1. History or historical discourse, as mediated discourse.
2. History as a 'followable story'.
3. History as an interpreted account.

It must be said at the outset that philosophers of history recognize a dual use for the term 'history'. 'History' may refer to 'a well-known

---

94. Brown and Steinmann call this 'pretence-of-reporting' rule, a genre rule, i.e. a convention, which is the one rule that distinguishes fictional from nonfictional speech-acts (see 'Native Readers', p. 152).

genus of researches and writings' or it may refer to 'the objects of
these researches and writings'. History, in this latter sense, stands 'for
what actually happened or what men actually did at certain particular
times and places'.[95] It comprises what might be described as the 'facts
of history' (particular events, personages, times and circumstances).
History, in the first sense, is the ordering of these facts into an acces-
sible, generally narrative, form. It is with the first use of the term
'history'—history as a narrative discourse—that we are concerned
here. History as narrative is the act of ordering the raw materials of
'fact'. This leads naturally into the first of the shared conventions.

History as Mediated Discourse
A work of historical narrative is, first of all, a reconstruction of the
events and happenings to which it refers. We cannot have direct access
to the past. We can only obtain that access more or less obliquely
through the detritus of a past age (where the interests of the archeo-
logist are especially concentrated) or the documents left behind by the
human inhabitants and observers of that age (and observers may include
those at one or several stages of remove from the actual events). The
historian, by painstaking research and careful testing, must reconstruct
the contours of past events mediated by time, artefact and document.
So much is self-evident. But there are two aspects of this which are
easily forgotten. First, when it comes to documentary evidence from
the past, particularly when it is a narrative account of events, we are
dealing with mediated material. In fact, we are handling literary speech-
acts which emanate from some source under the constraints of a
particular viewpoint. Second, the historian is also part of the process
of mediation as he or she selects, and orders the material to arrive at a
coherent account. In this respect, the historian stands in something of
the same relation to the historical 'facts' as an implied author, through
a narrator, stands to the *fabula*, the story stuff and story world, of the
fictional narrative.[96]

95.   W.B. Gallie, *Philosophy and the Historical Understanding* (London: Chatto
& Windus, 1964), p. 51.
96.   '*Fabula*' is the Russian Formalist's term for the raw material of the story
'awaiting the organizing hand of the writer'. See R. Selden, *A Reader's Guide to
Contemporary Literary Theory* (London: Harvester Wheatsheaf, 2nd edn, 1989),
p. 13 and cf. Martin, *Recent Theories*, pp. 107-109. As for the raw material of
history, there is scarcely such a thing as a 'bare historical fact' for everything must be

History as a 'Followable Story'

The work of an historian is not simply that of selecting and ordering material; it is selecting and ordering with a particular end in view. W.B. Gallie, to whom I am indebted for the description, describes 'following a story' as a 'teleologically guided form of attention'.[97] We follow a story by traversing 'a series of incidents, and outcomes, which are unpredictable yet acceptable, toward an anticipated and expected conclusion'.[98] The conclusion, though expected, is always open and the way to the conclusion is across 'any number of contingent, surprising events' which yet turn out to be acceptable because the retrospective viewpoint shows the essential connection of one event to the next.[99] The conclusion of a story guides our attention almost from the start because we want to know how things will turn out for the characters in the end. We follow a story to find out 'what happens': we persist in following a story because of the intrinsic human interest of the story and because of the way our sympathies are engaged with the characters.

History shares something of the characteristics of story—indeed, it can be said to be a 'species of the genus Story'[100]—because, unlike the natural or social sciences, but 'like all stories and all imaginative literature, [it] is as much a journey as an arrival, as much an approach as a result'.[101] That is to say, whereas the systematic sciences present us with hypotheses based on logically derived laws and predicted results which are either confirmed or refuted by testing, history presents us with a process or succession of contingencies which lead to a conclusion which is expected even though it cannot necessarily be predicted from what has gone before. Every genuine work of history is read as a followable story; 'a story followed in the light of its promised or adumbrated outcome through a succession of contingencies'[102] because its subject matter is felt to be worth following in its compelling human interest.

---

mediated through the interpretative grid of human report (including, of course, eyewitness report) and analysis. This remains true no matter how many video or film cameras might capture an event.

97. Gallie, *Philosophy*, p. 64.
98. Gallie, *Philosophy*, p. 29.
99. Gallie, *Philosophy*, p. 65.
100. Gallie, *Philosophy*, p. 66.
101. Gallie, *Philosophy*, p. 67.
102. Gallie, *Philosophy*, p. 67.

Histories then become followable stories through their succession of 'essentially contingent' developments, the directedness of this succession towards an inevitable end, and the human interest of their subject matter which 'pulls' the reader along in an act of following.[103] They also become 'followable stories' through the act of history writing by which historical events are configured or 'emplotted' into a coherent whole by the historian. As Hayden White shows, what comes to the historian is a congerie of historical events (or facts) furnishing the story-elements which are made into a story by the superimposition of a given plot-structure.[104] The historian seeks to 'refamiliarize' his audience with a given set of events (made unfamiliar by historical and cultural distance) by providing a 'set of culturally provided categories' (perhaps metaphysical or 'metaphorical' concepts, religious beliefs, or story-forms) against which the events may be understood. In particular, the historian shows how the way in which a structure of events develops, conforms 'to one or another of the story types we conventionally invoke to make sense of our own life-histories'.[105]

Following Northrop Frye, White suggests that histories are emplotted against the archetypal myths of 'pregeneric plot-structures' of Romance, Comedy, Tragedy, or Irony. Thus a given set of historical events, say those of the French Revolution, may be set against a comic plot-structure (the evolution of a new society through the revolutionary activity of the lower classes) or a tragic (the decline and fall of the *ancien regime*) depending on the particular class perspective adopted by the historian. 'The historical narrative', White states, 'thus *mediates* between events reported in it on the one side and the pregeneric plot structures conventionally used in our culture to endow unfamiliar events and situations with meanings, on the other.'[106] In addition, by a process of selecting and rejecting from the 'domain of facts' which is on hand for possible inclusion in the narrative, the historian chooses one of a number of possible 'sets of relationships' under which the events can be subsumed.[107] 'Most historical sequences can be emplotted in a number of different ways, so as to provide

---

103. See Gallie, *Philosophy*, p. 48 and *passim*.

104. H. White, 'The Historical Text as Literary Artifact' in his *Tropics of Discourse* (Baltimore: John Hopkins University Press, 1978), p. 84.

105. White, 'Historical Text', pp. 86-87.

106. White, 'Historical Text', p. 88.

107. See White, 'Historical Text', pp. 90-91.

different interpretations of those events and endow them with different meanings.'[108]

As I shall argue below, the reason for the differences which appear between the Fourth Gospel's version of the history of Jesus' life and ministry and those of the Synoptics arises because of the particular way in which the story has been emplotted. It may be that we can also discern the particular pregeneric plot-structure (or plot-structures, as there may indeed be a variable pattern of plot-structures) against which the story is told.[109]

History as an Interpreted Account

History is not simply made 'followable' by the fact that a succession of contingencies are structured towards an end which, in retrospect, gives them coherence, nor because our sympathies are engaged by the 'compelling human interest' of the events. A second salient feature of history, states Gallie, is that 'we are quite prepared to have any incident on the road to that conclusion explained to us, or justified, not simply by the production of appropriate evidence, but by all manner of general considerations and arguments'.[110] Elsewhere, Gallie describes a trend or tendency in history as a 'pattern-quality of particular events' disclosed when the narrative of those events is 'arranged in such a way that, roughly speaking, they move in some easily described relation to some fixed point of reference'.[111] In other words, an historical account is an interpreted account. The events are arranged into a particular 'pattern-quality' in accordance with the overall point of view or perspective of the historian, and the particular 'fixed point of reference' derived from the historical pressures and outcomes which the historian descries and seeks to illuminate or illustrate, and the background ideology and beliefs, historical or personal, from which the events arose, and against which the historian arranges his account.

This understanding of history as an interpreted account we may correlate, I believe, with Louis Mink's contention that narrative belongs to a configurational mode of comprehension. That is, a story provides

---

108. White, 'Historical Text', p. 85.

109. For reasons of space I do not pursue this particular line of enquiry. Stibbe discerns a tragic pre-generic plot structure in the Fourth Gospel; see *John as Storyteller*, pp. 129-38.

110. Gallie, *Philosophy*, p. 89.

111. Gallie, *Philosophy*, p. 70.

a mode of understanding in which the whole is 'grasped together' in a total act: the elements to be understood are configured into 'a single and concrete complex of relationships'.[112] Providing the narrative of a succession of historical events is like observing a river 'in aerial view, upstream and downstream, seen in a single survey'.[113] As Mink puts it elsewhere, '[t]he cognitive function of narrative form, then, is not just to relate a succession of events but to body forth an ensemble of interrelationships of many different kinds as a single whole. . . '[114]

But 'narrative form in history, as in fiction, is an artifice, the product of individual imagination'.[115] There is no such thing as the untold story of the past waiting to be discovered, there are only past facts waiting to be 'described in a context of narrative form'.[116] There are no simple or bare 'events' as such, but only 'events *under a description*', events which are redescribed in the construction of a given historical narrative.[117] Indeed we can go as far as to say, I think, that past historical events remain simply incomprehensible bits of data until they are placed within a context which places some sort of interpretation upon them. Thus the questions 'When?' and 'How?' are always followed quickly by the question 'Why?'. And without the 'Why?', 'When?' and 'How?' are of no real intrinsic interest to us. As Mink rightly says, we make the past determinable by placing the significance of past occurrences within an ensemble of interrelationships grasped

112. L. Mink, 'History and Fiction as Modes of Comprehension', *New Literary History* 1 (1970), pp. 551-55. Mink takes issue with Gallie over the concept of following a story (*idem.*, pp. 544-46; cf. also his, 'Philosophical Analysis and Historical Understanding', in B. Fay, E.O. Golob and R.T.Vann (eds.), *Louis O. Mink: Historical Understanding* (Ithaca, NY: Cornell University Press, 1987), pp. 134-37), but I think misunderstands and misrepresents Gallie's position as appropriate only to a 'naive', first time reader. I believe Gallie's dynamics apply even on second and subsequent readings. Contingencies remain contingencies except that now the reader knows the *particular* end to which they will lead. Even in life, events may still remain fortuitous even when we know the outcome. See also, P. Ricouer, *Time and Narrative* (ET: K. McLaughlin and D. Pellauer; Chicago: University of Chicago Press, 1984), I, pp. 158-61.

113. Mink, 'History and Fiction', p. 555.

114. L. Mink, 'Narrative Form as a Cognitive Instrument', in B. Fay, E.O. Golob and R.T. Vann (eds.), *Louis O. Mink: Historical Understanding*, p. 198.

115. Mink, 'Narrative Form', p. 199.

116. Mink, 'Narrative Form', p. 201.

117. See Mink, 'Narrative Form', pp. 199-200 (italics his).

in the construction of narrative form.[118]

These, then, are conventions which draw historical narration into a contiguity with fictional narration. The process of reconstruction, the selecting and ordering of facts, the casting of these into a coherent, followable narrative, shaped and patterned by the particular 'conclusion' to which the historian believes the events and their tendencies point, is of a similar sort to the process of narration in fiction. In a sense, historical narrative is mediated and plotted just as much as fiction. Conventions of historical writing demand that the 'mediation' is hidden behind a detached, abstracted style of presentation. The plotting of events must bear some relation to the actual chronological order of events as they happened, or are believed to have happened. At least the causality of the events must be logically and chronologically explained. But arguably, a work of history would not necessarily be a less reliable or excellent historical narrative if, in the interests of some rhetorical purpose, the historian began by describing some event seen as central to a complex of events before analyzing the process of events which led up to it, as well as detailing those which flowed from it. (By the same token, a source available to the historian for the work of historical reconstruction, a Gospel for example, is not rendered entirely worthless by the reconfiguration of events, as is the case with the Fourth Gospel's handling of the Temple cleansing.)[119] Sometimes the catalytic quality of an event has the effect of casting into fresh perpective and of reordering the significance of events which precede it. Historical discourse arises through a process of retrospective patterning as well as prospective (causal) patterning. Very often the conclusions drawn about the relative importance of events, or more usually, the ideological and conceptual ideas by which events are analyzed, determine the shape which the narrative of those events takes. This may also be the case with the historical trends which these events are taken to constitute.

Narrative as a Continuum of Genres

We have seen that there are no linguistic markers which, of themselves, definitively or exclusively signal that a particular piece of discourse is fictional. It is true that, following Hamburger, certain features will

118. Mink, 'Narrative Form', p. 202.
119. See chapter 7.

suggest a fictional mode to the reader. However, this may have much to do with the conventional expectations of modern readers who know that these features are most often found in fictional works. That they are not exclusively the preserve of fiction may be seen from an analysis of certain types of autobiography and journalistic history. Indeed, approaching the issue from the side of fiction, we note that some types of historical novel can blur the edges of both reality and fiction.[120]

It would seem, therefore, that a distinction between history and fiction on the lines of some sort of differentiation between poetic and nonpoetic language, or fictional and 'ordinary', nonfictional discourse, is not possible. On the contrary, speech-act theorists would positively assert the lack of such intrinsic difference. Can we, then, decide the issue on the basis of whether or not the author of a particular discourse has entered into a pretence whereby the world or reality to which the discourse refers is an imagined rather than a real one? We would then decide the question of fiction or nonfiction on the basis of what kind of speech-acts are found in the discourse, that is, on whether or not the illocutionary force of these speech-acts is suspended by the 'pretence' hypothesis. This line of approach seems more promising. But, as has been shown, we will need to make a prior decision regarding the genre to which we will assign a given discourse before we can be entirely sure of the status of the speech-acts present.

Readers will find this task made easier in the cases where the genre is specifically designated on the title page or in the dustjacket 'blurb', or identified by a preface, or by the category to which the work is assigned for bibliographic purposes. However, our discussion of the conventions shared by history and fiction, together with the lack of formal differentiation between poetic and nonpoetic discourse, leads to the suggestion I will now develop—that, in fact, the varied genres

120. As an autobiographical example, see Laurie Lee's personal evocation of the Spanish Civil War in *A Moment of War*. The writings of Dominic Lapierre and Larry Collins provide good examples of 'journalistic' history; see, for instance, *O Jerusalem* or *Freedom at Midnight*. An interesting example of an historical novel is Pat Barker's *Regeneration*, which concerns the real-life encounter between R.H. Rivers, an army psychologist, and the poet, Siegfried Sassoon. The author adds an appendix to the novel to help the reader distinguish what is factually based from the imagined. Without such an account, this reader, at least, would have judged the descriptions of the method used by one of the medical professionals to treat a shellshocked soldier as 'fictional'.

which comprise the genus 'Narrative' are best seen as points along a continuum of narrative types.

Understanding narrative discourse as forming a continuum, or spectrum of genres, means that the boundaries between these narrative genres is open and, in many cases, hard and fast distinctions between the points along the continuum are not always possible. Indeed, might it not be possible, and in fact more precise, if we were to provide a model of narrative discourse in the form of a 'typological circle'? I shall pursue this suggestion shortly.

As part of a discussion of the 'poetics of point of view', Susan Lanser offers a series of 'axes' by which the status of a narrator may be determined. One of these axes relates to 'the implied or overt claim a narrator makes for the referential status of the tale'.[121] Her 'axis of reference' provides a useful starting point for constructing a continuum of narrative discourse. It is reproduced below:

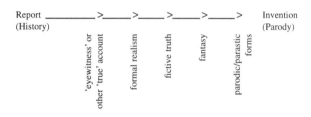

Figure 7

Lanser applies this axis to fictional texts. It will be simplest to give her own account of the axis.

> [T]he mode closest to the axis of report is the fictional text that insists on its historical truth by claiming to be a factual document, a biography or eyewitness account. Moving toward the pole of invention is the text that does not insist on its factual truth but applies the conventions of formal realism to present the illusion of a document. The term 'formal realism', used by Ian Watt in *The Rise of the Novel*, describes 'a set of procedures' that create the implication 'that the novel is a full and authentic report of human experience' (p. 32). The use of actual dates and place names is one convention of formal realism. At a midpoint [on the axis of reference] are texts that accept and communicate a sense that the story is fictively 'true' but not necessarily tied to historical reality. Moving toward the pole of invention is the text that stresses or suggests a status as fantasy; finally,

121. Lanser, *Narrative Act*, p. 163.

the extreme pole of invention is the parody, the parasitic text dependent
for its meaning not on the real world but on the conventions of literature
itself.[122]

In order to incorporate a wider range of narrative discourse onto the
'axis of reference', I shall extend Lanser's diagram. In this way I
include nonfictional narrative texts as well as fictional.

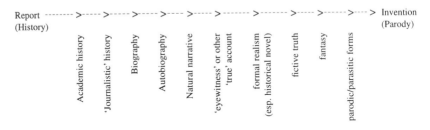

Figure 8

Display texts represent a category of narrative discourse which encompasses or 'straddles' a number of the genres. As a category it brackets
together a number of points on the axis, for example, from natural
narrative through to parody. There is, of course, an element of 'display'
in other forms of narrative as well, particularly autobiography and
memoir. Biography and even works of history may also include
elements of display, inasmuch as they may seek to 'entertain' and
engage the reader's sympathies with their subject as well as to inform.
However, as the verbal display of a state of affairs is seen by Pratt to
be the main characteristic of display text, a feature which subjugates any
didactic element to the aesthetics of 'display', it is, perhaps, as well to
confine the description to genres more at the 'invention' pole of the axis.

As a further refinement of the model, I propose that the continuum
of narrative discourse, which is comprised of various points along an
axis of reference, be converted into a typological circle of narrative
discourse.[123]

122. Lanser, *Narrative Act*, pp. 163-64. I have incorporated a footnote into the
text itself.
123. It should be noted that while the inspiration for this typological model comes
from Stanzel's typological circle of narrative situations, there is no intention that this
model should correlate the types or genres of narrative discourse with Stanzel's
narrative situations. It may be possible to argue that, broadly speaking, discourse of
an historical or reporting kind is found in an authorial, third-person mode of narration; and much fiction, especially modern fiction, locates in the reflector mode. It

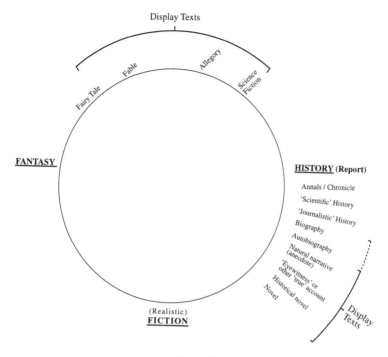

Figure 9

would be difficult, however, to make any correlation between Fantasy (Invention) and the first-person narrative situation. In any case, the two typological circles aim at schematizing entirely different aspects of narrative point of view. Stanzel's represents the formal, functional operation of the point of view of the narrator, the way in which the discourse is mediated. My typological circle schematizes the stance taken by an author, or implied author, as regards the referential status of the discourse.

I have provided a three-fold idealization of types (major categories of genre). However, I have substituted the term 'Fantasy' for Lanser's term 'Parody'. In many respects, of course, the genres subsumed under Fiction and Fantasy are of the same general type: and, in a bi-polar schema, works of fiction and fantasy gravitate toward the same end of the spectrum or axis (i.e. Invention). Conventionally, these genres all tend to be gathered under a broad type of narrative discourse labelled 'Fiction'.

However, a tri-partite schematization provides for a certain flexibility. Also, it is arguably the case that certain types of 'Fantasy' sit closer to the 'report' or history end of the axis than polarization along a unilinear spectrum might suggest. I am primarily interested in the sector of the circle between the 'History' and 'Fiction' types. A full schematization would see genres of the type 'biography', 'autobiography', and 'journalistic history' occupying the space between history and fantasy as well, e.g. histories of an 'apocalyptic' nature, or works of science fiction which are parasitic on the real world and real science. In other words, some types of narrative could be placed around the top half of the typological circle.

This typological circle presents a schematization of narrative types which fall into three broad sectors: History, Fiction (being imaginative discourse of a realistic type) and Fantasy (imaginative discourse of a fantastical, 'other-worldly' nature). The boundaries of these sectors may be minimally distinct or may overlap. Individual works may occupy a number of different points within a sector or even cross the boundary between two sectors. Hence, just as there may be a degree of dynamization possible in the mediation of a discourse's narrative situation (as suggested by Stanzel), so also there may be a certain flexibility in the classification of the genre of a given work. In some cases, too, one might wish to identify a subsector which encompasses a number of genres along the arc of the circle. I suggest that display texts form a subsector which encompasses genres including natural narratives, realistic fictional narrative, and fantasies (or parodies) as well.

An objection which might immediately be put forward is that this schematization turns what *should* be a polarity, that between History and Invention, into something a lot less differentiated. I suggest that, on the one hand, the polarity between history and invention might, at times, be less real than imagined; and that certain forms of narrative discourse might be seen as 'invented' history. Also, we should not forget that the reconstructive nature of historical discourse, based as it is on positing hypotheses about the past, admits of a degree of 'invention' anyway. On the other hand, it is possible that polarized schemas derive from some deep structural principle of human thinking, or are conventionally formed, so that an axis or bi-polar model is simply one that is more easily grasped than a circular one.

There are, I think, certain advantages to be gained in presenting the genres of narrative discourse in the form of a typological circle rather than as an axis or continuum of polarized forms. As has already been said, the boundaries between the different genres, and the formal and functional characteristics of these genres, are often less clear or fixed than conventionally thought. In the second place, specific examples of narrative discourse may, in fact, occupy various points around the circumference of the continuum. Indeed, a given discourse may move in and out of various genres, or display features of one genre at a given point in the discourse, and those of another at a different point. Yet it will still be possible to locate a given work within one of the broad sectors. An historical novel may occupy the border region between history and fiction, yet be read as a fictional discourse. A work of history, say of the 'journalistic' type or an academic history which includes attempts at psychological insight, may take on features which are more or less fictive (i.e. imaginative and 'poetic') yet remain accepted as historical discourse.

The Fourth Gospel and Chariton's Chaereas and Callirhoe

Before we attempt to place the Fourth Gospel on the typological circle of narrative discourse, we will examine it in relation to another form of ancient display text, the Greek romance or novel.[124] This narrative type must certainly be placed in the fiction sector of the circle, or, on Lanser's axis of reference, somewhere between formal realism/fictive truth and fantasy. I have chosen to compare the Gospel with Chariton's *Chareas and Callirhoe* as this work almost certainly predates, or was roughly contemporaneous with the Gospel. It is generally dated from 100 BCE to the end of the first century CE.[125]

A comparison between the gospels and ancient Greek romances is important partly because this form of popular literature has generally

124. There is, however, no formal generic name for this type which derives from ancient literary classification. Like the Gospels, they were too populist in nature to attract the attention of ancient literary critics. The modern terms 'novel' and 'romance' are used more or less interchangeably by scholars. See M.A. Tolbert, *Sowing the Gospel* (Minneapolis: Fortress Press, 1989), p. 62 n. 46. For further discussion, cf. T. Hägg, *The Novel in Antiquity* (ET: Oxford: Basil Blackwell, 1983), pp. 3-4; Perry, *The Ancient Romances*, p. 3.

125. See T. Hägg, *Narrative Technique in Ancient Greek Romances* (Stockholm: Svenska Institutet i Athen, 1971), pp. 14-15, esp n. 1. Cf. Reardon, *Collected*, p. 5; Perry, *The Ancient Romances*, pp. 243-46 n. 12, and p. 350. n. 15; E.L. Bowie, 'The Greek Novel', in P.E. Easterling and B.M.W. Knox (eds.), *The Cambridge History of Classical Literature* (Cambridge: Cambridge University Press, 1985), I, p. 684. See Tolbert's early dating, *Sowing*, p. 62: 'Chariton is usually dated between 100 BCE–50 CE; Xenophon, 50 CE–263 CE.' Her dating may well be right for Chariton, but scholars generally give Xenophon a later *terminus a quo*. Of the five complete Greek novels which have come down to us, three are too late to be brought into consideration (being dated from the late second century CE to the fourth century). However, as a generic type, the Greek novel certainly came into existence some time in the two centuries before Christ, as the existence of numerous papyrus fragments testifies. *Ninus*, dated about 100 BCE, which is in a very fragmentary state, is generally taken as the earliest example of the genre. A pagan Greek prototype, upon which the Pseudo-Clementine Latin romance *Recognitiones* is based, is also thought to fall within the pre-100 CE era (see Perry, *The Ancient Romances*, p. 291).

been ignored by scholars in their study of the gospel genre.[126] More-over, the existence of the Greek novel demonstrates that fictional invention of the realistic type was possible in the first century CE. Inasmuch as the Gospel shows some formal affinities with Chariton's work, there is an argument for allowing a degree of fictive invention in the Gospel. At the least, the comparison may influence the decisions taken by scholars on the Gospel's genre.[127] However, the Greek novel is itself generically difficult to 'fix' and early examples such as Chariton's are indebted to ancient historiography (as we shall see below). This provides further support for taking a flexible approach to determining the relationship both of Chariton and the Fourth Gospel to 'history' and 'fiction'. Finally, the Gospel's motivation as the elaboration of an historical person's theological significance is quite other than Chariton's invention in pursuit of entertainment. Thus, noting how the Gospel differs from the ancient novel enables us to define more clearly how and why it gravitates towards the history sector of the circle. Basing my study upon T. Hägg's analysis of *Chaereas and Callirhoe* in his *Narrative Technique in Ancient Greek Romances*, I note the following structural and formal correspondences between this novel and the Fourth Gospel.

Both Chariton and the Gospel's implied author operate under a prin-ciple of selection, choosing only certain incidents from amongst a much greater number of possible ones.[128] Both begin their stories *in medias res*: Chariton, from the time his hero and heroine first meet; the Fourth Gospel (excluding the semi-philosophical parts of the prologue) from the time of John the Baptist's witness. Both confine themselves to

---

126. To my knowledge M.A. Tolbert, *Sowing*, represents a pioneering attempt to draw analogies between ancient romance and, in her case, the gospel of Mark. This neglect has been paralleled by, and perhaps due to, a corresponding neglect of the ancient novels by classicists, though this is changing (cf. Reardon, *Collected Ancient Greek Novels*, p. 6). Pervo, *Profit with Delight*, draws analogies between the book of Acts and ancient romance.

127. I am, of course, concerned mainly with modern readers' attitudes to the Gospel: in this case, critically informed readers. We may, however, allow that ancient readers familiar with the Greek novel, may also have noted the affinities.

128. This feature is not confined to these genres, of course. For a description of Thucydides' selective procedure, see W.R. Connor, 'Narrative Discourse in Thucydides', in Department of Classics, Stamford University, *The Greek Historians* (Saratoga: ANMA Libri & Co., 1985), pp. 1-17.

a restricted period in the lives of their chief protagonists, ostensibly two to three years.

In terms of the plot structure, and the ratio of story time to discourse time (that is time it takes to tell the story), the tendency is to present the action in concentrated blocks of events which appear to be temporally related.[129] These blocks of action, or we might say collections of scenes, are linked with (and separated from) each other by narrative in which temporal notices are more generalized or even absent. Often these transitional passages also involve a journey or physical movement from one place to another. Tomas Hägg analyses *Chaereas and Callirhoe* for what he calls the 'day-and-night phases' or sequences of action which may be conceived as taking place on one day or night, or a series of consecutive days and nights. It is noted that these account for a large proportion of discourse time (i.e. extent of text) while covering a proportionately small amount of story time. On the other hand, there are portions of the narrative where a greater amount of story time is covered by a smaller amount of discourse time. The action is viewed from a greater distance and takes on an iterative-durative aspect (that is, the narration conveys the sense of repeated or continuous action over a period of time). The function of these narrative phases is to introduce or conclude a 'day-night' (i.e. concentrated) phase of action and to provide 'transitional passages between two scenes or sequences of scenes'.[130] Analysis of a segment of the text of *Chaereas and Callirhoe* shows that '25% of fictional time takes up 93% of narrative time';[131] that there are both individual scenes embedded within narration and at several points 'sequences of scenes conglomerate forming a larger "day-and-night" group'.[132]

We may note a similar pattern of blocks of concentrated action covering either one day (and a single event) or a series of days (and a number of events) within the Fourth Gospel. For example, John 1.19–2.11 covers a period of days (many commentators say it is seven or a week) which deal with John's witness, the 'call' of some disciples, and a wedding at Cana (closely allied with what precedes it by the temporal

129. Hägg uses the term 'narrative time' for that which I subsume under the term 'discourse time'.
130. Hägg, *Narrative Technique*, p. 40.
131. Hägg, *Narrative Technique*, p. 31.
132. Hägg, *Narrative Technique*, p. 34, and see also pp. 26-49, 84-85.

note Καὶ τῇ ἡμέρᾳ τῇ τρίτῃ). There follows a series of more or less discrete, individual scenes: the cleansing of the Temple, the visit of Nicodemus, the witness of John, Jesus and the woman of Samaria, the healing of the official's son which are each separated by brief transitional passages and narrator's comment. From ch. 6 onwards we find more concentrated sequences of action to which often extensive passages of discourse are attached. John 6.2-71 tells of the feeding of the five thousand, the walking on the water that night and a discourse on the Bread of Life the next day. After a brief transitional passage in which Jesus' brothers challenge him to show himself publicly in Jerusalem at a Jewish festival, there follows a couple of discourses (one in the middle and the other on the last day of the festival), general discussion amongst the crowd about Jesus and an attempt by the authorities to arrest him. This is closely followed by the healing of a blind man and a discourse on the Good Shepherd (7.14–10.21).[133] Two further 'day-and-night' sequences are found in the Gospel: the meal at Bethany, followed by the triumphal entry and the approach of some Greeks to see Jesus (12.1-36a) and the Passion narrative (beginning with the footwashing incident, including the long farewell discourses and ending with Jesus' appearance to Thomas (John 13.1–20.29). The transitional passages which separate these 'day-and-night' phases often involve notice of Jesus' movements, or a description of some iterative-durative activity (2.12, Jesus goes to Capernaum and stays there a few days; 3.22, Jesus goes with his disciples into Judaea, presumably somewhere near Aenon where John is, and baptizes; 4.43-45, Jesus travels from Samaria to Galilee; 7.1, Jesus travels around in Galilee; 10.40-42, cf. also 11.54).

The Fourth Gospel shares with Chariton a preference for scenic depiction along with the use of a great deal of direct discourse, either of dialogue or monologue. Another feature is the use of anticipations and recapitulations: that is, narrative comments or summaries which look forward to or foreshadow future events; or those which summarize or recall earlier events.[134] Neither of these features, particularly

---

133. Within a given 'day-and-night' phase, a narrative may show temporal density (cf. Hägg, *Narrative Technique*, pp. 35-38). An example of this is Jn 9 where we have a highly detailed incident in seven scenes.

134. There are two major recapitulations in Chariton, one at the beginning of book five: ref. Reardon, *Collected* (= R.), p.75; G. Molinié, *Chariton*, (Budé = B.), p. 131; and the other at the start of book eight (R., p. 110; B., p. 181-82). In the latter

recapitulation, are used as extensively in the Gospel as in Chariton. However, examples of anticipations in the Gospel may be found at Jn 2.22, where Jesus' death is anticipated; Jn 6.70, 71, anticipating the betrayal by Judas; Jn 7.33, 34, where Jesus foreshadows his departure; and Jn 11.11, 23 where the raising of Lazarus is directly referred to prior to the event. Some anticipations are not fulfilled within the narrative, or at least only by the interpretive activity of the reader (e.g. 1.51). As is the case with Chariton's love story, the Gospel concludes with a couple of anticipations which project the reader forward into the world beyond the story. At 20.29 Jesus refers to future believers who will believe in him without having seen him (amongst whom the reader who accepts the implied author's speech-acts may be counted). I believe that 21.23 may be understood as a form of anticipation suggesting both the continuation of faithful witness (and it is one of the intents of this narrative to provide that continuing witness) and possibly the return of Jesus (expected to be imminent?). As an example of recapitulation, we may note that the first major section of the book (known as the 'Book of Signs') ends at 12.37-50 with a summary statement of the reasons for the failure of Jesus' mission amongst 'his own people' as well as a summary declaration of his revelatory mission.

A stylistic feature in which the Gospel resembles Chariton's novel is the way in which quotations from earlier works are taken up directly into the narrative. In the case of *Chaereas and Callirhoe* the author draws upon the works of Homer (amongst others), often times weaving the quotations seamlessly into the web of the narrative,[135] though at other times making direct reference to Homer.[136] An episode in book five where Callirhoe appears before the Persian people, and the ensuing trial scene, contain allusions to Xenophon of Athen's *Cyropaidea* and his *Anabasis*.[137] Generally speaking, the Gospel details the quotations it uses as coming from 'the Scriptures', or 'the prophets' or 'the Law' (ref. 1.23; 2.17; 6.31, 45; 10.34; 12.15, 38, 40; 13.18; 15.25; 19.24, 36) though occasionally the quotation is taken up into the narrative

---

case the recapitulation gives way to an anticipation which foreshadows the book's happy ending.

135. Cf. G. Molinié, *Chariton*, I.1.14 (B., p. 52, R., p. 23); I.4.6 (B., p.56, R., p. 26); II.9.6 (B., p. 88, R., p. 47); III.4.4 (B., p. 101, R., p. 56).

136. II.3.7 (B., p. 77, R., p. 41); V.5.9 (B., p. 141, R., p. 82).

137. Cf. Reardon, *Collected*, p. 79 n.79.

without such notice much in the manner of Chariton's use of Homer (ref. 1.51; 12.13; 12.27).

As for the motifs which characterize Chariton's novel, those of the journey, the 'death' and 'resurrection' of a character, the final recognition scene (where the lovers are reunited) and the central turning point, find their echoes in the Fourth Gospel.[138] The motivation of these motifs is different in each case: the journeys of Jesus in the Gospel are more intentionally conceived (e.g. Jesus wishes to escape the malice of the Jews) than the somewhat random or fated wanderings and movements of the young lovers. Death and resurrection in the Gospel are to be taken as instances of real death and real resurrection, not merely the apparent death and later resuscitation of a hero or heroine. The recognition of Jesus is a spiritual recognition of his real identity, though chapters 20 and 21 provide actual recognition scenes. The latter involves the reunion of Peter with Jesus and his subsequent reinstatement as a disciple. One wonders whether readers familiar with the Greek novels may not have perceived a 'parodying' and reworking of these motifs by the Gospel's implied author.

Finally, there are generic similarities in that both the gospel form and the ancient romance originate as popular literature, written in *koine* Greek,[139] with their roots in historiography.[140] The early romances such as Chariton's or the *Ninus* fragments draw upon historical persons and, in some cases, historical incidents for their inspiration. Chariton, in particular, draws upon historical personages and events, but reworks them so that the historical framework becomes vague and anachronistic and the main characters are more imaginative than factual in conception and depiction. Yet it may still be described as an 'historical novel'.[141]

Furthermore, the ancient romances bear in their outward form the stamp of historiography and from this 'the romancer derived a large

138. See here also Tolbert, *Sowing*, pp. 64-66.

139. Though perhaps the Fourth Gospel's Greek would not be described, as is Chariton's, as 'straightforward literary *koine*', see Reardon, *Collected*, p. 20. Cf. G.L. Schmeling, *Chariton* (New York: Twayne Publishers, 1974), pp. 24, 25.

140. On the ancient Greek novels as popular literature, see Perry, *The Ancient Romances*, p. 48; also his 'Chariton and and His Romance', *American Journal of Philology* 51.2 (1930), p. 95, n. 5.

141. See Reardon, *Collected*, p. 18, Perry, *The Ancient Romances*, pp. 137-40. On the relationship of the ancient novel with historiography see Perry's careful discussion in *The Ancient Romances*, pp. 32-43; also, Reardon, *Collected*, p. 8; Hägg, *Novel*, pp. 111-14.

part of his manner and method in writing'.[142] Again, Chariton consciously 'followed the rules for Hellenistic historiography, in composition as well as style'[143] and models the form of his opening sentence upon those of Herodotus and Thucydides.[144] Gareth Schmeling writes, '[f]ew pages go by without Chariton imitating the three great Greek historians, Herodotus, Thucydides, and Xenophon. . .'[145]

The affinities with historiographical writing are greater in the earlier romances such as *Chaereas and Callirhoe* and *Ninus* than in the later ones. That this is so suggests that first-century romance lies closer to the pole of *historia* than the later romances and this fact must be taken into account when placing them on a typological circle. It also means that the same will apply to a work such as the Fourth Gospel which may seem to approximate to the romance form in some of its features. Of course, ancient forms of historiography drew a less clear distinction between 'history' and 'fiction' than we do in this century. Legendary and traditional material was regarded as in some manner historical, or taken up into a work of historiography without a sense of incongruity. Realistic, credible invention and literary embellishment, the creation of speeches to put in a character's mouth, for instance, were permitted for aesthetic and educative purposes.[146] This means that ancient genres will display a greater flexibility than modern ones and there will be a tendency for the boundaries between genres and 'ideal' typological poles to be more open.

Despite the formal parallels which the Fourth Gospel shares with the ancient novel, in terms of function and purpose it springs from a completely different motivation. As 'display texts', the primary purpose of the display or elaboration in the Greek novels is that of entertainment. Their purpose is artistic and creative fulfillment on the part of the author, and aesthetic enjoyment and uplift for the reader. Sentiment, the love of adventure, and the portrayal and exploration of the psychological and physical experiences of the characters also play a part.[147] Despite psychologizing touches in the Gospel worthy of an

142. Perry, *The Ancient Romances*, p. 38, cf. p. 78.

143. Hägg, *Novel*, p. 114.

144. Reardon, *Collected*, p. 18.

145. Schmeling, *Chariton*, p. 24.

146. See here Hägg, *Novel*, p. 18; and especially Perry's important and subtle discussion in *The Ancient Romances*, pp. 66-69, 72-78.

147. Cf. Perry, *The Ancient Romances*, pp. 34-36.

ancient romancer (Judas presented as a thief, the Samaritan woman as a quick-witted interlocutor and enquirer after truth, Pilate as urbane cynic or compromising politician following the path of expediency) its intent is plainly the theological, and even moral, instruction of the reader. The implied author also has a case to make for Jesus, an historical figure, as having the status of the Christ.

However, scholars in discussing the cultural and social conditions which gave rise to the romance genre, point up a feature of their motivation which is certainly also applicable to the Fourth Gospel's purpose. The novels, it is said, spoke to the individual's sense of isolation and helplessness in the face of Fate (τύχη) or the gods. They witness to a search for salvation and security. They arise in the midst of an 'open society', a milieu of 'conflicting desires and centrifugal tendencies' where people were 'rootless, at a loss, restlessly searching'.[148] The Gospel tells the story of one who as 'Lamb of God' and 'Saviour of the world' brings hope of eternal life. The narrative is written so that the reader 'may have life in his name' (20.31). It tells of numerous 'seekers' after truth and life (Nicodemus, the Samaritan woman, the blind man) with whom some readers will have identified. Hence, the Gospel would appeal to the same human feelings and needs as do the novels, while providing a completely different solace.

The Fourth Gospel on the Typological Circle of Narrative Discourse

It is as well to rehearse some of the broad lines of the argument so far. It has been proposed that any attempt to determine the status of a given discourse as fictional or nonfictional on the ground of a 'poetic' language or certain supposedly distinctive fictional features is difficult and misplaced. The most we can say is that certain grammatical and linguistic features will *tend* to suggest a fictional mode of discourse to the reader, though in some cases, lacking a clear specification of genre, there will be a margin of uncertainty. Also, we need to consider whether conventional expectations derived from familiarity with modern fictional discourse might not affect the way in which modern readers read ancient literature as well.

---

148. Hägg, *The Novel in Antiquity*, pp. 89, 90. On the social context which gave rise to the novel, see further Hägg, *The Novel in Antiquity*, pp. 81-90; Reardon, 'The Greek Novel', *Phoenix* 23.3 (1967), pp. 291-309; Perry, *The Ancient Romances*, pp. 45-49. Cf. also Pervo, *Profit*, pp. 111-13.

I would concur with speech-act theorists of literature that there is no set of linguistic properties shared by all works of fictional discourse which definitively mark out such discourse as being fictional. Furthermore, the use of language in fictional discourse is the same as that in nonfictional, ordinary discourse. Within that discourse the rules for speech-acts operate in the same way. Pratt has shown in an examination of natural narrative, in which the field of reference is the real world, that structurally ordinary discourse shares the same features as does literary discourse.

What may be said with confidence is that the *context* within which speech-acts are found is not the same in fictional as in nonfictional discourse. In fictional discourse, the context is an imagined, pretended world; the discourse is not *situated* as that between a real speaker and a real addressee and, hence, the illocutionary force of an assertion, as it would apply in the real world, is suspended. Establishing the context of a given narrative discourse is partly a matter of identifying its genre: and partly a question of the status a reader confers, or is led to confer, on its speech-acts. We consider the matter of the Fourth Gospel's genre here. We examine the status of its speech-acts in the next section.

The Fourth Gospel may be broadly described as a display text which shares some resemblances in aspects of its discourse to natural narrative (see above pp. 189-93). It also has features which are characteristic of realistic (fictional) narrative (see above pp. 176-85). We have noted how some of its formal features draw it into contiguity with an ancient romance such as *Chaereas and Callirhoe*. At the same time, other features would bring it into association with biography and history (and we have seen that early forms of the ancient novel also moved on the borders of historiography).[149] Of course, modern readers would also consider that it contains elements of the fantastic. Whether readers prior to the Enlightenment would have done so as well is a question

149. Burridge, *What are the Gospels?*, chapter 9, includes the Fourth Gospel along with the Synoptic gospels as a Βίος Ἰησοῦ on the grounds of mainly formal but some functional correspondences with Greco-Roman *bioi* (Cf. also C.H. Talbert, *What is a Gospel?* [London: SPCK, 1977], chapter 3, for another generic parallel i.e. *katabasis-anabasis* mythology). For the Fourth Gospel's affinities with Hebrew narrative (arguably a form of ancient historiography) see Alter, *The Art of Biblical Narrative*, pp. 52-57, 72, 93-96, 182-83, on use of type-scenes, the tendency of narrative to gravitate towards dialogue and dialogue scene, restriction to two characters per dialogue-scene, contrastive dialogue, and use of key words and recurrent motifs. Unfortunately, space precludes elaboration of how these appear in the Fourth Gospel.

which can only be answered by attention to the reactions (in so far as we have the evidence to gauge these) of real readers in the pre-Enlightenment period. In the majority of cases, one would suspect that they did not.[150] But a tendency to read biblical narrative typologically or allegorically makes this point difficult to establish in all cases.

I would place the Fourth Gospel somewhere on an arc falling within the radii of the genres 'biography' and 'realistic narrative' (or, 'formal realism'). More precisely, it would occupy a point on the circle somewhere between the points occupied by a natural narrative and 'eyewitness' account (as shown in Fig. 10 below).

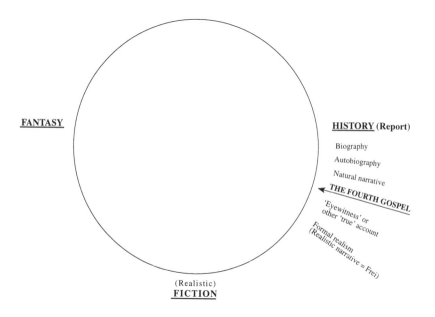

Figure 10

My reasons for placing the Fourth Gospel here are dependent upon what I take to be the status of its speech-acts, as well as the stance taken by the implied author to his material. Both these indicate that the implied author's motivation is not to write a piece of fiction, for he claims to be writing about matters for which he has good 'eyewitness' authority. But features of resemblance to the genres contiguous with it, suggest that the Gospel must be placed in a position of dynamic tension between the poles of history and fiction.

150. See Frei, *Eclipse*, p. 1.

We are, of course, discussing the issue on the basis of modern genre types. In other words, we have plotted the Fourth Gospel's situation in relationship to genre types whose formal and motivational characteristics have been arranged against a background grid of modern conceptions of 'history', 'realistic fiction' and 'fantasy'. However, it would be possible to plot a typology of ancient genres—*hypomnemata, bios, aretalogy* and so forth—where the types most relevant to the gospel type would be situated on a typological circle.[151] In all probability, these genres would be found, more or less, in contiguity with one another and inhabiting an arc within the same sectors of the circle. In the ancient world there would, perhaps, be more latitude in placing works displaying features of 'realistic narrative' in the direction of the history (report) ideal than much modern scholarship or readership would allow. We would, at the least, need to take cognizance of the different conventions by which ancient types were formed in our construction of a typological circle. Any correlations between ancient and modern genres would have to bear these differences in mind.

The description of the Fourth Gospel as a display text is helpful as long as one recognizes that the motivation from which the Gospel arises is different from that of a fictional display text. The theological motivation of the implied author has an important bearing on the nature of the 'display'. The Gospel might best be described as an historically based, theological display text. In other words, the motivation behind the display is not entertainment, nor the mere imparting of information about the narrative's chief character. Rather, the narrative provides a *theological elaboration* upon an historical substratum: selected aspects of the story of the historical Jesus are recounted in order to lay bare the inner theological truths of the significance of his being and of his life, death and resurrection. We shall expand upon this point in an examination of the implied author's speech-acts.

The Status of the Fourth Gospel's Speech-Acts

Placing the Fourth Gospel on the typological circle of narrative discourse in the position outlined above, carries with it certain implications for an understanding of the nature of its speech-acts. It means, I suggest, that we cannot properly describe the illocutions as 'pretended'. The implied author does not intend that readers adopt the stance that

151. See Appendix, p. 273 (esp. Fig. 11).

the world referred to within the Fourth Gospel is an imagined or 'pretended' one. There is a real and genuine reference to actual historical events, characters and circumstances. This is not to say that the discourse is historical in every particular, or that every item of reference to event and action had its counterpart in the actual, historical life of Jesus. What it does mean is that, to recall the statement of Brown and Steinmann, the Fourth Gospel is *situated* discourse. The implied author speaks the discourse *in propria persona*. That is to say, the implied author's illocutionary acts are ones to which he is committed and to which we may apply the appropriateness rules. When the implied author, through the medium of the narrator, relates Jesus as saying, 'I am the way, the truth and the life, no one comes to the Father, but by me' (14.6), or 'I am the resurrection and the life...' (11.25, 26), or 'For the bread of God is that which comes down from heaven, and gives life to the world' (6.33), he is making assertions which operate under the appropriateness rules for illocutions in the real world. Thus when we say that the implied author speaks *in propria persona*, the implication for the status of his speech-acts is that he stands behind these statements. The implied author asserts that these claims made of Jesus are true, whether or not Jesus actually said them. He is saying, in effect, 'I am claiming that Jesus is the way, the truth and the life'. The implied author stands behind the truth value of the statements made about Jesus in his narrative, both in that he asserts what he believes to be true and in that he provides evidence in support of the truth of his assertions.

Now there may be an element of 'pretence' in that the implied author could be putting words into the mouth of Jesus, but there is no pretence about the truth value of these words or that Jesus is the one to whom they refer. He may say, as it were, 'Let us suppose that Jesus said, "I am the way, the truth and the life...".' He does not say, 'Let us imagine that Jesus is the way, the truth and the life' (or the resurrection and the life, or the bread of God), nor is he inviting the reader to enter into an imagined world where there is an imagined character, called Jesus, who says, or about whom it is claimed, that he is the way, the truth and the life. The pretence, if it is such, lies in the origin of the performative (implied author's words in character's mouth) but not in the context within which the performative occurs.

But if the assertions made are real assertions about a real person, in what sense may it yet be possible that the implied author can put words into the mouth of Jesus, as a novelist puts words into the mouth of one of his characters, and yet not transgress the boundary between illocutions which operate in a context of reality and those which do not? How may the implied author produce discourse which is feigned, yet not be taken as fictional?

It should be noted, of course, that we cannot entirely rule out the possibility that the implied author was, or believed he was, reporting the actual words of Jesus. The overall context of the discourse suggests that this is how he intends the reader to take them. What is more the case in terms of his strategy is that some of the Gospel's reported speech is an elaboration upon remembered words of Jesus, or sayings received from the tradition, which have been reworked in this discourse. The ἀμὴν ἀμὴν sayings may be a case in point: a traditional saying is taken up and becomes the basis upon which further dialogue is developed in the spirit of Jesus.[152]

It is possible, I believe, to discern a theological motivation in the Fourth Gospel which maintains the integrity of the implied author's illocutionary acts vis-à-vis the real world, while at the same time allowing an element of 'fictivity'. It might perhaps be better, in view of our discussion of the Gospel as a display text, to describe this element of 'fictivity' as arising out of the Gospel's *elaboration* on a state of affairs which has its basis in the real world, than to speak of it as a tendency to fictionalization. The motivation which permits this elaboration is, as I have said, a theological one: the implied author seeks to bring before his implied reader what he understands to be the real and true significance of the historical Jesus. Moreover, his understanding of the post-resurrection relationship of the believer to the Risen Christ, his theology of the role of the Paraclete in providing development yet continuity between pre-Easter and post-Easter understandings of Jesus, and the retrospective point of view from which he sees the life and ministry of Jesus, allows for a creative refiguring upon the historical tradition. It also permits a perspective which sees a continuation of the works and words of Jesus into the present of the implied author (cf. 14.12, 13; 15.26, 27; 16.13-15).

This elaboration on events in the life and ministry of Jesus (including some elaboration on his teaching) is a result of the merging of two horizons and the bringing together of two historical times. It is a merging of the 'event then' (or to borrow a term from J.L. Martyn,

152. Cf. Lindars, *John*, p. 48.

the *einmalig* time, historical 'once upon a time') with the time of the discourse, the time of the writing or telling of the tale and of theological, and scriptural, reflection upon it. It is important to keep in view the basic theological motivation and orientation of the discourse, for it is this motivation which makes the nature of the elaboration, the kind of 'display' it is, *of a different sort* from that which gives rise to the 'world' of fictional discourse. The theological perspective brings to bear upon the real world a dimension and aspect of reality which gathers up the real world of human event and time-bound circumstance into a world of divine and eternal truth. Fictional discourse engages a world that is mimetic of, imitative of the real world. Theological discourse engages a world (a reality) that is contingent upon the real historical world but which also expands the boundaries of that world. In so far as the eternal impinges upon the world, the narrative genre (historical narrative even) provides a useful and necessary mode of discourse. Inasmuch as theological truth transcends the 'real, historical world' (but not necessarily reality), it lies beyond the reach of mere scientific historical analysis and discourse. Lying thus beyond the reaches of mere scientific historical discourse, it requires the use of elaboration and takes on the qualities of a display text. The Fourth Gospel might be described as a theological display text, that is, theological elaboration upon history. It is a believer's 'display' of the true significance of an historical person.

As such, the illocutionary acts of the implied author are governed by the appropriateness rules which apply in the real world. But the perlocutionary acts require the reader to move into the realm of faith. When the implied author says, 'These are written that you may believe...', it follows that the perlocutions required of the reader derive not from historical knowledge pure and simple, but from theological perception and spiritual receptivity. The claims made for Jesus as the Christ are predicated upon the historical substratum of the narrative. But the 'pattern-quality' of the narrated events is determined by a theological and supernatural perspective. It is a view 'from above'. In other words, the Gospel presents a history of Jesus seen in theological perspective. It is a believer's view of history: not that of the modern secular historian. This is not to say that it is not 'historical'; rather, it is history of a different sort, namely, *theologized history*. Since the Enlightenment it has been the habit of historical research to bracket out this type of history. It is a temptation even for Christian historians to put history and theology in some sort of subtle contra-distinction to each other, so that, when the empirical tools of historical research prove no longer able to provide a full description, then we move by a subtle change of gear to something called theology. Thus, it is all too easily forgotten that to acknowledge a theological (and *ipso facto* supernatural) reality is immediately to bring a new dimension to bear upon the real historical world. If this is not the case, then views of the world which posit theological causes and events, and a supernatural reality, belong with fictional worlds in the realm of the imagined.

It is important to recognize that, by the very act of casting the dis-course into narrative form, the implied author has created difficulties for a clear-cut distinction between history and fiction. The mediated character of narrative, whether historical or fictional, draws the two genres into a contiguous relationship and sets up a 'curious, unmarked frontier'[153] between them. But to read the Gospel narrative as 'realistic narrative', as 'history-like', or as 'poetic history' does not mean to set it in absolute contradistinction to history. Frei appears to set history-like and historical in opposition to each other, thereby continuing the polarity which has long dominated scholarly thinking on this issue. 'What actually happened' has been set in opposition to what is written about what happened, as if the 'facts of history' are recoverable from the narrative as the kernel may be extracted from the shell of a nut. All historical narrative and understanding remains, at a fundamental level, discourse which treats historical facts 'as they must have happened', or, 'as they might have happened'. To this extent, histori-cal narrative may take on elements of fictivity just as fictional narra-tion may be mimetic of reality. On the other hand, we cannot take the Gospel narrative simply as literal historical record. The merit of Frei's book is the inference it contains that a narrative reading of the Gospel will be a much more subtle enterprize than the discussion and concern about its ostensive reference to history, both from a liberal and a conservative perspective, would suggest. Where a speech-act approach is particularly helpful is in bringing a clearer recognition of the fact that the speech-act *context* is important in determining the nature of the exchange as well. Questions of the illocutionary stance of the implied author, the illocutionary force of assertions made and the perlocutionary effects of these statements must also be kept in view.

153. Cf. Frei, *Eclipse*, p. 150.

The overall speech-act context which motivates the discourse, that is whether it is fictional ('pretended'), or historical-theological, must also be considered.

Though the relationship of the Fourth Gospel's discourse to the question of the historicity of its content is problematic, it is possible, I think, to define a plausible relationship between the structure of the narrative and the traditions and historical data, some of it shared with the Synoptics, to which the implied author had access. When we understand something of the theological motivation which informs the enterprise, we may be able to see how and in what way the historical data has been refigured to provide the 'followable story' which is this Gospel. The issue will be approached through a consideration of the cleansing of the Temple.

Chapter 7

HISTORY IN THEOLOGICAL DISPLAY: THE CLEANSING
OF THE TEMPLE AND HISTORICAL RECONSTRUCTION

The Issues

The question of the relationship of the Fourth Gospel as a narrative about Jesus and the historical life and ministry of Jesus are posed sharply in the pericope of the 'cleansing' of the Temple. For here we have an incident recorded in all four gospels. Furthermore, in the broad outline of the incident, all four agree. Jesus entered the Temple and disrupted the normal course of its commercial activity. This brought him into conflict with the Jewish authorities: and according to Mark and Luke put him in jeopardy (Mk 11.18; Lk. 19.47). Matthew defers narrating the desire of the authorities to arrest Jesus until later (21.46, par. Mk 12.12 // Lk. 20.19) and gives this a slightly different motivation,[1] while, as we shall see, the Fourth Gospel implies a direct link between the Temple act and Jesus' death. Yet when we put the Fourth Gospel's account alongside those of the Synoptics, it is found to differ significantly at a number of points. In brief, these differences can be marshalled under three headings.

First, there are differences in matters of detail. While the Synoptics do not agree entirely on matters of detail, it is fair to say that their terse descriptions largely correspond.[2] The Fourth Gospel, on the other hand, elaborates on the incident and provides a vivid scene.

---

1. The authorities are reacting to the parable of the vineyard told against them. Their reaction at the time of the action in the Temple is muted: Jesus is apparently able to continue with a healing ministry directly after his demonstration (21.14). They simply challenge Jesus on account of the reaction of children to him and his apparent failure to correct them (21.15, 16).

2. For instance, Luke omits the overturning of the seats of the moneychangers and pigeon sellers (19.45). Mark adds the information that Jesus refused to allow anyone to carry anything through the Temple precincts (11.16).

Jesus sees (Gk. 'finds') the merchants with their livestock, sheep and oxen; he makes a whip (φραγέλλιον) and drives them all out—presumably this means the merchants, along with their animals (as RSV).[3] The implied author uses a different word from that employed by the Synoptics to describe the moneychangers. Though he describes Jesus' action in overturning their tables (as do Matthew and Mark), he adds that he scattered their coins (2.15). Where Matthew and Mark have Jesus upsetting the seats of those who sell pigeons as well, the Fourth Gospel merely informs us that Jesus tells them to take the birds away. Most significantly perhaps, the logion ascribed to Jesus in the Synoptics does not appear. In its place, the Fourth Gospel's narrator makes Jesus say, 'Take these things away: you shall not make my Father's house a house of trade' (2.16 cf. Mt. 21.13 // Lk. 19.46; Mk 11.17).

Next, there is a major discrepancy between the Synoptics and the Fourth Gospel on the question of chronology. The Synoptic gospels indicate that Jesus made one visit to Jerusalem near the close of his ministry. On the day of his triumphal entry into the city (Mt. // Lk.), or the day after (Mk), he carried out his dramatic act of protest.[4] The

---

3.   In the Greek the sense is difficult. Many scholars point out that 'all' (πάντας) refers to the men, and that τά τε πρόβατα κτλ. . . is in poor apposition to it (as in Barrett, *John*, p. 197; Brown, *John*, p. 115; Lindars, *John*, p. 138; Schnackenburg, *John*, I, p. 346). It is thought by some to be an editorial addition. Haenchen, *John*, p. 183, on the contrary, understands 'all' as referring to the sheep and oxen, as he is reluctant to think that Jesus used the whip on people.

4.   Many scholars place this within the last week before Jesus' death. The Synoptics do not necessarily support this conclusion. While they agree in placing the 'cleansing' of the Temple after the triumphal entry, a precise date for the latter is not given. It is, in fact, Johannine chronology that puts the triumphal entry five days before the Passover (12.1, 12). 'Day after day, I taught in the Temple. . . ' (Mt. 26.55 // Mk 14.49) suggests that Jesus spent some time in and around Jerusalem after his arrival there. The only incidents to be precisely dated in the Synoptics are the plotting of the authorities, the anointing at Bethany, Judas' agreement with the Jewish leaders to betray Jesus, and the last supper (Mt. 26.1, 2 // Mk 14.1) where the accounts state that it was 'two days' before the Passover. Only Luke fixes precisely the date of the last supper, which he places on 'the day of Unleavened Bread' (Lk. 22.7). The Church's calendar and some scholarly comment derive from harmonization of the Fourth Gospel's account with those of the Synoptics. On the evidence of the Mishnah, R. Bauckham, 'Jesus' Demonstration in the Temple', in B. Lindars (ed.), *Law and Religion* (Cambridge: James Clarke, 1988), p. 75, argues that the most likely time for the incident in the Temple would not have been in the week prior to the Passover, but about three weeks earlier. This is because the moneylenders set up

Fourth Gospel sets the incident when 'the Passover of the Jews was at hand' (2.13), but this apparently was not the Passover at which Jesus was crucified. At any rate, the Gospel appears to refer to three separate Passovers (2.13, 23; 6.4; 11.55, cf. 12.1) and possibly four if the feast mentioned at 5.1 is to be taken as a Passover.[5] It is on the first of these that Jesus enters the Temple and 'cleanses' it. It is difficult to get any sense of the chronological length of Jesus' ministry from the Synoptics (especially from Mark). But none appear to support the Fourth Gospel which indicates an apparent length of at least two years. This ministry begins with a dramatic act in the Temple, and ends two years later with the death of Jesus on the eve of the Passover. The questions posed for historical reconstruction by these discrepancies are (a) when did the Temple cleansing incident take place, early or late in Jesus's ministry and (b) were there, in fact, two such incidents?[6]

A third set of discrepancies (related to the two above) has to do with the wider context or implications of the incident. In the Synoptics, Jesus' action in the Temple is not followed immediately by a challenge from the authorities in which they ask for a justification from Jesus for his behaviour. Rather, the interrogation comes later: Matthew and Mark place it on the following day (Mt. 21.18, 23; Mk 11.19, 20, 27, 28)[7] and Luke at some less specific time (Lk. 20.1). The incident does however appear to intensify their desire to do away with Jesus, and shortly thereafter he is brought to trial, where among the evidence brought against him is a saying he is alleged to have uttered about the Temple's destruction (Mt. 26.61 // Mk 14.58; not Lk.). In the Fourth Gospel, Jesus' act in the Temple is followed immediately by a challenge from 'the Jews' (probably meaning the Jewish authorities) and in reply Jesus utters the saying about the destruction of the Temple. But the trial of Jesus is far removed in discourse time (and in chronological time): and, indeed, the formal trial before the Jewish Sanhedrin as reported in the Synoptics, drops out of the narrative. How, if at all,

their tables at this time, and they remained up for a week (from 25 Adar to 1 Nisan) by which time the Temple tax was supposed to have been paid; cf. Carson, *John*, p. 178.

5. See the discussion in Brown, *John*, p. 206; Barrett, *John*, pp. 250-51; Carson, *John*, pp. 240-41.

6. It is not my purpose to explore these questions in this chapter, on which see the commentaries. For reasons, see below p. 232.

7. Cf., however, Mt. 21.15, 16: on this see n. 1 above.

are these discrepancies to be reconciled? Associated with the wider questions of cause and effect, is the question of Jesus' motivation for the act: was it an act signalling the destruction of the Temple or its purification?

All of these divergencies and discrepancies raise questions regarding the relationship of the Fourth Gospel to matters of ostensive historical reference. At one level, and in relation to the Synoptic accounts, are questions about which accounts are closest to the bedrock of historical event. Can and should they be reconciled and if so, how far and at what points? At another level, there is the question of whether the Fourth Gospel should be read as 'history' at all; or, more generally, how should it be read?

These are large and complex questions and it will be as well to point out at this juncture what will be attempted here as regards our consideration of Jesus' Temple act. What I will not engage in is a full-scale reconstruction of the Temple cleansing which will seek to discover from the text, and in comparison with the Synoptic accounts, a description of what happened and why. In other words, the approach at the first level is largely set aside. We are not seeking an historical reconstruction of the Temple act which will then enable us to ask how accurate the Fourth Gospel account is in relation to this reconstruction. What we are attempting here has to do more with the second level of question: how should the Fourth Gospel be read?

To put the matter in terms of the argument developed in the last chapter: if the Fourth Gospel is theological elaboration of an historical substratum, how are we to understand the nature of that theological elaboration and display? Put in other terms, which gather up some of the other issues in this study, how has the history been 'refigured' to provide a followable story? This approach itself yields two sets of related questions. At the level of the story world we might ask: given that the story presents us with refigured history, can reliable historical data be drawn from it? If so, how might we go about determining the historical data? At the level of the discourse, we might ask: *how* might the implied author have refigured history?

It might be objected that these questions take us back to issues which have to do with 'what happened?', rather than 'what is the nature of this discourse?'. Of course, at a fundamental level, these issues cannot be entirely separated. For to ask 'How might the implied author have refigured history?' or, 'How has he produced a theological elaboration

upon an historical substratum?' presupposes that we have some reasonably firm grasp on the historical data (the details of the event) which
has been refigured or elaborated upon. To this extent, there is always
going to be both an element of circularity and a degree of ambiguity
in the discussion.[8] Nevertheless, I believe it is possible to sketch out, to
a greater or lesser degree, a profile of this narrative as an historically-
based, theological display text. It involves doing two things in the
analysis of the cleansing of the Temple. First, attention will be paid to
the types of illocutionary acts being performed, and in particular, to
what is being asserted both by direct statement and by the implicatures
set up in the narrative. This will be addressed in the section to follow.
Second, the literary and narrative structure of the pericope will be
noted; that is, the way in which motifs and themes are introduced and
developed in the pericope and also to its place in the narrative as a
whole. Also a note will be made of any particular markers or indications which suggest that certain words or phrases (including temporal
notices or physical settings) are being used in elaboration of themes
rather than to provide a strictly chronological or scientifically historical
account.

The Implied Author and his Speech-Acts

One way, then, to arrive at an understanding of the way in which the
Fourth Gospel is to be read, is to enquire after the status of the implied
author's speech-acts. Do these give us any clues as to his purposes which
will help the exegete determine how far the material is to be used as a
source for historical reconstruction, as well as how it may be read as a
theologically motivated narrative?

The implied author makes the narrator give two assertions which
suggest that the Temple cleansing episode as a whole is seen largely in
the light of the death and resurrection of Jesus. These are the statements
in 2.17 and 2.22 that the disciples remembered a text of scripture,
and the words of Jesus respectively. The second of the two explicitly
states that the understanding which the disciples arrive at is a post-

8. As we have already seen, historical discourse itself, in its reconstructive
capacity, bears within it the elements of refiguration and elaboration. Also, inasmuch
as historical events must be given a particular 'pattern-quality', or set against an
interpretative grid (be it Marxist or Christian, secular or theological), history itself
retains an ambiguous, hypothetical character.

resurrection understanding: 'When, therefore, he was raised from the dead, his disciples remembered that he had said this; and they believed the scripture and the word which Jesus had spoken.' The 'word' of Jesus referred to here is, of course, the logion of 2.19 which 'the Jews' misunderstand but which the narrator flatly states Jesus meant as a reference to his body.

The first of these assertions (2.17) is presented in such a way that it is not clear whether the disciples' recall of scripture occurs at the time they witness the action of Jesus in the Temple, or later, after the resurrection. We shall see below that this is a deliberate narrative ambiguity which enables the implied author to use this scripture as a 'sign' at two levels: that of the story and that of the discourse. The text itself comes from Ps. 69.9, this psalm being one 'most frequently drawn upon for testimonies to Jesus'.[9] In the early church the psalm was used as a Passion proof text[10] and understood as messianic.[11] It may be, then, that the implied author intends the reader to understand that as they observed Jesus cleansing the Temple, an action which brought to mind this text, the disciples had the first glimmerings of insight into his messianic status. However, in the latter part of 2.22 the implied author associates this scripture and the word which Jesus spoke subsequent to his action in the Temple with a post-Easter act of belief on the part of the disciples. This undoubtedly means that both acts of remembrance are to be understood as post-resurrection events.

A second feature of the implied author's speech-act here is that the Temple incident is associated with the death of Jesus by the implied author's implicative strategy. Most obviously this is done by the explicit interpretation of the logion which Jesus speaks in 2.19 as a reference to his death. The 'temple' which will be destroyed is not the actual Temple, as the Jews suppose, but the 'new temple', Jesus himself. We need also to note that what the Synoptics place in varying forms upon the lips of 'false witnesses' and mocking bystanders, the Fourth Gospel's implied author places on the lips of Jesus. That Jesus made some such statement, either on this occasion or upon some other, seems certain given the strength of the attestation. I shall argue below that the implied author has probably preserved the authentic statement, but, for the

9.   Brown, *John*, p. 119; cf. C.H. Dodd, *Historical Tradition in the Fourth Gospel* (Cambridge: Cambridge University Press, 1965), p. 159.
10.   Lindars, *John*, p. 144.
11.   Schnackenburg, *John*, p. 347.

present, we need only observe that by placing the logion in the context of the Temple cleansing, and thereby providing an entirely plausible setting for the saying, the implied author has made a link between the incident, for which this saying is Jesus' 'defence' and rationale, and his death.

This linkage of the incident of the Temple cleansing with the death of Jesus implied by the interpretation of Jesus' saying as a reference to his body is further strengthened by the comment that the disciples remembered this saying *after Jesus was raised from the dead* (2.22a). In other words, it is from the vantage point of the end point of story time (when Jesus has been crucified and raised) that the disciples are able to understand the true significance of his saying, and to perceive that it is, in fact, entirely appropriate to understand it as a reference to his death. Furthermore, as commentators have noted repeatedly, the scripture that the disciples remember, in the form in which it is quoted by the implied author, has an ambiguous ring to it. Just as the psalmist finds himself in an invidious position on account of his zeal for the Lord's house, so Jesus' action on behalf of '[his] Father's house' will lead to his destruction. It is not clear whether the disciples recognize the import of Jesus' action at the time as a portent of coming doom, or only after his death are they able to understand the part played by this incident in his eventual trial and condemnation. But in terms of the flow of the narrative, the use of the future tense here (καταφάγεται) is entirely appropriate and probably intended. Word of Jesus and word of scripture are brought together by the narrator's comment to locate the Temple act in the overall pattern quality of this story as an event, *par excellence*, which led to Jesus' death and confirmed his messianic status.

The Narrative Dynamics of the Temple Cleansing

The implied author's speech-acts link the incident in the Temple with the death of Jesus. They also suggest that this is one of the signs by which the characters in the story world should have come to know of Jesus' true status. Some did, of course, but the implied author allows an ambiguity to remain over whether the disciples recognized the implications of this sign for an understanding of Jesus' identity at the time of the event, or only later. This arises through the tension between the retrospective point of view of the discourse and the perspective of the disciples as characters within story time. Certainly, the event functions as a sign for the implied reader within the discourse-act as a whole. I said above that the way in which motifs and themes are introduced and developed in the relation of parts of the narrative to the whole is important for understanding how these parts operate as an elaboration of the theological argument. A given event may be placed within the narrative for thematic purposes rather than to provide a strictly chronological or scientifically historical account.

In this respect, several aspects of this episode may be noted. The narrative has already established the claim that Jesus is the Messiah in, for instance, the testimony of John (1.19-27), Andrew (1.40-41) and Philip (1.45); and that he is the son of God (cf. Nathanael's testimony, 1.49; and the Prologue). When the reader reaches the end of the story, he/she will be told that a selection of signs has been provided to support the claims made for Jesus' status (20.30, 31), thus, by the way, fulfilling Grice's maxims of quantity and quality.[12] That this incident is intended to function as one of the signs is, I think, implied and confirmed by three narrative strategies.

First, 2.23 speaks of Jesus doing signs at the Passover feast, but the only activity specifically narrated is the cleansing of the Temple. The implication is that this, at least, is one of those signs. Second, the Jews are described as asking for a sign (2.18): the word is already beginning to function as a thematic marker. The disciples are said to recall a scripture which speaks of someone being consumed by zeal for the Lord's house. This statement is made immediately after the narrator has recounted Jesus' act in the Temple, the implication being that this scripture comes to mind as they observe Jesus' actions. Taken together, these narrative statements recounting the disciples' remembrance of scripture and the Jews' request for a sign, imply that the Jews have already received their sign in Jesus' act of protest, but fail to recognize it. The disciples, however, do recognize it as such for they realize that the one they have just watched acting with messianic zeal is the one spoken of in scripture. Ironically, Jesus offers another sign but its significance cannot be grasped until it has been fulfilled in his death and resurrection, and then only by those who can make a believing connection between event, word of scripture and word of Jesus.

Third, the incident operates as a sign (one amongst others) of the truth of the implied author's claims. The reader is invited to share the

12. For Grice's maxims, see above pp. 74-75.

disciples' post-resurrection perspective which sees the significance of the Temple incident both in terms of the 'event then' (Jesus' act was a messianic act in fulfilment of scripture) and the now of discourse time. In the early church, this scripture operated as a *testimonium* to Jesus' messianic status. The implied author, by using it here, implies that Jesus fulfilled the expectation that when the Messiah came he would display zeal for the Lord's house. Also, the reader shares the wider perspective that what the incident did, above all, was to set the course for the destruction of Jesus, the true temple of God.

Thus the incident operates as a sign at two levels. In terms of story time, it is a sign to the Jews (who fail to see it) and the disciples (who, the implied author indicates, recognized it as such) that Jesus is indeed the Messiah. In the development of the narrative, it is the second act witnessed by the disciples by which they come to believe in Jesus (cf. 2.11). V. 22 and the use of the future tense at v. 17 establishes that later in story time they also came to understand that the event had an even greater significance. It was a catalyst for the process of events which led to the eventual replacement of the old Temple with the new temple, Jesus himself. It was the event which set in train the build up of opposition to Jesus by the authorities, and the rejection of him by his own people, which led him to his 'hour'. At the discourse level, the incident becomes a sign for the implied reader. Jesus is proved to be the Christ for here he is shown as one who came doing the works of God (seen in zeal for the Lord's house); hence he fulfilled the messianic programme. But the event is also part of a larger picture; it is part of the pattern of events which led to the death of *the* Passover Lamb.

Words and phrases, including temporal notices, may also be used in elaboration of themes rather than as indices of temporal progression. Thus the phrase, 'the Passover of the Jews was at hand' (2.13) may be a thematic marker signalling to the reader that what we have in the Fourth Gospel is not a chronologically motivated placement of Passovers, but a thematic development of the crucial significance of one particular Passover. It focuses attention on the Passover at which Jesus is crucified, when as 'the Lamb of God', he took away the sins of the world (1.29).

Modern narrative theory provides us with the insight that time in narrative may be presented in different ways. There is straightforward 'story time', the progress of a plot from event to event, incident to incident, in a temporally progressive chronological order, for example, the story of a person's life from birth to death. But in any given discourse, this story time may be patterned and ordered by narrative devices such as repetition, gapping, projection and retrojection.[13] Put simply, any narrative event can be told several times (repetition), it can be told before its proper chronological position vis-à-vis story time (i.e. projected forward in time, prolepsis) or after (retrojected, analepsis). An event in story time can also be omitted from the discourse. When this happens the reader generally becomes aware of a gap in the story or a sense of dislocation of some sort. In the narrative locale of the Temple incident, for instance, the statement is made that Jesus performed a number of signs which led some to believe in him and Nicodemus to enquire about Jesus' source of authority. Unless the reader is to understand that the Temple cleansing and the changing of the water into wine are the signs to which these narrative statements refer, he/she must assume that the implied author has chosen not to have all these signs narrated.[14]

In a sense, in this story, the Passover is always at hand and the implied author works out his theme of the significance of the 'Lamb of God' in the shadow of this Jewish feast. What clues are there that the phrase, 'the Passover of the Jews was at hand' may function as a thematic marker? It appears three times in an almost identical fashion at 2.13, 6.4 and 11.55. However, in the first two instances there is very little interest shown in the feast itself. Indeed, in the second instance, the Passover that is said to be 'at hand' never arrives. The implied author chooses not to narrate anything about the Passover itself; rather the narrative moves from the temporal indication of its approach (6.4)—the phrase is thrown into the narrative almost gratuitously— to relate, at 7.2, Jesus' teaching activity at another feast, Tabernacles. However, the phrase does introduce a sign, the feeding of the five

---

13. For these latter two devices, Genette has coined the neologisms, 'analepsis' and 'prolepsis'.

14. The changing of the water into wine will surely be ruled out by the reader as it is located at Cana in Galilee. The use of the plural here (τὰ σημεῖα) may linger in the reader's mind to provide a narrative echo effect with the 'many signs' referred to in 11.47, thus providing a narrative bridge between these two parts of the narrative; or, it may underline the selective process (cf. 20.30). Alternatively, it may make this narrative statement into a general one which applies to the total discourse-act (see below pp. 238-40). These possibilities presume a second reading.

thousand, and a discourse, on Jesus as the Bread of Life, for which a Passover setting is entirely appropriate.[15] It is a theological use of the Passover setting, where details of the story and the discourse are used to undergird a messianic theme, drawing on items important to Jewish Passover traditions (manna, a prophet like Moses, the messianic banquet).[16] In addition, the discourse on Jesus as the Bread of Life with its strong eucharistic undertones, brings it into thematic contiguity with the final Passover, seen from the perspective of the Christian tradition.

There is little focus on the Passover feast at 2.13-25, though it is mentioned again at 2.23 so that, in this case, the reader has the sense of the arrival of the Passover but only in order for the narrator to make a very general comment about the signs Jesus performs while in Jerusalem at the feast. It is only when the third and most important of the Passovers is narrated that the story begins to give specific temporal indications of the Passover's nearness. Indeed, now the reader is reminded several times of the proximity of the Passover. Following the general reference at 11.55, a specific time frame is supplied in 12.1 as the reader is told that it is six days before the Passover. Then at 13.1 reference is made to Jesus' hour and the narrator informs the reader yet again that it was πρὸ (δὲ) τῆς ἑορτῆς τοῦ πάσχα. All this suggests that the implied author's gaze is fixed upon the Passover at which Jesus died right from the outset of the narrative, even if he looks across two prior Passovers to the third and final one. As has been often noted, the final Passover is carefully plotted to gain a maximum of symbolic interplay between the death of Jesus and the slaughter of the Passover lambs. We might note in passing that in this Gospel much of the action takes place around a Jewish feast of one sort or another, and the discourses of Jesus often resonate with imagery and symbolic teaching which is pertinent to the feast at which it is delivered. This suggests a thematic rather than a chronological significance to these temporal markers.[17]

Furthermore, 2.23-25 functions as a kind of summary statement by the narrator, linking Passover with the theme of acceptance and belief in Jesus and threat to Jesus. 'Passover' is a thematic tag around which

15. Cf. Barrett, *John*, pp. 273-74; Carson, *John*, p. 268.
16. See here G.A. Yee, *Jewish Feasts and the Gospel of John* (Wilmington, DE: Michael Glazier, 1989), pp. 64-67.
17. On this see Yee, *Jewish Feasts*.

the reactions to the Passover Lamb cohere. The signs which Jesus performs at this (first) Passover evoke in many an inappropriate, mistaken form of believing, which causes Jesus to distance himself from them (2.24). Note that the implied author follows up the sign done at the next Passover (i.e. the feeding of the five thousand), with this same pattern of inappropriate 'belief' on the part of the witnesses to the sign; rejection of their response and withdrawal on the part of Jesus (6.14, 15; cf. 6.26-29). Passover is the time of threat to Jesus and perhaps the menace inherent in 2.25 is a preparation for, and a proleptic evocation of, the 'evil in man' which is most clearly in evidence at the Passover occurring at the end of the implied author's narrative.

The suggestion being made, then, is that when the narrator says that 'the Passover of the Jews was at hand', the reader is invited not to take this only as a temporal marker of a particular Passover (discovered by reading on to be the one two years earlier than the final, climatic Passover), but also as a thematic one that foregrounds Passover and all its associations as significant for understanding who Jesus is, and as the temporal locale, *par excellence*, where reactions to Jesus, for and against, coalesce. To adopt this kind of reading is to place the narrative against a literary grid rather than an historical one. Even as a *narrative* reading, it can only remain tentative for, as has already been stated, a straightforward reading of the narrative suggests a story time of three Passovers. Given that the implied author creates the impression of a temporally sequential ordering of the plot (in some respects even more tightly defined than the Synoptics), generations of readers have taken it at face value.[18] 'Story time', writes Powell, 'refers to the order in which events are conceived to have occurred by the implied author in creating the world of the story'.[19] Once the narrator of the Fourth Gospel begins the story of the earthly Jesus, story time appears to span three Passovers. Of course, in the case of this story, there is also a 'story time' situated in history, the progress and contours of

18. I have in mind, for example, the way in which the narrator uses the adverbial phrase, 'after this' (μετὰ τοῦτο/ταῦτα); the apparent precision of temporal recording suggested by the use of 'the next day' (1.29, 35, 43; 6.22) not to mention other relatively precise markers such as 'on the third day' (2.1), 'after two days' (4.43), 'six days before the Passover' (12.1), 'It was the feast of the Dedication at Jerusalem, it was winter' (10.22) and so forth. All this gives the reader the sense of time moving forward.

19. Powell, *Narrative Criticism*, p. 36.

which may well have been different from that presented by our implied author. We have the Synoptics to suggest how this story might be otherwise reconstructed. We cannot be certain whether the first readers did as well, or whether in fact the implied author may have constructed his story against a knowledge of the Synoptics. If he did, then the suggestion might be made that he played his story time against that of the Synoptics to gain an effect such as that outlined above. It seems certain that the implied author shared some of the same stream of tradition with the Synoptics. How this influenced the construction of his story or what use he made of it, particularly in the thematic development of his discourse, we cannot be entirely certain.

The Temple Cleansing in its Immediate Narrative Context

We have seen that in terms of the total discourse-act, the Temple cleansing is set where it is to highlight the fact that the incident, seen in retrospect, was a major contributing factor to Jesus' death. Set near the Passover, it also foregrounds the thematic significance which Passover will have in this Gospel, especially when understanding the meaning of Jesus' death.[20] But we must also note that it is placed in the narrower context of two sets of narrative doublets. We noticed earlier that the implied author is fond of repetition and overlapping movements; to this we must add his fondness for pairing.[21] Thus this incident forms part of a series of two signs (the miracle at Cana, the Temple cleansing) which are followed by two significant encounters, one with a Jew (Nicodemus), the other with a Samaritan woman.

Throughout these linked narrative units flow a number of interwoven themes which have already been introduced in the narrative's prologue. One of these is the replacement (or fulfillment) motif: Jesus is the one in whom the Jewish religious system is renewed or replaced. Hence water drawn from pots provided for Jewish purification rites becomes wine of superior quality; the Temple is replaced by a new temple, Jesus' body; a new centre or mode of worship (worship in spirit and in truth, 4.23, 24) replaces both Jerusalem and Mount Gerizim (4.20). Allied with this is the theme of Jesus as the giver of new life

20. It may also indicate that the Fourth Gospel retains a connection with the tradition shared with the Synoptics.

21. See above pp. 104-105, 108. Pairing also applies to the way in which sign is paired with discourse.

and birth from above. He is the source of the superior wine;[22] he can offer living water. In his 'lifting up' will new life and birth from above be found; the 'lifting up' is also the occasion of the destruction and resurrection of the 'temple' of his body. Linked with the wedding at Cana, and the two encounters, Jesus' dramatic act in the Temple and his enigmatic statement (2.19) point to the narrative climax, his death and resurrection, from which all the possibilities of renewal and new life flow.

These units are also linked by another narrative movement. Jn 4.54 states that the healing of the official's son (4.43-54) was the second sign Jesus performed after coming from Judaea into Galilee; this second sign is specifically linked with the first by being located at Cana-in-Galilee (4.46). Thus John 2–4 is bracketed by two signs, both involving a domestic crisis and both ones in which the resolution of the problem is brought about by a word from Jesus, who remains distanced from the physical outcome of the miracle.[23] It is in order to bracket these events that the healing is described as a 'second sign' (πάλιν δεύτερον σημεῖον)[24] and not in order to 'count off' the signs.[25]

The physical movement from Judaea to Galilee is paralleled by

22. No one knows the origin or destination of the Spirit from whom new birth derives (3.8), just as the steward of the feast does not know where the good wine has come from (2.9).

23. To speak of Jn 2–4 as bracketed by two signs does not mean that these chapters form a self-contained unit which can be marked off from the rest of the narrative. The only really self-contained unit is the narrative itself, which to use traditional Aristotelian terms, has a beginning, a middle and an end. Within the beginning and the end there will be a continual narrative flow, and all the parts will be interrelated. Thus any attempt to demarcate units within a narrative may have a use for heuristic purposes but will break down upon structural analysis. Any patterns and structural units (chiasms, dramatic acts, even 'books') discovered within the narrative must be subsumed under the overall structure of the narrative, which is a dynamic, free-flowing entity which thrives much on gaps and indeterminacies filled by the reader, as well as networks of themes and motifs. The structural patterns and devices discovered by Johannine scholars of all hues, including those who employ narrative criticism, are not inherently wrong, but they must not become procrustean beds.

24. See on this, F.J. Moloney, *Belief in the Word* (Minneapolis: Fortress Press, 1993), pp. 177, 189. Yee, *Jewish Feasts*, p. 30, follows Brown, *John*, pp. 95-96, in designating Jn 2–4 a section entitled 'From Cana to Cana'.

25. Too many scholars confuse the issue of signs in the Fourth Gospel by attempting to determine the presence of seven signs in the narrative. A sign in this narrative is anything which acts as an index of Jesus' true status.

another movement in these chapters; that in which Jesus moves from among his 'own' who do not receive him, or whose response he rejects as mistaken (2.23, 24; cf. 4.48) to those whose true belief bears fruit. At the same time these incidents and encounters illustrate a variety of responses to Jesus (Jesus' mother, the disciples, the Jerusalem crowd, Nicodemus, the Samaritan woman, the Samaritan villagers, the official) along a spectrum of possibilities which are finely modulated. Taken as a whole, John 2–4 serve to illustrate the theme adumbrated in 1.9-13. To examine adequately how the narrative achieves this would require more time and space than we can allow here. The point I wish to establish is that the Temple cleansing incident is part of a narrative which has been plotted in order to develop a complex of theological themes rather than simply to provide a chronological story. Its setting in the narrative is governed by the implied author's narrative art in attempting to elucidate these themes and to lead the implied reader to the story's overall perlocutionary intent; namely, that the reader believes that Jesus is the Christ, the Son of God and finds life in his name.

Narrative Art, Act and History

We have seen that the event of the Temple's cleansing has been plotted within the overall narrative under the constraints of the implied author's art. This narrative art seeks to present the incident as a sign which points to the new regime (the kingdom)[26] inaugurated in the coming of Jesus the Messiah, the Passover Lamb, whose death and resurrection provides the foundational event for this new reality. Sign is brought into contiguity with sign providing an illumination of the way in which the old issues onto the new: encounter follows encounter in which different responses to the Jesus who establishes the new community are explored. Later, especially in John 5–11, sign paired with discourse, or discourse set in the context of a Jewish feast, will explicate the theological realities of belief in Jesus.

At the same time, the implied author's speech-acts indicate that this is a believing perspective rendered possible from the post-resurrection

---

26. This Synoptic motif is found in the Fourth Gospel only in the dialogue-discourse which follows the Temple incident (3.3, 5). References to 'the kingdom' in the scenes where Jesus appears before Pilate are much more in the Johannine mode of thought.

vantage point informed by *anamnesis* and scriptural reflection. (This point is reiterated at 12.16.) Also, in terms of plot development, the Temple cleansing provides a rationale for one of the story's plot lines. It helps to make the account of the growing opposition by 'the Jews' and the eventual rejection of Jesus by 'his own people' followable. The question which remains is, given that the Gospel is written with theological themes to the fore and from a definite post-resurrection believing perspective, is it nevertheless still available as a source for historical reconstruction? Moreover, is there any sense in which its followable story may also be called historical?

As a preparation to answering these questions, two aspects of historical reconstruction and historical narrative must be borne in mind. The first is that, as we have seen already,[27] providing a coherent historical narrative is a matter of reconstructing a 'followable story' of past events from the historical data available from the past. Now it has become popular among literary critics to describe the historical-critical method as one by which the gospel stories are used as 'windows' through which the historian looks to recover historical data. As the text is the product of an evolutionary development from historical event to written deposit of the event, this will require the careful analysis of the various stages through which the text has evolved in order to recover the original stratum, or the primitive historical situation.[28] Theoretically, the more surely one is able to discern an earlier stage in the development of a tradition, the more confidence one can have in gaining a clearer view onto the actual historical situation.

This is true to some extent. But I would argue that in fact this is only a part of the historian's task, and the current emphasis put upon the 'window' aspect of the textual data leads to a misapprehension of the true nature of the situation. The observable practice of biblical criticism, moreover, suggests that the case is otherwise than simple recovery of an historical substratum. The historical task involves not just looking *through* the followable stories to the historical event; the historical event must be reconstructed *out of* and *alongside* the data recovered from the text. Indeed, the historian must reconstruct his or her own 'followable story' against which the accounts offered in the gospels may be set and analyzed for their coherence as sources of

27. Above pp. 203-205.
28. See Petersen, *Literary Criticism*, pp. 11-19. Cf. Powell, *Narrative Criticism*, pp. 8-9.

historical data. Thus, the gospel narratives are set within and against their context in the first, and early second, century where Palestinian Judaism, the particular ambience of the Greco-Roman world, the clues proferred by archeology and non-canonical documentation, all provide the backdrop against which they are interpreted. These sources outside the gospels also provide the raw materials from which the historian constructs the framework of a 'followable story' into which the data provided by the gospel narratives will be fitted.

Thus historical data must be interpreted, and it must be ordered if it is to become 'history'. The historian may need to interpret and reorder the data of each gospel in order to arrive at a plausible reconstruction of the incident in the Temple. In pursuit of this it may not be helpful to prefer one account above another as somehow more 'primitive' but to assess the evidence of each against considerations and probabilities derived from a broad background of information gained from a variety of sources. Then a coherent picture may be reconstructed out of and against each gospel account.

All this means that such historical data as is available in the gospels is weighed and tested against criteria and hypotheses arrived at *on other grounds* (plausibility in terms of what is known of social and cultural conditions of the day, general psychological plausibility, and so forth) than simple preference of one account over another. Aspects of each gospel account may yield data which will contribute to the overall picture. This, I suggest, is what happens in practice in the historical reconstruction of gospel events, though it remains often unrecognized and unacknowledged in theory.

Thus we may ask, for instance, is it likely that a challenge from the Jewish authorities would have followed immediately upon Jesus' Temple act and would it have been generated in specific response to his action? If so, then we may prefer the Johannine account over the Synoptics, where the response is delayed and the sense that the challenge is specifically related to the Temple cleansing is blurred (cf. Mt. 21.23; Mk 11.27, 28; Lk. 20.1, 2). Is it likely that an act such as this would have led to the arrest of the perpetrator, and his death, within a relatively short space of time as the Synoptic accounts seem to indicate, or after a period of two years as the Fourth Gospel apparently indicates?[29] On this matter, many prefer the Synoptic chronology,

---

29. We must bear in mind, as not all scholars do, that the Synoptics are vague about when exactly the Temple cleansing occurred in relation to the Passover; and

though here, as on every aspect, there are possibilities for plausible counter-hypotheses.[30]

On specific details, the historian may have to make a more or less arbitrary decision on grounds of plausibility, or simply pronounce something unable to be resolved on present evidence. This is the case, for instance, on whether or not the presence of sacrificial animals within the Temple precincts was likely.[31] The question of how much Jesus would have been able to get away with is another issue where the balance of probabilities swings uncertainly on questions of the exact nature of the action (a large demonstration or a smaller 'prophetic' act?) and *realpolitik* (how much the Roman authorities would have allowed such action at a time of possible tension, the extent of popular support for the action which may have made the authorities cautious in their response, the element of surprise and the moral force of Jesus' personality, and so forth). Thus, in terms of the yield of reliable historical data that the Fourth Gospel's account is believed to provide, the issue will depend to a large extent upon the general framework of plausible reconstruction the historian builds against which to test the details.

But there is another level at which historical reconstruction is required to be coherent. Not only does the historian seek a coherent account of what happened (i.e. a followable story which makes sense of the data), but in order to be fully understood as an historical account, some sort of explanation as to why an event happened and what it meant must also be provided. What led up to this event, what flowed from it, and what does it mean in the wider scheme of things? Thus the event must be understood in the light of a particular 'pattern-quality', an interpretation which provides a plausible rationale of the motivations, causes and effects which lay behind and within the event.

how much time Jesus spent in and around Jerusalem before his eventual arrest. In terms of discourse time (i.e. the time a reader spends reading the narrative) quite a period elapses between the account of the cleansing of the Temple and Jesus' arrest. In the absence of critical awareness, this also tends to suggest an elapse of quite some story time.

30. See, for example, F.M. Braun 'L'Expulsion des Vendeurs du Temple', *Revue Biblique* 38 (1929), pp. 196-97, who argues that the witnesses at the trial who attempt to recall Jesus' words against the Temple, have difficulty both in remembering the exact words and in being consistent precisely because some time has elapsed since the event when the words were uttered.

31. See on this Brown, *John*, p. 119.

This amounts to providing the retrospective viewpoint which configures event and interpretation into the followable story which is at the heart of historical explanation.

It is at this level that the Fourth Gospel's account of the Temple cleansing may offer the historian some valuable assistance. We have seen that the implied author connects this incident with the death of Jesus. The use of the future tense of the verb καταφάγειν and the ambiguity of meaning ('consume/destroy') implies that the event is a direct cause of Jesus' death. The double-entendre of Jesus' saying against the Temple is emphasized by the narrator's comment at v. 21. If we consider the Fourth Gospel's account in the light of what we learn of the arrest and trial of Jesus (before the Jewish authorities) as recounted in the Synoptics, we note the following points.

First of all, by bringing together Jesus' act in the Temple with the saying against the Temple (2.19), the Gospel provides a plausible context for a saying which the Synoptics accounts show to have had an important role in the attempt to secure a conviction for Jesus. This saying against the Temple, which Matthew (26.61) and Mark (14.58) report is brought against Jesus at his trial by false witnesses, is not given a definite context by them: the Fourth Gospel supplies the context. If Jesus never did say anything of the sort, that is it was a pure fabrication, then it is difficult to account for the mockery of the passers-by reported by both Matthew and Mark (Mt. 27.40; Mk 15.29).[32]

The narrator tells us that when Jesus was asked to give the Jews a sign which would legitimate or show that he had the authority to do what he did, Jesus replied, 'Destroy this Temple and in three days I will raise it up' (2.19). Here the implied author may well give us a form of the saying which, of all the variants, comes closest to what Jesus might originally have said. Even if the words are not the *ipsissima verba* of Jesus, the form and the import of the saying might well represent that of the original.

As to form, it might well be described as a riddle,[33] perhaps even a

---

32. One might hypothesize that somehow the fabricated testimony, having been made to stick, then became generally known among the bystanders at the cross and, wittingly or unwittingly, taken as something Jesus actually said. One is still left with the difficulty that what Mark reports the false witnesses as saying Jesus said (14.58) does not tally with what the passers-by thought Jesus said.

33. See on this B.F. Meyer, *The Aims of Jesus* (London: SCM Press, 1979), pp. 181-85.

prophetic *mashal*[34] that is typically cryptic and enigmatic. As such it is not immediately understood and could easily give rise to the sort of misunderstanding and misreporting witnessed to by Matthew and Mark. That some such riddle was spoken by Jesus is almost certainly established by the wide attestation in the tradition, and particularly by the discrepancy between Mark 14.58 and 15.29. That it was open to interpretation is shown by the fact that the false witnesses in Matthew give the saying in quite a different form from that in Mark. Mark's version (14.58) suggests that it might well have been understood something along the lines of the interpretation that the Fourth Gospel's implied author suggests for it, that is that the Temple would be replaced by another form of 'temple' (one Mark describes as 'not made with hands'). Of course, Mk 14.58 may well be due to Christian interpretation of the original saying, so that any correspondence in interpretation as between Mark and the Fourth Gospel does not necessarily indicate how the saying was received in the context in which it was first heard.[35] Everything points to the original saying having been an enigmatic statement which all the original hearers (including initially the disciples) had difficulty understanding. The Johannine form, 'Destroy this Temple. . . ', an imperative with the force of a condition, attests to its age and originality[36] and perhaps its character as a prophetic *mashal*,[37] while the use of the verb ἐγείρειν contributes to its enigmatic character. It is difficult to conceive of Jesus having said, 'I will destroy this Temple. . . ' (as reported by Matthew and Mark) but easy to understand how, given that he claims to be able to rebuild it in three days, he could also be represented, either through malice or misunderstanding, as saying he would destroy the Temple. Its enigmatic character coheres with the tendency of the Synoptic Jesus to meet critics and opponents with a riddle (Mt. 16.4; cf.12.39-42) or an evasive answer (Mt. 21.24-27; Mk 11.29-33; Lk. 20.3-8).[38]

Finally, in his description of the scene, in the words spoken by Jesus to the sellers of pigeons (2.16) and in the cited scripture, the implied

34. See Schnackenburg, *John*, I, p. 349.

35. One would think that the Christian redactor of Mk 14.58 might have done better not to have put this Christianizing addition onto the lips of a false witness!

36. As in Dodd, *Historical Tradition*, p. 302 n. 1; Brown, *John*, p. 115.

37. See Bultmann, *John*, p. 125.

38. Cf. Meyer, *Aims*, p. 181; cf. his reinterpretation of Mk 4.11, 12: 'To those outside [God] imparts everything in riddles' (p. 185).

author preserves vestiges of Jesus' initial motivation for the act. When these features of the story are set alongside the Synoptic accounts, and especially in comparison with the defence given by Jesus there for his action (Mt. 21.13 // Lk. 19.46; cf. Mk 11.17), the historian is able to confirm that the original act was not done to sweep away the sacrificial system or as a portent of the Temple's destruction, so much as out of concern for the purity and right use of the Temple, with perhaps an underlying attack against corruption. The concern of the Johannine Jesus is with the right use of his 'Father's house' (compare the Markan prohibition against carrying profane vessels across the sacred space, Mk 11.16).[39] The implied author strengthens the force of Jesus' action against the moneychangers (as compared to Matthew and Mark): he not only overturns the tables but scatters the coins as well. Might this point to an objection to the rates of exchange or exorbitant profits being made by these traders? At the same time, he softens the action against the pigeon sellers. Does this perhaps reflect the attitude Jesus took to them, recognizing that pigeons were the item most in demand amongst the poorer members of the Temple's clientele? They are merely told to remove themselves; they can sell elsewhere but the Temple is not to be an οἶκος ἐμπορίου.[40]

Nonetheless, the implied author has also lifted the incident onto a new plane of interpretation by making the event speak of his themes of the messiahship of Jesus and the replacement of the old religious order with a new one inaugurated by Jesus and centred in him. Thus Jesus' words in 2.16, and the incident itself, recall Zech. 14.21 where it is said that 'On that day, there shall no longer be any merchant in the house of the Lord'.[41] This is followed by the remembered scripture of zeal for the Lord's house, a zeal of messianic proportions. Thus, the inference is that this action by Jesus is a sign that the eschatological moment has arrived. The implied author then develops the theme of replacement by referring the saying about the Temple's destruction to a new temple: Jesus himself. This aspect of historical reconfiguration may, indeed, be developed out of his own historical perspective on the Temple act. That is, he now understands that in that saying Jesus was

39. Lindars, *John*, p. 138.
40. Though Jesus may well have objected to the price being charged for the birds. See Bauckham, 'Jesus' Demonstration', p. 77, on this point, and for an interesting parallel from the Mishnah.
41. Cf. Meyer, *Aims*, 198, on this as a signal of a 'restoration' theme.

also speaking of a day when Temple worship would give way to new forms inspired by spirit and truth (4.23, 24) and centring not on a place but on a person (cf. 9.38; 20.28).[42]

The Temple Incident: History, Theology, and Narrative Form

The implied author has taken up an incident from the life of the historical Jesus and refigured it to suit his own literary and theological purposes. But this does not mean that his material is of no value as a source for historical reconstruction. There are elements of the pericope which may in fact provide us with some of the best historical information we have. For example, placing the saying about the destruction of the Temple in the context of the incident provides a plausible setting for it. Moreover, by bringing together the elements separated by the Synoptics, the cleansing of the Temple, the protest against the subversion of the Temple's integrity as a place of worship and prayer, and the saying about the destruction of the Temple, and by associating these clearly with the death of Jesus, the implied author has highlighted the significance of this incident for Jesus' eventual fate. In other words, he has given the incident a weighting which may be historically quite accurate. Indeed, though E.P. Sanders, in *Jesus and Judaism*, prefers to draw on Synoptic material in his reconstruction of this incident, does he not share a Johannine perspective in placing the incident in a position of central importance for understanding the historical Jesus?[43]

At the same time, the implied author has placed upon the incident the impress of a longer perspective. The event is gathered up into the 'pattern-quality' of his overall story of the significance of Jesus as the Christ, the son of God, whose life, death and resurrection has brought to birth a new era. His post-resurrection perspective, informed by

---

42. Lindars, *John*, p. 136, states that '[t]here is a possible hint of an original connection with Jesus' activity in the Temple in the allusion to "our place" (11.48) in the complaint of the chief priests'. This is a perceptive comment. However, I think that the connection is not only possible but almost certain, and that what we have in 11.48 is an narrative echo effect which links 2.13-22 with the plot. It indicates that the Temple act led to this response by the authorities as surely as did the raising of Lazarus. In the light of the situation at the time the Gospel was written, one cannot help pondering the ironic possibilities of a pun in 11.52. Those who, because of their allegiance to Jesus the Christ, are made ἀποσυνάγωγοι (16.2; cf. 9.22) are, nevertheless, because of the death of Jesus, gathered into one by him (συναγάγῃ εἰς ἕν).

43. See E.P. Sanders, *Jesus and Judaism* (London: SCM Press, 1985), chapter 1.

believing *anamnesis* and scriptural reflection, yields a theological history in which sign is brought into contiguity with sign. In this narrative, historical data is refigured in the interests of theological display and the elaboration of a complex of themes.[44] This makes the value of the historical data for a reconstruction of the event in the life of the historical Jesus, and the overall shape and meaning of the historical display, in terms of modern, scientific history difficult to determine. The details of the Fourth Gospel's account of the Temple cleansing may be more or less accurate, in whole or in part. Or they may be, in the manner of a display text, an elaboration upon an historical event, with a view to providing a vivid, and to a degree imaginative, reconstruction. The driving out of all the animals, for example, and the scattering of the coins, serves to highlight the zeal of the protagonist. They also throw into sharp relief the eschatological significance of the act, the danger into which it was bound to put Jesus and the inevitable end to which it was to lead.

Again, the chronological placing of the Temple's cleansing at the beginning of the ministry may provide a plausible 'pattern-quality' for the shape of the ministry as a whole (assuming that we accept the Gospel's temporal notices of the Passover at face value). Jesus begins his public ministry during a Passover visit to Jerusalem with a dramatic, prophetic act in the Temple. This event, indeed, propels an unknown Galilean 'rabbi' into the public eye and begins to establish his reputation as a 'prophet'. A ministry of at least two years follows, based in Galilee but including several trips to Jerusalem, mostly at the time of a feast, when Jesus engages in teaching in the Temple as well as performing acts of healing. Opposition grows among the authorities and comes to a head around the time of another Passover, when at last the authorities move to eliminate Jesus.[45]

On the other hand, the placing of the incident may be motivated by

---

44. This, of course, applies *mutatis mutandis* to the Synoptic Gospels as well.

45. Such a reconstruction as that offered here depends in part upon the data supplied by the Synoptics as the Fourth Gospel only hints at a Galilee ministry. A number of permutations are possible, of course, one being a framework based on the Synoptics which would involve a relatively brief ministry, concluding with one fateful visit to Jerusalem, but which included some time spent in and around the Temple and city before the Passover. On this schema we might posit that the Fourth Gospel presents, in the main, the Judaean ministry with Galilean episodes retrojected into the story.

narrative dynamics which seek to make the story 'followable' by providing a catalyst for the theme of rejection of the Messiah by his 'own'.
As far as this story is concerned, the response of the Jews to Jesus
from the outset is a fulfillment of the Isaianic prophecy (12.38-40).
The many signs simply produce unbelief (12.37) and opposition and
panic amongst the authorities (11.47, 48).[46] It also serves the implied
author's thematic development of the 'replacement' of one dispensation
with another. Moreover, in 2.22 the implied author provides an interpretative key for reading his narrative. He asserts that the perspective
of the narrative is fundamentally a post-resurrection, believing stance.

The implications of the preceding argument have a bearing on the
question of the Fourth Gospel and historical reference. The Gospel
ought not to be neglected as a source for historical reconstruction,
even if it must be used with caution and with an understanding of its
function as a display text. While it is true that in recent years there has
been a renewed respect amongst scholars for the historical worth of
the Gospel, it still remains generally true that it suffers from scholarly
neglect, if not hostility, when it comes to using it as a source for
reconstruction. I want to suggest two reasons why the Fourth Gospel
ought to be part of the picture in any reconstruction of the historical
Jesus.

In the first place, the Fourth Gospel may provide a useful model of
how, in each of the Gospels, history has been refigured under theological contraints. The historian is helped in the task of sifting the data
from the theological process because the implied author's illocutionary
acts are more clearly defined than those of the Synoptic authors and
his purpose is made clear. Most obvious is the way in which he states
clearly that a principle of selectivity is in operation which admits of a
reordering of the material and that the narrative presents a retrospective post-Easter point of view. Arguably the display is more evident and
the elaboration clearer. The historical distance enables the interpreter
more clearly to recognize the particular pattern quality that has been
superimposed upon the data and has determined the way the traditional
material has been reworked. The Synoptic Gospels may contain more
traditional material but it may be quite arbitrarily arranged or under
equally strong theological motivation.[47] Because the Fourth Gospel is

46. Including, significantly, in terms of the time of discourse, the Pharisees
(12.18, 19).

47. For example, one reason why Jesus' action in the Temple has become detached

so different from the Synoptics, where it appears to share something of the same tradition, it may provide a form of 'control' on the Synoptic accounts, enabling the historian to test for authenticity in the interaction one with another and to refine the historical reconstruction.

I have suggested above how this may work in determining an appropriate context for the saying against the Temple, and for determining the nature and form (enigmatic riddle/prophetic *mashal*) of the saying, if not indeed, the actual wording. I reiterate, in passing, that the tendency of many scholars to place the Temple cleansing within the last week prior to the Passover at which Jesus was crucified is actually a result of a (conscious or unconscious) harmonizing of the Synoptics with the Fourth Gospel. The Synoptics provide us with the order of events, 'triumphal entry' followed by Temple cleansing, but it is the Fourth Gospel which locates the triumphal entry five days before the Passover (12.1, 12).

Furthermore, the Fourth Gospel is important to the historian in the task of historical reconstruction in that it provides useful material to enable the historian to analyze the motivation of Jesus, and that of his opponents. Thus the interpretation put upon Jesus' Temple act by the Fourth Gospel as an act of zealous concern for the right use of his 'Father's house' undergirds a reading of the incident as portrayed by the Synoptics as an act of cleansing and protest at what is considered to be corrupt practices and a denigration of the Temple's true purpose as a worship centre, rather than as a portent of the Temple's destruction. In the manner of an Amos (ref. Amos 5.21-24; cf. 9.1; cf. with 9.11-15), Jesus seeks a renewal of Israel's devotion to God.[48] In support of this, the Synoptics show on several occasions that Jesus often castigated the religious leadership for hypocrisy and empty show. At the centre of the nation's religious life stands the Temple, now like a fig

from the Jewish authorities' response in Matthew and Mark is because each has inserted the 'parable of the fig tree' (Mt. 21.18-22 // Mk 11.12-14, 20-25). This is in order to provide a vivid illustration of the emptiness of the Temple worship and to point towards its replacement (this is especially the case in Mark where the Temple cleansing is bracketed by the acted parable). In a sense, this aligns their perspective on the event with the Johannine interpretation, though they have also added some teaching on prayer which tends to dilute the impact of the parable as a symbol of the corruption of current Temple worship.

48. Cf. Bultmann, *John*, p. 125 n. 4, where he correlates Jesus' 'prophetic style' saying against the Temple with Amos 4.4. Cf. also Hos. 6.2 with the second part of this saying.

tree which is all leaf and no fruit (Matthew/Mark). In the Fourth Gospel's terms it is more an emporium than a place for the worship of God. It becomes the setting for a dramatic act of protest; a sign of the Galilean prophet's messianic zeal. It is an eschatological act signalling the arrival of the kingdom.

The Fourth Gospel's implied author recognizes the crucial part this event played in the eventual 'destruction' of Jesus. Later in the narrative, the motivation of the authorities is presented more fully as a concern for the status quo (11.45-53). They will destroy the 'new temple' to preserve the old. From the perspective of the time of the discourse (post-resurrection and post-70 CE), the implied author savours the irony of this. The temple cleansing was a sign that the Messiah had come and a new era was to be inaugurated. The enigmatic reply Jesus gives to the Jews, when they challenge him to demonstrate his authority for taking this action, points to the inauguration day (the 'hour') of that new era. In the destruction of the temple of his body and its resurrection three days later lies the birth of a new form of temple; a new locus for the true worship of God. The implied author is concerned with the community of the new era, a community which itself represents a new centre of worship, while the old Temple, which the Jewish leaders strove to protect, lies in ruins.

Above all, however, the historian is provided with an understanding of the implied author's motivation in including this incident from the tradition with which he works. By underlining the wider significance of this Temple incident as a trigger for the death and resurrection of Jesus, the Passover event above all others upon which he wishes to focus, the event is gathered into his collection of signs. These signs both tell the story of the 'Lamb of God who takes away the sin of the world' and provide the necessary appropriateness conditions for the assertion that Jesus is the Christ, the son of God.

Finally, there are the implications of reading the Fourth Gospel as a theological display text, where history is refigured under the constraints of narrative art, for a broader understanding of the nature of historical knowledge and interpretation. Biblical scholarship needs to discover a more nuanced approach to the question of history and what it is. For too long has it fallen under the spell of an Enlightenment thinking which reduces the understanding of history to one form only, namely, scientific history. A Christian view of reality which admits theological truths (the activity of God in the world, for instance) which intersect with the real historical world, immediately opens up a form of history which moves beyond that for which a merely empirical approach is adequate. For want of a better term I would call this form of history theologized history. To describe the Fourth Gospel's narrative as a theological elaboration upon an historical substratum is not to deny that it is history, but rather that it is of a particular sort. It is history interpreted under the impress of a particular understanding of the historical Jesus. It is a story—the story of an historical figure— made followable by placing it within the context of a promised Messiah who, so the story asserts, was also God dwelling in flesh among his own people; who was rejected and killed, but who rose again and in whom all who believe receive power to become children of God. The 'ensemble of interrelationships' which makes this narrative comprehensible includes causes and effects deriving from that which is of heaven (τὰ ἐπουράνια) as well as that which is of the earth (τὰ ἐπίγεια).

Chapter 8

CONCLUSION:
NARRATIVE ART, ACT AND MEANING IN THE FOURTH GOSPEL

Narrative Point of View

The point of view established by the discourse is one in which the implied author is portrayed as having a close personal connection with the Gospel's story world. Not only is this because he is personally committed to the truth of his account but also because he lays claim to having had first-hand access to at least some of the events described. The discourse establishes this by the mediacy of the narration which, over the course of the story, moves increasingly from an authorial to a figural narrative situation. The figural narrative situation is particularly channelled through the characterization of the beloved disciple who functions as a reflector-character. He is brought to the fore as a privileged participant in the story and, in a concluding statement, declared to be *the* witness and authoritative source for it.

The manner in which the narrative is mediated means that it takes on the status of a first-hand report. This status is supported by a number of features. In the first place, the implied author, through his narrative persona the narrator, is brought into proximity with story time. Thus the narrator's claim to have seen Jesus' glory and to have received from the fullness of his grace (1.14, 16) is undergirded by the presence in the narrative of an anonymous disciple. This anonymous disciple materializes with increasing specificity of characterization under the epithets of 'the disciple whom Jesus loved' and 'the other disciple', to take on the role of a disciple who occupies a place of privileged access to the events unfolding as Jesus approaches his 'hour'. The reader identifies him as a character who has a central place in the circle of Jesus' disciples, able to act as a percipient and reliable witness of Jesus' words and actions and functioning as an ideal and faithful disciple who 'remains' until the end. The reader discovers in the narrative statement of 21.24 that this disciple's reliable witness is carried forward into the time of discourse as he is identified as the authoritative source upon whose testimony the narrative is based. Thus the reader may retrospectively identify him as a disciple who has been with Jesus from the beginning and who may, as a member of the band of disciples, legitimately claim a share in his grace and a vision of his glory. The narrator-cum-implied author is identified with this disciple, not only by direct assertion (21.24) but because the narrative situation has increasingly been one in which he shares the beloved disciple's perspective.

The movement from authorial to figural narrative situation serves, in John 3, to create a perspective whereby the voice of the narrator merges with that of Jesus. As the discourse identifies the narrator with a disciple who has been with Jesus and shares in the gift of the Holy Spirit, he may be accepted as able to transmit the words of Jesus reliably. John 3.11 then, becomes a statement which refers not only to the situation of Jesus but also to that of the implied author and those for whom he speaks (i.e. his community). He, like Jesus, speaks of what he knows.

The effect of this narrative mediacy is to present the reader with a discourse in which the illocutions take on the force of first person belief statements. This is the case not only because some of the illocutions either directly (1.14, 16), indirectly (19.35), or by implication (3.11, 21.24) have the effect of first person belief statements but also because the discourse as a whole is spoken *in propria persona*. In other words, the implied author has a direct subject-object relationship with the story and the characters of whom he writes. The speech-acts are not 'pretended', for the context in which they occur is not a story world which springs wholly from the imagination of the implied author. Rather, the narrative events have a connection with tradition (which is corroborated at those points where the Fourth Gospel corresponds to a Synoptic-like tradition) and with historical persons.

The status of the narrative as based upon eyewitness and first-hand report receives further support from certain other features in the discourse. One such is the fact that in structure and tone the discourse takes on the aspect of a natural narrative. This is the case in the formal structuring of a number of the narrative units which are framed by orientation and coda. The use of the historic present not only gives the narrative a vivid aspect, but also suggests a connection with reminiscence and oral anecdote. It may be that the somewhat disjointed style of some of the narration betrays a 'spiral effect' which occurs in oral discourse, where items of information are brought into an anecdote out of sequence (cf. 1.35-42, especially v. 40, where the narrator reverts to the fact that Andrew first called Peter before going with Jesus to see where he lived).

While the narrative point of view is that of an implied author who has a close connection with the events narrated, speaks *in propria persona*, and lays claim to eyewitness authority, *at the same time* it is a perspective which sets the time of discourse at some distance from story time. The manner of narrative mediacy reflects this in the movement between an authorial and a figural narrative situation, so that even when the figural situation predominates, the narrator may suddenly revert to an authorial, omniscient perspective. Thus the narrative perspective is also a post-resurrection one, where the events of story time are refracted through the grid of reminiscence (*anamnesis*) and scriptural reflection under the inspiration of the Holy Spirit. This post-resurrection perspective means that the chief protagonist, Jesus, may now be seen in the light of a faith which has grasped the full import of his δόξα. By the same token, the distance from story time allows for the selective interpretation which can see John in his role primarily as fore-runner and first witness to Jesus' identity.

This perspective sets up a certain tension between *then* and *now*: between story time and time of discourse. The tension is brought out explicitly in the discourse as in, for instance, direct comments by the narrator that the disciples were unable to fully comprehend the significance of the events or come to a true belief in Jesus until after the resurrection (2.22; 12.16); and in the light of scriptural insight (20.9). It is conveyed implicitly by a curious disjunction between the anonymous disciple's persona as one of the disciples who shares with the others their lack of knowledge and understanding, and his role as the beloved disciple, who is idealized as a percipient, faithful follower, placed in a position of privileged insight and responsibility. Hence, the beloved disciple combines pre-and post-resurrection perspectives, which he shares with the narrator/implied author. We might say that as 'the other disciple' the implied author appears as his story time self; as 'the beloved disciple' he appears as his self at the time of discourse, and as he places himself in retrospection within story time. He is the faithful witness whose testimony is true and continues beyond story time.

The implied author's view of Jesus is theologically informed so that he is able to see his subject both 'from above' and 'from below'. His is an omniscient vantage point from which he is able to share with the implied reader, from the outset, his insight into the true significance and identity of Jesus. The story begins with a rich catalogue of titles and descriptions for Jesus. The protagonist is 'the Logos become flesh', 'the Light of the world', 'the Son of God', 'the only begotten of the Father', 'the Lamb of God', 'the King of Israel', 'the Christ'. Nonetheless, it is also a view 'from below' in that it is the story of the earthly Jesus that is told. The implied author's chief character is a human person to whom the designations of Logos, Light, and son of God may fitly and rightly be applied. The δόξα of Jesus is seen in and through the historical and earthly events of his life. These constitute the 'signs' by which believing observers can perceive his true identity. By the same token, it is possible for the observer to fail to truly 'see' or to fail to comprehend the meaning of the 'signs'.

It is in the events of one fateful Passover in particular that Jesus' δόξα is fully realized and made plain. Until that 'hour' no one, not even the most percipient observer, can fully comprehend him. Seen in retrospect, the death and resurrection of Jesus throw a clear light upon the whole story. The implied author's perspective is also 'from above' because it has the advantage of historical hindsight. He is able to get above the congerie of disparate events and perceive them in a total act of comprehension.

The disciples who have been with Jesus from the beginning may, thereby, be witnesses to his true status for they have seen and heard the evidences for this status in deed and word. The narrative provides, however, a further theological rationale for why such a role is possible for them. As they have come to believe in him (their belief having its first stirrings before Easter, but now come to full fruition in their encounter with the Risen Christ, and under the impress of scripturally-informed remembrance), so now they remain in him and, thereby enjoy the gift of the Holy Spirit.

This παράκλητος enables the disciples to remember Jesus' words, and to grasp his true significance. This 'Helper' will continue the revelation of, and witness to Jesus into the future (16.14; 15.26). The Paraclete makes effective in the life of the believer the historical event. The implied reader can be assured of the reliability and validity of the implied author's witness because it resides in the connection

made between historical memory and Spirit-inspired development and interpretation. The Holy Spirit, by activating the disciples' memories, also enables them to pass on and extend the tradition (14.26, 16.12-15).

Narrative Art and Act in the Gospel: Implications for Meaning

The fact that theological meaning in the Fourth Gospel is found in a narrative form has certain implications for reading the Gospel. In the first place, it creates a narrative unity in which even gaps and indeterminacies are subsumed under the overall coherence and pattern of the story. The story, in its beginning, middle and end, pulls the reader along and enables him or her to receive the work as the product of a single entity, the implied author. It also means that the reader finds that in reading the narrative, part speaks to part. Part is illuminated by the whole, and the whole is made coherent in the configuration of the parts. In the second place, the narrative form presupposes the selection and ordering of material in order to fulfill the implied author's purpose, that of elaborating on the theme of the true identity and status of Jesus. This selectivity and purpose is confirmed by the narrator's direct assertion made at 20.30, 31. At the same time, the narrative is a dynamic system of gaps that invites interpretation. In part this arises because of the selective process: not everything is told that might be told. More often it is a result of artistry.

The meaning of the narrative is formed by the structural and formal patterning of the discourse. The overall structure of the discourse-act conveys the Gospel's message in a series of thematic 'waves' and in two major movements. The first movement (1.1-12) confirms Jesus' identity in a series of signs and discourses. It largely *confirms* rather than establishes who Jesus is, for the prologue and the initial scenes (1.19-51) leave the reader in no doubt as to Jesus' status. It portrays a variety of responses to him which supply the implied reader with a continuum of response types. On the one hand, in the reaction of 'the Jews', it illustrates the theme that the Messiah came to his own people and they did not receive him. On the other, it shows that there were those who did receive him and who believed in his name, e.g. *inter alia*, the Samaritan woman and her compatriots (4.4-42), the official from Capernaum (4.46-53), and the blind man (ch. 9). Even though the response of 'the Jews' taken *en masse* is largely negative, and the response of many individual characters is positive, the implied author indicates that in the world of the story, there is much that is imperfect and ambiguous in the response to Jesus. Implicit in this is a challenge to the implied reader to weigh his or her own response to the story of Jesus. The events of the first movement take place in the public arena. It ends with an apologetic rationale for the failure of the Jews to recognize and receive their Messiah and follows this with a proclamation to the public who will hear or read the narrative: they are challenged to receive Jesus' (and the narrative's) message.

The implied author's attention turns in the second movement to the inner band of disciples, those who are truly Jesus' 'own'. The nature of discipleship is explored, mostly in a long farewell discourse that looks to the disciples' life of faith and witness beyond the confines of story time. At the same time, the Passover 'hour' arrives, to which the narrative has been leading. In keeping with the 'private' tenor of this movement, the settings for the final confrontation which will establish Jesus' universal kingdom are mainly indoor or enclosed: a garden, the high priest's courtyard, Pilate's praetorium.[1] Even the crucifixion, in contrast to the Synoptics, is a curiously intimate affair; there are no mocking crowds, in the main only a handful of soldiers, some women, and the beloved disciple. The focus of attention is very much upon individuals, so it is perhaps appropriate that the beloved disciple should materialize here.

In the story's 'double ending', the implied author brings together two challenges: the challenge to believe (represented in Jesus' encounter with Thomas) and the challenge to follow (Jesus and Peter). The theme of the disciples' witness in the world and the continuation of that witness predominate. The disciples receive the Holy Spirit and are sent by Jesus to continue his ministry; the beloved disciple and his book take over the testimony of John. As the narrative opens with the witness of John in story time, so it ends with the witness of the beloved disciple (the 'implied author'), whose testimony extends into the time of discourse. At 20.30, 31 the implied author rounds out the themes of the first movement by turning once more to the implied reader, as he had at 12.44-50, and inviting belief in Jesus. At 21.24, 25 he rounds out the themes of the second movement by implicitly challenging the implied

---

1.   Other indoor, 'enclosed' or 'private' settings are: the location of the supper (from where Judas, the opponent on the inside, departs), the garden and the tomb, the locked room where the disciples meet on the first Easter evening, and again eight days later, and the private fishing party by the lake.

reader to faithful discipleship, and by affirming the trustworthy nature of the narrative.

Supporting the double movement of the narrative as a whole are the repetitions and pairings; the interweaving, interlinking, and even the juxtaposition of themes and motifs, theme-words and images. Within the overall plot-structure of the story, the implied author has created narrative units which illuminate a theme or cluster of themes at one level, while at another forming part of the forward movement of the plot. Thus, for example, John 2–4 is a narrative unit which brings together a series of paired narrative events, specifically two signs, followed by two encounters between Jesus and another character. Here the themes of the replacement of previous forms of ritual and worship, and worship-centres, and of new life, are explored. In addition, the journey from Judea, through Samaria, to Galilee, illustrates the progress of the Gospel message from among Jesus' own people, who misunderstand or reject him, to the wider world, where are found those who do receive him and 'believe in his name', that is the Samaritan villagers (4.42), and the official and all his household (4.53). This journey anticipates the narrative's double movement from Jesus' public activity among his own people to the more private revelation among those who are truly 'his own'. Yet again, the two signs point towards the hour of Jesus' death and resurrection and so contribute to the narrative's wider plot development. The cleansing of the Temple, for instance, provides a proleptic indicator of the central significance for this story of Jesus' Passover 'hour'. The wedding at Cana, held 'on the third day', points toward the climatic sign, the resurrection.

The juxtaposing of events and of characters is a narrative device which would bear greater examination. We have considered the juxtaposition of the beloved disciple with Peter as a 'foil' to Peter's preresurrection understanding and discipleship. To give but one further instance, and to indicate that this device extends to aspects of the narration not dealt with in this study, we note that in the prologue, the entry of John into the story world is juxtaposed with that of Jesus. At 1.6 John is brought into view in a somewhat abrupt manner. By contrast, Jesus appears almost obliquely, and under cover of a series of images, notably that of the Logos and of light. It is not until 1.17 that his name is revealed. This strategy has the effect of piquing the reader's curiosity about the identity of this mysterious figure. At the same time, Jesus is firmly identified as another human character who appeared in history and in story time after John, yet whose origins transcend history, and thus extend discourse time (and momentarily, story time) back to a beginning 'with God'. It is a view 'from above' and 'from below' of which much ironic play is made in the story which follows.

At the surface level of the discourse, the story contains a series of assertives, issuing both from the narrator and many of the characters, which support the summary assertive that Jesus is the Christ, the son of God. At a deeper level, the operations of the co-operative principle serve to bring implicature into play so that overt speech-acts are bolstered by implicit confirmations and influences. We have seen how the link between the beloved disciple and 'the other disciple' establishes in the implied reader's mind the presence of an unnamed, elusive disciple who, as a member of the band of disciples, is implicitly an unseen, silent observer of all the narrative events. This is important for assuring the reader of the story's validity. The process of implication extends to other elements in the discourse such as the recurrence of certain theme words or phrases. The repetition of the phrase, 'the Passover of the Jews was at hand', for example, is a device used to mark out the events and discourses which follow as important to the theme of Jesus as the 'Passover Lamb'. Again, because Jesus is identified as ὁ λόγος in the prologue, a resonance attaches to this term which creates an echo effect with the prologue's sense when it is used elsewhere in the discourse. This is especially the case where the immediate context suggests that it might well be an oblique reference to Jesus as well as serving the surface meaning or attaching to the obvious referent (see, in particular, 6.60; 7.36; 8.37; 10.35; 12.48; and 17.17 where, in each case, the nominative form is found).

Speech act, narrative art, and the implicative operations of both these, all work together to establish the implied author's illocutionary intent and to achieve the story's perlocutionary effect. That intent is to present Jesus in his true identity and status as the Christ and son of God: that effect aims to persuade the reader to accept this claim and come to faith in Jesus. The implied author's purpose is to fulfill the appropriateness conditions for his assertions. In the dynamics of narrative mediacy and the accumulation of overt speech-acts he commits himself to the truth of the proposition being asserted. In the 'signs' he has selected to recount, and in the discourses, he presents the required evidence. His characterization of Jesus, and the narrative of response to him, creates a story of relevance to a wide readership. A true knowledge of the Jesus presented here requires expanded horizons of understanding. Firm faith in Jesus leads to a committed, faithful discipleship which gives itself to service and witness in the world. The implied author seeks not simply to bring the implied reader to faith in Jesus, but to build up and strengthen such faith as already exists.

Narrative Form and Historical Discourse

The Fourth Gospel is a theological display text. The implied author seeks to display an 'unusual and problematic state of affairs', namely, the true δόξα of the historical Jesus, seen in theological and cosmic perspective. He seeks to enable the implied reader to share his estimation of Jesus and take up the same stance of belief in him. The story has its basis in history, but as a historical discourse it is not only configured from a retrospective point of view (as all historical discourse must be), but is also shaped under the impress of theological reflection and narrative art.

The implication of this is that it is not scientific history in that it adheres in every detail to the 'facts' as they must have been and as they occurred chronologically. Rather, the data of history have been refigured and interpreted in the interests of theological display. Thus consideration of the accuracy of the historical data must be balanced by attention to the theological intent and narrative shaping of the story. Over and above the provision of such historical data as the Gospel might afford, we find the implied author's purpose to be the elaboration and exposition of Jesus' true identity.

In addition, he seeks to provide the necessary appropriateness conditions for his assertions by supplying a selection of signs which will undergird the claims made. The provision of these signs is necessary to give weight to the illocutions but is not a sufficient condition to secure the perlocutionary effect sought by the implied author. He wishes to induce faith in the implied reader and recognizes that the mere provision of signs is not enough. That is why the narration of the signs is accompanied by a narrative of response to the signs, and the elucidation, in the discourse, of the inner meaning of the signs.

In order for the signs to be effective, they must first be understood correctly and then appropriated. That is, those who witness the signs must believe in the one to whom they point. This requires an act of self-involvement. Thus the narrative is a theological display which, in setting forth the state of affairs it represents, seeks an affective response. This response is not to be at the level of aesthetic enjoyment but of belief and self-involvement in the 'world' which is represented in the story. As the state of affairs displayed has to do with events and persons in the real world, and as the illocutionary stance taken by the implied author does not fall under the rubric of a pretence, the narrative comes within the generic field of nonfiction rather than fiction. As such, its illocutions are subject to the appropriateness conditions which obtain for assertions in the real world. We have already seen that the narrative is intended to fulfill the appropriateness conditions for the implied author's view of Jesus as the Christ, the son of God.

Here we might note a comment by Brown and Steinmann that '[a] discourse is fictional because its speaker or writer intends it to be so. But it is *taken* as fictional only because the hearer or reader *decides* it is so.'[2] The same might be said of nonfictional discourse: something given as nonfiction might be taken as fiction. In chapter 6 I considered some of the textual indications of fiction which may induce readers to take the Fourth Gospel as such. Questions of the clash of culture-texts (pre-scientific/post-scientific), and the problem of attempting to get a generic 'fix' on an ancient text, also arise here. These are large issues which, no doubt, have been only superficially and inadequately touched on. The aim of the study has been to examine some of the grounds on which we must address the questions and to attempt to avoid both a false distinction between history and theology and too simple an affinity between theology and fiction. The question is not simply one of how theological discourse is related to historical discourse but also of how it is related to fictional discourse.

Thus, the thrust of this study in its second part has been to examine the status of the Gospel as a *form of* historical discourse. This puts the issue beyond the question of mere usefulness or reliability as a source for scientific historical data. We ought not to confuse the assessment of the yield of historical data in the Fourth Gospel with the task of understanding the Gospel as a form of historical discourse. Nor should we restrict historical discourse to one *form* of discourse, namely scientific historical discourse. Rather, we must ask whether there are other forms of historical discourse, not strictly scientific, which may nevertheless yield interpretations which are true with regard to the

2.   Brown and Steinmann, 'Native Readers', p. 149 (italics theirs).

assertions made about events in the real historical world.

To take the first issue: the historical data of an account may be found to be, or perceived to be, mistaken in detail, but this does not mean that the account is necessarily worthless in its overall historical import. For instance, the Gospel's account of the Temple incident may be chronologically inexact. The form of the display, as I have attempted to show, may mean that the historian will have to understand this detail under a literary rather than a scientifically historical rubric. The reference to Passover may have been generalized to take on a thematic rather than a chronological function. The incident may have been plotted to serve the implied author's wider narrative purposes. However, the implied author may yet preserve a historical perspective by showing the importance of the Temple incident as a cause of Jesus' death. But even so, he subsumes this perspective under the wider historical-theological display of Jesus as the one who brings in a new 'temple' and another kingdom.

This leads to the second issue: that of the Fourth Gospel as a *form of* historical discourse. I have argued that all historical discourse must be understood as the interpretation of events under the pressure of a given 'pattern quality'. That is, the historical data is configured or refigured in a particular way to make it into a followable story and to give it the coherence which amounts to historical explanation. As discourse, then, history does not present itself as an immutable chunk of data, but as a collection of *forms* of historical discourse by which the historical data is made followable and comprehensible. The form of historical discourse predominating depends to a large extent upon existential and pragmatic decisions taken by a given interpretative community or individual. This is why history can be 'rewritten'. We might consider, for instance, how the history of Columbus's discovery of the 'new world' may be reinterpreted from the perspective of the original inhabitants of that world.

The Fourth Gospel's implied author refigures the tradition about the historical Jesus, as it is remembered and as it is handed on, in order to produce a story which, as he sees it, will elucidate the true significance of the historical Jesus and the 'real meaning' of his life and death. I have called this refiguration a theologized history because it brings to bear on historical person and historical event an interpretation which is rooted in a theological perspective upon the real world. The stance is that of a believer, one committed by an act of self-involvement to the truth of the assertions made about Jesus. It requires an act of self-involvement on the part of the reader, who must adopt the same believing stance as the implied author. In order to accept it as the historically based, theological display text the story purports to be, the reader must accept the particular 'pattern-quality' of the events and accept the validity of the interpretative grid against which the historical data have been configured. The narrative must be 'taken as' a form of historical discourse. But it might equally be taken as something else, for example, a fictional account.

In a very real sense the implied author recognizes this. As well as stressing the validity of the witness, therefore, he provides in the story's double ending two pericopes which set forth the type of belief and the act of self-involvement required. In the first (20.24-31), Thomas's need for physical and empirical evidence is superceded by the blessedness of those who believe not on the basis of sight, but on the basis of the implied author's assertions, and on the written evidence supplied in his narrative. In the second (21.15-25) the command to follow is absolute. What matters for the implied reader, as for Peter, is not the fate of the implied author who supplies the continuing witness to Jesus, but that the implied reader should be assured that this witness is true, and may and must be trusted. In appropriating the Jesus of this story for him or herself, the implied reader will know the truth and find eternal life.

The Fourth Gospel as Narrative and Issues in Johannine Scholarship

Narrative and History
The debate about the form of historical discourse found in the Fourth Gospel will and must continue. Further refinements may be required in order to find an adequate descriptive term to encapsulate this form. Perhaps, no one term will do and a range of descriptions such as 'fictionalized history', 'poetic or charismatic history', or 'theologized history' may serve: provided always that we are as clear as possible about what is intended in the description. If, on the issue of the relationship of the discourse to matters of historical reference, I have not provided definitive answers to the pertinent issues, I may have at least contributed to the discussion in the following ways.

First, this study shows that a narrative-critical approach to the Gospel does not necessarily nor inevitably require the bracketing out of historical questions. Thus, it seeks to mitigate a tendency within the discipline of narrative criticism to downgrade concerns of the historical-critical method, and to consign the Gospel to some sort of 'fictional' category. By the same token, in a fruitful interchange with the approach of narrative critics, practitioners of the historical-critical method may be able to revitalize and review some of its basic presuppositions and operations.

Second, in providing a broad description of the Fourth Gospel as an historically based theological display text, I wish to mitigate what I perceive as a tendency to place history in opposition to theology. Much discussion of the relationship of the Gospel's discourse to history sees it in terms of being not history but theology. But theological discourse may also be historical discourse, as I have attempted to argue, to the extent that it places historical interpretation under the cover of a theological understanding of the real historical world. It is the text's status as a *display*, and as an elaboration on events in the interests of the theological understanding, that allows for the creative refiguring and reordering of historical data. It is the Gospel's nature as a theological display text which pushes it into the border region between history and fiction. It is evocative historical discourse, and, putting the matter in terms of modern genres, is like some forms of autobiography, biography, or historical novel (or, to change media, docu-drama). Its motivation is not fictional, but historical report with theological display. Thus, it is not wholly referential by the canons of scientific history. The question is, does it take us further from or closer to the essence of the historical Jesus?

Third, I intend my typological model of narrative genres to allow for an open, flexible approach to the Gospel's genre. In particular, this may free research from overly dogmatic or rigid attempts to correlate it with any one generic type. A recognition of the range of formal and functional features it contains may provide the option of a more nuanced view of what the Gospel may be 'taken as'. To place the Gospel under the broad description of a display text is to recognize that the form of display, as well as formal correspondences with other types of representational narrative, means that it will appear on the typological circle of narrative discourse at a mid-point between fiction and history. Some latitude in either direction will be necessary in determining the historical value of any given part of the discourse.

More research is required to determine the place of the Fourth

Gospel amongst the various types of ancient narrative genres. The question of first-century readers' understanding of what might be taken 'for true' and of what constituted fictional and nonfictional forms of discourse, as well as the expectations by which decisions on these matters were made, remains an issue where more light needs to be shed. As regards the Gospel's own theological display, other aspects of the narrative, e.g. the discourse with Nicodemus, or the material on John, might fruitfully be explored to discover the way in which the implied author has elaborated upon historical tradition.

Implied Author and Real Author
We have seen that the narrative situations in the Gospel vary so that the implied author may appear in the guise of an omniscient narrator who may also withdraw behind the persona of a reflector-character. The beloved disciple, in particular, appears within the story world as the character with whom the narrator/implied author may be identified. From the first appearance of the beloved disciple as an identifiable character, the narrator adopts a point of view which might well be that of the beloved disciple. This remains the case until the close of the story when he specifically identifies the beloved disciple as the authoritative source upon whose testimony the narrative is based.

This has important implications for the reader's understanding of the real author's identity. The way in which the personae of the narrator and the beloved disciple merge suggests that either the author has pretty nearly anticipated a form of fictional narration found in many modern novels, or that the motivation for this springs from some other source. It is unlikely that the former is the case. Given that the discourse maintains the subject-object relationship that characterizes nonfictional discourse, the explanation for the form of mediacy adopted must be that the real author has *a close association with the beloved disciple*.

There is no doubt, on the basis of 21.24, that the real author intends the reader to understand that the beloved disciple is the 'author'. But we are not able finally to determine whether this means he is to be identified as the real author or as the one on whose initiative the narrative was promulgated. Nevertheless, the way the story is told and the nature of the illocutions leave us with only two options. The real author was either the beloved disciple, or someone who *knew* the beloved disciple. If the latter is the case, then the real author will have derived at least some of his material from the beloved disciple, and claimed him as his authoritative source.

To accept that the beloved disciple is the real author is to take the implications of narrative mediacy and the overt illocutions of 21.24 at their face value. From this the conclusion can be drawn that the author was Jesus' contemporary. He was a disciple who witnessed at least some of the events recorded in the narrative. We may also infer that he was a Jew. He was probably native to Palestine, but had or had developed a good understanding of hellenistic thought and culture. In this study, I have several times referred to the beloved disciple's status as 'eyewitness'. Again, the mediacy of the narrative as well as a locution such as 19.35 indicate that this is regarded by the author as a legitimation of the account. But the import of this status is that here is a reliable purveyor of tradition, whether this comes from first-hand experience, or out of familiarity with early oral or written *paradosis*. 'Eyewitness' status need not preclude familiarity with, and use of, a tradition shared in common with the Synoptics. His own memories will certainly have had their part to play, and whatever sources he had in addition to these, he was able to combine them in a narrative of powerful theological unity.[3]

The second possibility is that the real author and the beloved disciple are two distinct persons. Aspects of the discourse, notably the use of the third person to refer to the witness, and the use of the first person plural (though only at 21.24), imply such a distinction. However, in this case, we must certainly infer that the author had a close association with the beloved disciple as a prime witness and source for his narrative. This need not be in contention, but what is difficult to determine in this case is the extent to which the real author shaped the material and drew upon other sources. Given the skill and intellectual coherence of the written discourse, the balance must tip in his favour as the major theological and literary genius behind the Gospel. If the Fourth Gospel can be shown to have a literary dependence upon one or more of the Synoptic Gospels, this will suggest but not absolutely confirm that the author is not the beloved disciple.

---

3. It is not impossible that, if the beloved disciple is the real author, he made use of an *amanuensis*. Further, 21.23-25 may, but need not, have been added after his death.

Readings and Readers: Implied, Intended, Ideal and Real

The implied reader presents a variegated personality which creates puzzles when it comes to determining the reader for whom the story is intended. On the one hand, the implied reader is surely steeped in the Jewish scriptures (even if only the LXX) and is well able to pick up quite subtle allusions. On the other, this reader requires translations of Aramaic and Hebrew words. The implied reader appears to have prior knowledge of the Christian tradition. Yet the implied author seems to work hard to supply the reader with evidence of Jesus' identity as the Christ, and provides a subtle apologetic which challenges both temptations to unbelief and any inclinations to secretive or superficial discipleship.

The dual movement of the narrative focuses on a readership wider than the believing community. Ironically, the double textual tradition which gives the option of either a present subjunctive or an aorist subjunctive at 20.31 (and at 19.35) supports a dual focus on insiders and outsiders. We must, I think, retain a broad and openminded approach to the question of the intended readers. Such an approach is required not simply as a ruse to allow one to 'hedge one's bets', but in recognition of two difficulties. In the first place, at this remove from the first century's 'culture-text' and the context of the Gospel's composition, we may be far less certain about the original *Sitz-im-Leben* than might sometimes be acknowledged. In the second place, somewhat paradoxically, scholarly readers may today be more aware of the broad intertextual canvas against which the narrative may be set, than were either the implied author or the intended reader. The implied reader reconstructed today may be a more *ideal* reader by far than the implied author ever knew! The advantage of a narrative display text is that, as a 'dynamic system of gaps' which retains large areas of indeterminacy, it can absorb a wide range of backgrounds and allow for many intertextual resonances, yet still be rendered coherent through its narrative unity.

The approach offered in this study is not necessarily incompatible with other approaches, nor need it displace them. However, it will tend to strengthen certain reading strategies and interpretative positions as against others. There are three tendencies, in particular, to which it adds its weight. First, it favours a unitive and anti-atomistic approach to the Gospel story, and, hence, tends not to favour theories of textual dislocation, or multiple redactions, except where, of course, the textual

evidence clearly points to instances of this, e.g. at 5.3b, 4 and 7.53–
8.11. When it comes to sources, particularly hypothetical ones such as
a 'Logos' hymn, the approach will stress that the implied author has so
taken up his source into the narrative that it has become his own.
Reconstructing it will be difficult, if not impossible, and may even be
destructive of good exegesis if source as conceived is set against the
text as it now is.

Second, it favours a conservative approach to the Fourth Gospel's
value for historical reconstruction. The word 'conservative' is used
here to indicate that scholarship ought to retain rather than discard the
Gospel for use, alongside the Synoptics, as a source for obtaining historical data. It is especially important for providing a perspective upon
the overall historical-theological interpretation of the historical Jesus,
and for providing an insight into the dynamics of the early church's
'effective historical consciousness'.

Finally, it would encourage an appreciation of the Gospel's narrative form, and urge its significance for interpretation and hermeneutics.
A story has been told. In the mediacy of its narration are found the
choices and strategies the implied author has chosen to guide the reader
toward his point of view. But the understanding, and hence the meaning
of the story, arises out of the interaction of author and reader, situated
in their respective contexts, and meeting on the common ground of
the text in the guise of their textual persona: the implied author and
the implied reader. In that interactive meeting lie the possibilities of
endless tellings and retellings of the story. The last word should go to
the Gospel's implied author, who was perhaps as aware as any that it is
possible to view Jesus from many perspectives. This possibility enables
limitless tellings of his story—'Were every one of them to be written,
I suppose the world itself could not contain the books that would be
written (RSV).'

Appendix

A TYPOLOGICAL CIRCLE OF ANCIENT NARRATIVE GENRES: A SKETCH

Space precludes expansion on this sketch to give an adequate description of the forms included here and a defense of their place on the circle. The Gospels form a generic subgroup in their own right (called here *euangelion*). Various types of Greco-Roman *bioi* would also find their place in contiguity with the Gospels.

The typological circle of ancient genres presented below is based upon the three categories into which ancient rhetoricians divided narrative.

1. *Historia*: (*alēthēs historia*) = 'accurate record of the memory of what happened'.

2. *Plasma (argumentum)*: (*hōs alēthēs historia*) = 'a story plot or imagined situation which could very easily have taken place'.

3. *Mythos (fabula)*: (*pseudēs historia*) = 'narrative which is neither true nor does it approximate to actual events'.[1]

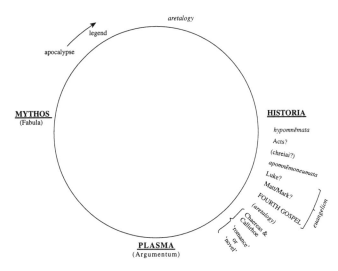

Figure 11

1.   Schmeling, *Chariton*, pp. 36, 37. Cf. D.E. Aune, *The New Testament in Its Literary Environment* (Cambridge, James Clarke, 1987), p. 83; Nelson, *Fact or Fiction*, p. 5.

BIBLIOGRAPHY

1. General: Literary and Narrative Theory, Speech-Act Theory, Narrative and History, General Biblical Works

Aarde, A.G. van, 'Narrative Point of View: An Ideological Reading of Luke 12.35-48', *Neot* 22 (1988), pp. 235-52.

Abrams, M.H., *A Glossary of Literary Terms* (Fort Worth: Holt, Rinehart, and Winston, 5th edn, 1988).

Achtemeier, P.J., 'Omne Verbum Sonat: The New Testament and the Oral Environment of Late Western Antiquity', *JBL* 109.1 (1990), pp. 3-27.

Achtemeier, P.J. (ed.), *Society of Biblical Literature 1980 Seminar Papers* (Chico, CA: Scholars Press, 1980).

Alter, R., *The Art of Biblical Narrative* (London: George Allen & Unwin, 1981).

—'How Conventions Help us Read: The Case of the Bible's Annunciation Type-scene', *Prooftexts* 3.2 (1983), pp. 115-30.

Alter, R., and F. Kermode (eds.), *The Literary Guide to the Bible* (London: Collins, 1987).

Arndt, W.F., F.W. Gingrich and F.W. Danker (eds.), *A Greek-English Lexicon of the New Testament and Other Early Christian Literature* (Chicago: University of Chicago Press, 2nd edn, 1979).

Aune, D.E., *The New Testament in its Literary Environment* (Cambridge: James Clarke, 1987).

Austin, J.L., *How to Do Things with Words* (ed. J.O. Urmson; London: Oxford University Press, 1962).

Backus, J.M., ' "He Came into her Line of Vision Walking backward": Nonsequential Sequence-Signals in Short Story Openings', *Language Learning* 15 (1965), pp. 67-83.

Bal, M., 'The Laughing Mice, or: On Focalization', *Poetics Today* 2.2 (1981), pp. 202-10.

—'Tell-Tale Theories', *Poetics Today* 17 (1986), pp. 555-64.

Barker, P., *Regeneration* (London: Penguin Books, 1992).

Barrett, C.K., *New Testament Essays* (London: SPCK, 1972).

Barton, S.C., *The Spirituality of the Gospels* (London: SPCK, 1992).

—*People of the Passion* (London: SPCK, 1994).

Bateson, G., 'A Theory of Play and Fantasy', in *idem*, *Steps to an Ecology of Mind* (London: Granada Publishing, 1973), pp. 150-66.

Beardsley, M.C., 'Intentions and Interpretations: A Fallacy Revived', in M.J. Wreen and D.M. Callen (eds.), *The Aesthetic Point of View, Selected Essays* (Ithaca, NY: Cornell University Press, 1982), pp. 188-207.

Berlin, A., *Poetics and Interpretation of Biblical Narrative* (Sheffield: Almond Press, 1983).

Blass, F., and A. Debrunner, *A Greek Grammar of the New Testament and Other Early Christian Thought* (rev. and trans. R.W. Funk; Chicago: University of Chicago Press, 1961).

Booth, W.C., *The Rhetoric of Fiction* (Chicago: University of Chicago Press, 1st edn, 1961).

Bowie, E.L., 'The Greek Novel', in P.E. Easterling and B.M.W. Knox (eds.), *The Cambridge History of Classical Literature*. I. *Greek Literature* (Cambridge: Cambridge University Press, 1985), pp. 683-99.

Bronzwaer, W.J.M., *Tense in the Novel: An Investigation of Some Potentialities of Linguistic Criticism* (Groningen: Wolters-Noordhoff, 1970).

Brown, R.L., and M. Steinmann, 'Native Readers of Fiction: A Speech-Act and Genre-Rule Approach to Defining Literature', in P. Hernadi (ed.), *What is Literature?* (Bloomington: Indiana University Press, 1978), pp. 141-60.

Burridge, R.A., *What are the Gospels?: A Comparison with Greco-Roman Biography* (Cambridge: Cambridge University Press, 1992).

Canary, R.H. and H. Kozicki, *The Writing of History: Literary Form and Historical Understanding* (Madison: University of Wisconsin Press, 1978).

Casparis, C.P., *Tense without Time: The Present Tense in Narration* (Swiss Studies in English, 84; Bern: Francke Verlag, 1975).

Champigny, R., *Ontology of the Narrative* (The Hague: Mouton, 1972).

Chatman, S. (ed.), *Approaches to Poetics* (New York: Columbia University Press, 1973).

Chatman, S., 'The Structure of Narrative Transmission', in Fowler (ed.), *Style and Structure in Literature,* pp. 213-57.

—*Story and Discourse: Narrative Structure in Fiction and Film* (Ithaca, NY: Cornell University Press, 1978).

—*Coming to Terms: The Rhetoric of Narrative in Fiction and Film* (Ithaca, NY: Cornell University Press, 1990).

Clines, D.J.A., D.M. Gunn and A.J. Hauser (eds.), *Art and Meaning: Rhetoric in Biblical Literature* (JSOTSup, 19; Sheffield: JSOT Press, 1982).

Cohn, D., 'Narrated Monologue: Definition of a Fictional Style', *Comparative Literature* 18.2 (1966), pp. 97-112.

—'The Encirclement of Narrative: On Franz Stanzel's *Theorie des Erzählens*', *Poetics Today* 2.2 (1981), pp. 157-82.

Cole, P., and J.L. Morgan (eds.), *Syntax and Semantics*. III. *Speech-Acts* (New York: Academic Press, 1975).

Collins, L. and D. Lapierre, *O Jerusalem* (London: Weidenfeld & Nicolson, 1972).

—*Freedom at Midnight* (London: Collins, 1975).

Combrink, H.J.B., 'The Structure of the Gospel of Matthew as Narrative', *TynBul* 34 (1983), pp. 61-90.

Connor, W.R., 'Narrative Discourse in Thucydides', in Department of Classics, Stamford University, *The Greek Historians*, pp. 1-17.

Crites, S., 'The Narrative Quality of Experience', *JAAR* 39.3 (1971), pp. 291-311.

Culler, J., 'Problems in the Theory of Fiction', *Diacritics* 41.1 (1984), pp. 2-11.

—*Framing the Sign: Criticism and its Institutions* (Oxford: Basil Blackwell, 1988).

Culpepper, R.A., 'Story and History in the Gospels', *RevExp* 81 (1984), pp. 467-78.

—'Commentary on Biblical Narratives: Changing Paradigms', *Foundations and Facets FORUM* 5.3 (1989), pp. 87-102.

Department of Classics, Stamford University, *The Greek Historians: Literature and History* (papers presented to A.E. Raubitschek; Saratoga: ANMA Libri, 1985).

Dodd, C.H., *About the Gospels* (Cambridge: Cambridge University Press, 1952).

Dolezel, L., 'The Typology of the Narrator: Point of View in Fiction', in *To Honor Roman*

Jakobson. I. *Essays on the Occasion of His Seventieth Birthday* (Janua Linguarum Series Maior XXXI; The Hague: Mouton, 1967), pp. 541-52.

—'Truth and Authenticity in Narrative', *Poetics Today* 1.3 (1980), pp. 7-25.

Dray, W.H., 'On the Nature and Role of Narrative in Historiography', *History and Theory* 10.2 (1971), pp. 153-71.

Eagleton, T., *Literary Theory: An Introduction* (Oxford: Basil Blackwell, 1983).

Eck, E. van and A.G. van Aarde, 'A Narratological Analysis of Mark 12.1-12: The Plot of The Gospel of Mark in a Nutshell', *Hervormde Teologiese Studies* 45.4 (1989), pp. 778-800.

Eco, U., 'The Role of the Reader', in V. Lambropoulos and D.N. Miller (eds.), *Twentieth-Century Literary Theory,* pp. 423-33.

Ellis, E.E., and E. Grässer, *Jesus und Paulus* (Festschrift für Werner Georg Kümmel; Göttingen: Vandenhoeck & Ruprecht, 1975).

Ely, R.G., R. Gruner and W.H. Dray, 'Mandelbaum on Historical Narrative: A Discussion', *History and Theory* 8.2 (1969), pp. 275-94.

Fackre, G., 'Narrative Theology: An Overview', *Interpretation* 37.4 (1983), pp. 340-52.

Fay, B., E.O. Golob and R.T. Vann (eds.), *Louis O. Mink: Historical Understanding* (Ithaca, NY: Cornell University Press, 1987).

Felman, S., *The Literary Speech-Act: Don Juan with J.L. Austin, or Seduction in Two Languages* (ET: C. Porter; Ithaca, NY: Cornell University Press, 1983).

Ferrara, F., 'Theory and Model for the Structural Analysis of Fiction', *New Literary History* 5.2 (1974), pp. 245-68.

Fish, S.E., 'How to Do Things with Austin and Searle: Speech-Act Theory and Literary Criticism', in *idem, Is There a Text in This Class?: The Authority of Interpretive Communities* (Cambridge, MA: Harvard University Press, 1980), pp. 197-245.

Fokkema, D.W., and E. Kunne-Ibsch, *Theories of Literature in the Twentieth Century: Structuralism, Marxism, Aesthetics of Reception, Semiotics* (London: C. Hurst, 1977).

Fowler, R.M., *Loaves and Fishes: The Function of the Feeding Stories in the Gospel of Mark* (SBLDS, 54; Chico, CA: Scholars Press, 1981).

—'Using Literary Criticism on the Gospels', *The Christian Century* (May 26, 1982), pp. 626-29.

—*Let the Reader Understand: Reader-Response Criticism and the Gospel of Mark* (Minneapolis: Fortress Press, 1991).

Fowler, R. (ed.), *Style and Structure in Literature: Essays in the New Stylistics* (Oxford: Basil Blackwell, 1975).

Fox, R., *The Unauthorized Version: Truth and Fiction in the Bible* (London: Viking/ Penguin, 1991).

France, R.T., and D. Wenham (eds.), *Gospel Perspectives: Studies in History and Tradition in the Four Gospels* (2 vols.; Sheffield: JSOT Press, 1981).

Frei, H.W., *The Eclipse of Biblical Narrative: A Study in Eighteenth- and Nineteenth-Century Hermeneutics* (New Haven: Yale University Press, 1974).

—*The Identity of Jesus Christ: The Hermeneutical Bases of Dogmatic Theology* (Philadelphia: Fortress Press, 1975).

Friedman, N., 'Point of View in Fiction: The Development of a Critical Concept', *PMLA* 70 (1955), pp. 1160-84.

Fritz, K. von, 'The So-Called Historical Present in Early Greek', *Word* 5 (1949), pp. 186-201.

Funk, R.W., *The Poetics of Biblical Narrative* (Sonoma, CA: Polebridge Press, 1988).

Gallie, W.B., *Philosophy and the Historical Understanding* (London: Chatto & Windus, 1964).

Genette, G., *Narrative Discourse* (ET: J.E. Lewin; Oxford: Basil Blackwell, 1980).

—*Narrative Discourse Revisited* (ET: J.E. Lewin; Ithaca, NY: Cornell University Press, 1988).

Gossman, L., 'History and Literature: Reproduction or Signification', in R.H. Canary and H. Kozicki (eds.), *The Writing of History*, pp. 3-39.

Green, G. (ed.), *Scriptural Authority and Narrative Interpretation* (Philadelphia: Fortress Press, 1987).

Grice, H.P., 'Logic and Conversation', in P. Cole and J.L. Morgan (eds.), *Syntax and Semantics*, pp. 41-58.

Hägg, T., *Narrative Technique in Ancient Greek Romances: Studies of Chariton, Xenophon Ephesius, and Achilles Tatius* (Stockholm: Svenska Institutet i Athen, 1971).

—*The Novel in Antiquity* (ET: Oxford: Basil Blackwell, 1983).

Hamburger, K., *The Logic of Literature* (ET: M.J. Rose; Bloomington: Indiana University Press, 2nd rev. edn, 1973).

Hauerwas, S. and L.G. Jones (eds.), *Why Narrative?: Readings in Narrative Theology* (Grand Rapids: Eerdmans, 1989).

Helm, J., *Essays on the Verbal and Visual Arts, Proceedings of the 1966 Annual Spring Meeting of the American Ethnological Society* (Seattle: University of Washington Press, 1967).

Hengel, M., *Studies in the Gospel of Mark* (London: SCM Press, 1985).

Hermerén, G., 'Intention and Interpretation in Literary Criticism', *New Literary History* 7.1 (1975), pp. 57-82.

High, D.M., *Language, Persons and Belief: Studies in Wittgenstein's Philosophical Investigations and Religious Uses of Language* (New York: Oxford University Press, 1967).

Hirsch, E.D., *Validity in Interpretation* (New Haven: Yale University Press, 1967).

Holub, R.C., *Reception Theory: A Critical Introduction* (London: Methuen, 1984).

Hutchison, C., 'The Act of Narration: A Critical Survey of Some Speech-Act Theories of Narrative Discourse', *Journal of Literary Semantics* 13 (1984), pp. 3-34.

Iser, W., 'Indeterminacy and the Reader's Response in Prose Fiction', in J.H. Miller (ed.), *Aspects of Narrative*, pp. 1-45.

—*The Implied Reader: Patterns of Communication in Prose Fiction from Bunyan to Beckett* (Baltimore: John Hopkins University Press, 1974).

Käsemann, E., *New Testament Questions of Today* (ET: W.J. Montague; London: SCM Press, 1969).

Kelber, W.H., *The Oral and the Written Gospel: The Hermeneutics of Speaking and Writing in the Synoptic Tradition, Mark, Paul and Q* (Philadelphia: Fortress Press, 1983).

Kermode, F., *The Genesis of Secrecy: on the Interpretation of Narrative* (Cambridge, MA: Harvard University Press, 1979).

Kingsbury, J.D., *Matthew as Story* (Philadelphia: Fortress Press, 1986).

Kort, W.A., *Narrative Elements and Religious Meanings* (Philadelphia: Fortress Press, 1975).

—'Narrative and Theology', *Journal of Literature and Theology* 1.1 (1987), pp. 27-38.

—*Story, Text and Scripture: Literary Interests in Biblical Narrative* (University Park: Pennsylvania State University Press, 1988).

Kurz, W.S., 'Narrative Approaches to Luke–Acts', *Bib* 68.2 (1987), pp. 195-220.

Labov, W. and J. Waletzky, 'Narrative Analysis: Oral Versions of Personal Experience', in J. Helm (ed.), *Essays on the Verbal and Visual Arts*, pp. 12-44.

Lambropoulos, V. and D.N. Miller (eds.), *Twentieth-Century Literary Theory: An Introductory Anthology* (Albany: State University of New York Press, 1987).

Lanser, S.S., *The Narrative Act: Point of View in Prose Fiction* (Princeton: Princeton University Press, 1981).

Lee, L., *A Moment of War* (London: Viking/Penguin, 1991).

Leitch, T.M., *What Stories Are: Narrative Theory and Interpretation* (University Park: Pennsylvania State University Press, 1986).

Lentricchia, F., *After the New Criticism* (Chicago: University of Chicago Press, 1980).

Lindars, B. (ed.), *Law and Religion: Essays on the Place of the Law in Israel and Early Christianity* (Cambridge: James Clarke, 1988).

Lindbeck, G.A., *The Nature of Doctrine: Religion and Theology in a Post-liberal Age* (London: SPCK, 1984).

Lotman, J.M., 'Point of View in a Text', *New Literary History* 6 (1975), pp. 339-52.

Louch, A.R., 'History as Narrative', *History and Theory* 8.1 (1969), pp. 54-70.

Mandelbaum, M., 'A Note on History as Narrative', *History and Theory* 6 (1967), pp. 413-19.

Martin, W., *Recent Theories of Narrative* (Ithaca: Cornell University Press, 1986).

Matera, F.J., 'The Plot of Matthew's Gospel', *CBQ* 49.2 (1987), pp. 233-53.

McConnell, F. (ed.), *The Bible and the Narrative Tradition* (Oxford: Oxford University Press, 1986).

Meier, J.P., *A Marginal Jew: Rethinking the Historical Jesus*, I (Garden City, NY: Doubleday, 1991).

Metzger, B.M., *A Textual Commentary on the Greek New Testament* (n.p.: United Bible Societies, 1971).

Meyer, B.F., *The Aims of Jesus* (London: SCM Press, 1979).

Miller, J.H., *Aspects of Narrative: Selected Papers from the ENGLISH INSTITUTE* (New York: Columbia University Press, 1971).

Mink, L.O., 'History and Fiction as Modes of Comprehension', *New Literary History* 1 (1970), pp. 541-58.

—'Narrative Form as a Cognitive Instrument', in B. Fay *et al.*, *Louis O. Mink: Historical Understanding*, pp. 182-203.

—'Philosophical Analysis and Historical Understanding', in B. Fay *et al.*, *Louis O. Mink: Historical Understanding*, pp. 118-46.

Molinié, G., *Chariton: Le Roman de Chairéas et Callihroé* (Paris: Société d'Edition 'Les Belles Lettres', Guillaume Budé, 1979).

Moore, S.D., 'Narrative Commentaries on the Bible: Context, Roots and Prospects', *Foundations and Facets FORUM* 3.3 (1987), pp. 29-62.

—*Literary Criticism and the Gospels: The Theoretical Challenge* (New Haven: Yale University Press, 1989).

Morgan, R., and J. Barton, *Biblical Interpretation* (Oxford: Oxford University Press, 1988).

Moule, C.F.D., *An Idiom-Book of New Testament Greek* (Cambridge: Cambridge University Press, 2nd edn, 1959).

Nelson, W., *Fact or Fiction: The Dilemma of the Renaissance Storyteller* (Cambridge, MA: Harvard University Press, 1973).

Neufeld, V.H., *The Earliest Christian Confessions* (Leiden: Brill, 1963).

Newton-De Molina, D., *On Literary Intention* (Edinburgh: Edinburgh University Press, 1976).

Niebuhr, H.R., *The Meaning of Revelation* (New York: MacMillan, 1941).

Nineham, D.E., *Explorations in Theology*, I (London: SCM Press, 1977).

Norton, D., *A History of the Bible as Literature*. II. *From 1700 to the Present Day* (Cambridge: Cambridge University Press, 1993).

Ohmann, R., 'Literature as Act', in S. Chatman (ed.), *Approaches to Poetics*, pp. 81-107.

—'Speech-Acts and the Definition of Literature', *Philosophy and Rhetoric* 4.1 (1971), pp. 1-19.

—'Speech, Literature, and the Space Between', *New Literary History* 4.1 (1972), pp. 47-63.

Ong, W.J., 'The Writer's Audience is Always a Fiction', in V. Lambropoulos and D.N. Millar (eds.), *Twentieth-Century Literary Theory*, 401-22.

Pascal, R., 'Tense and Novel', *The Modern Language Review* 57.1 (1962), pp. 1-11.

Pavel, T.G., 'Ontological Issues in Poetics: Speech-Acts and Fictional Worlds', *Journal of Aesthetics and Art Criticism* 40 (1981), pp. 167-78.

Perry, B.E., 'Chariton and His Romance from a Literary-Historical Point of View', *American Journal of Philology* 51.2 (1930), pp. 93-134.

—*The Ancient Romances: A Literary-Historical Account of Their Origins* (Berkeley, CA: University of California Press, 1967).

Pervo, R.I., *Profit With Delight: The Literary Genre of the Acts of the Apostles* (Philadelphia: Fortress Press, 1987).

Petersen, N.R., *Literary Criticism for New Testament Critics* (Philadelphia: Fortress Press, 1978).

—'The Reader in the Gospel', *Neot* 18 (1984), pp. 38-51.

Petrey, S., *Speech-Acts and Literary Theory* (New York: Routledge, Chapman & Hall, 1990).

Petzer, J.H., and P.J. Hartin, *A South African Prespective on the New Testament: Essays by South African New Testament Scholars presented to Bruce Manning Metzger during his visit to South Africa in 1985* (Leiden: Brill, 1986).

Poland, L.M., *Literary Criticism and Biblical Hermeneutics: A Critique of Formalist Approaches* (Chico, CA: Scholars Press, 1985).

Porter, S.E., 'Why Hasn't Reader-Response Criticism Caught on in New Testament Studies?', *Journal of Literature and Theology* 4.3 (1990) pp. 278-92.

—*Idioms of the Greek New Testament* (Sheffield: Sheffield Academic Press, 1992).

Powell, M.A., compiler, with C.G. Gray and M.C. Curtis, *The Bible and Modern Literary Criticism: A Critical Assessment and Annotated Bibliography* (New York: Greenwood Press, 1992).

Powell, M.A., *What is Narrative Criticism?* (Minneapolis: Fortress Press, 1990).

Pratt, M.L., *Toward a Speech-Act Theory of Literary Discourse* (Bloomington: Indiana University Press, 1977).

Press, G.A., *The Development of the Idea of History in Antiquity* (Kingston & Montreal: McGill-Queen's University Press, 1982).

Prince, G., *Narratology: The Form and Functioning of Narrative* (Berlin: Mouton/ de Gruyter, 1982).

Rabinowitz, P.J., 'Truth in Fiction: A Re-examination of Audiences', *Critical Inquiry* 4.1 (1977), pp. 121-41.

Reardon, B.P., 'The Greek Novel', *Phoenix* 23.3 (1969), pp. 291-309.

—*The Form of Greek Romance* (Princeton: Princeton University Press, 1991).

—*The Form of Greek Romance* (Princeton: Princeton University Press, 1991).

Reardon, B.P. (ed.), *Collected Ancient Greek Novels* (Berkeley, CA: University of California Press, 1989).

Resseguie, J.L., 'Reader-Response Criticism and the Synoptic Gospels', *JAAR* 52.2 (1984), pp. 307-24.

Ricoeur, P., *Time and Narrative* (ET: K. McLaughlin and D. Pellauer; 3 vols.; K. Blamey and D. Pellauer; Chicago: University of Chicago Press, 1984, 1985, 1988).

Rimmon-Kenan, S., *Narrative Fiction: Contemporary Poetics* (London: Methuen, 1983; London: Routledge, 1989).

Ritschl, D. and H.O. Jones, *'Story' Als Rohrmaterial der Theologie* (München: Chr. Kaiser Verlag, 1976).

Rhoads, D., 'Narrative Criticism and the Gospel of Mark', *JAAR* 50.3 (1982), pp. 411-34.

Rhoads, D. and D. Michie, *Mark as Story: An Introduction to the Narrative of a Gospel* (Philadelphia: Fortress Press, 1982).

Russell, D.A., *Criticism in Antiquity* (London: Duckworth, 1981).

Sanders, E.P., *Jesus and Judaism* (London: SCM Press, 1985).

—*The Historical Figure of Jesus* (London: Allen Lane/The Penguin Press, 1993).

Schmeling, G.L., *Chariton* (New York: Twayne Publishers, 1974).

Schneiders, S.M., *The Revelatory Text: Interpreting the New Testament as Sacred Scripture* (San Francisco: HarperCollins, 1991).

Scholes, R. and R. Kellogg, *The Nature of Narrative* (New York: Oxford University Press, 1966).

Scobie, A., *Aspects of the Ancient Romance and its Heritage: Essays on Apuleius, Petronius, and the Greek Romances* (Meisenheim am Glan: Verlag Anton Hain, 1969).

Searle, J.R., *Expression and Meaning: Studies in the Theory of Speech-Acts* (Cambridge: Cambridge University Press, 1979).

—'The Logical Status of Fictional Discourse', in *idem, Expression and Meaning,* pp. 58-75.

Segbroeck, F. van, *Evangelica: Gospel Studies, Collected Essays by Frans Neirynck* (BETL, 60; Leuven: Leuven University Press, 1982).

—*Evangelica II: 1982-1991, Collected Essays by Frans Neirynck* (BETL, 99; Leuven: Leuven University Press, 1991).

Selden, R., *A Reader's Guide to Contemporary Literary Theory* (London: Harvester Wheatsheaf, 2nd edn, 1989).

Shuler, P.L., *A Genre for the Gospels: The Biographical Character of Matthew* (Philadelphia: Fortress Press, 1982).

Smith, B.H., *On the Margins of Discourse: The Relation of Literature to Language* (Chicago: University of Chicago Press, 1978).

Solomon, J., 'Fictional Questions: Illocutionary Force in Literary Communication', in J. Hay and M. Maclean (eds.), 'Narrative Issues', Special Issue of AUMLA, *Journal of the Australasian Universities Language and Literature Association* 74 (1990), pp. 83-103.

Spencer, R.A. (ed.), *Orientation by Disorientation: Studies in Literary Criticism and Biblical Literary Criticism* (Pittsburgh: The Pickwick Press, 1980).

Stanzel, F.K., *Narrative Situations in the Novel: Tom Jones, Moby-Dick, The Ambassadors, Ulysses* (ET: J.P. Pusack; Bloomington: Indiana University Press, 1971).

—'Teller-Characters and Reflector-Characters in Narrative Theory', *Poetics Today* 2.2 (1981), pp. 5-15.

—*A Theory of Narrative* (ET: C. Goedsche; Cambridge: Cambridge University Press, 1984).

Sternberg, M., *Expositional Modes and Temporal Ordering in Fiction* (Baltimore: John Hopkins University Press, 1978).

—*The Poetics of Biblical Narrative: Ideological Literature and the Drama of Reading* (Bloomington: Indiana University Press, 1987).

Stroup, G.W., 'A Bibliographical Critique', *TToday* 32.2 (1975), pp.133-43.

—*The Promise of Narrative Theology* (London: SCM Press, 1st edn, 1984).

Stuhlmacher, P., *Das Evangelium und die Evangelien: Vorträge vom Tübinger Symposium* (WUNT, 28; Tübingen: Mohr, 1983).

Talbert, C.H., *Literary Patterns, Theological Themes and the Genre of Luke–Acts* (SBLMS, 20; Missoula, MT: Scholars Press, 1974).

—*What is a Gospel? The Genre of the Canonical Gospels* (London: SPCK, 1977).

Thiemann, R.F., *Revelation and Theology: The Gospel as Narrated Promise* (Notre Dame: University of Notre Dame Press, 1985).

Thiselton, A.C., *New Horizons in Hermeneutics* (London: HarperCollins, 1992).

Tolbert, M.A., *Sowing the Gospel: Mark's World in Literary-Historical Perspective* (Minneapolis: Fortress Press, 1989).

Uspensky, B., *A Poetics of Composition: The Structure of the Artistic Text and Typology of a Compositional Form* (ET: V. Zavarin and S. Wittig; Berkeley, CA: University of California Press, 1973).

Vanhoozer, K.J., *Biblical Narrative in the Philosophy of Paul Ricoeur: A Study in Hermeneutics and Theology* (Cambridge: Cambridge University Press, 1990).

Vorster, W.S., 'The Historical Paradigm: Its Possibilities and Limitations', *Neot* 18 (1984) pp. 104-23.

—'The New Testament and Narratology', *Journal of Literary Studies* 2 (1986), pp. 52-62.

Warner, M. (ed.), *The Bible as Rhetoric: Studies in Biblical Persuasion and Credibility* (London: Routledge, 1990).

Weinrich, H., 'Narrative Theology', *Concilium* 5.9 (1973), pp. 46-56.

White, H., *Metahistory: The Historical Imagination in Nineteenth-Century Europe* (Baltimore: John Hopkins University Press, 1973).

—'The Historical Text as Literary Artifact', in *idem, Tropics of Discourse: Essays in Cultural Criticism* (Baltimore: John Hopkins University Press, 1978), pp. 81-100.

—'The Value of Narrativity in the Representation of Reality', *Critical Inquiry* 7.1 (1980), pp. 5-27.

White, H.C., 'Speech-Act Theory and Biblical Criticism', *Semeia* 41 (Decatur, GA: Scholars Press, 1988).

Wreen, M.J., and D.M. Callen (eds.), *Monroe C. Beardsley: the Aesthetic Point of View, Selected Essays* (Ithaca, NY: Cornell University Press, 1982).

Wright, N.T., *The New Testament and the People of God* (London: SPCK, 1992).

Wright, T.R., 'Regenerating Narrative: the Gospels as Fiction', *RelS* 20.3 (1984), pp. 389-400.

—*Theology and Literature* (Oxford: Basil Blackwell, 1988).

2. The Fourth Gospel

A. *Commentaries*

Barrett, C.K., *The Gospel according to St John* (London: SPCK, 2nd edn, 1978).

Beasley-Murray, G.R., *John* (WBC, 36; Waco, TX: Word Books, 1987).

Brodie, T.L., *The Gospel according to John: A Literary and Theological Commentary* (Oxford: Oxford University Press, 1993).

Brown, R.E., *The Gospel according to John* (2 vols.; The Anchor Bible 29, 29A; Garden City, NY: Doubleday, 1970; London: Geoffrey Chapman, 1971).

Bultmann, R., *The Gospel of John: A Commentary* (ET: G.R. Beasley-Murray; Oxford: Basil Blackwell, 1971).

Carson, D.A., *The Gospel according to John* (Leicester: Inter-Varsity Press/Grand Rapids: Eerdmans, 1991).

Ellis, P.F., *The Genius of John: A Composition-Critical Commentary on the Fourth Gospel* (Collegeville: The Liturgical Press, 1984).

Haenchen, E., *John: A Commentary on the Gospel of John* (2 vols.; ET: R.W. Funk, Hermeneia; Philadelphia: Fortress Press, 1984).

Hoskyns, E.C., and F.N. Davey (ed.), *The Fourth Gospel* (London: Faber & Faber, 2nd rev. edn, 1947).

Lindars, B., *The Gospel of John* (New Century Bible Commentary; London: Marshall, Morgan & Scott, 1972).

Marsh, J., *The Gospel of St John* (The Pelican New Testament Commentaries; Harmondsworth: Penguin Books, 1968).

Morris, L., *The Gospel according to John* (NICNT; London: Marshall, Morgan & Scott, 1971).

Sanders, J.N., and B.A. Mastin (ed.), *The Gospel according to St John* (London: A. & C. Black, 1968).

Schnackenburg, R., *The Gospel according to St John* (3 vols.; ET: K. Smythe; London: Burns & Oates, 1968; New York: Crossroad, 1990).

Sloyan, G. *John* (Interpretation; Atlanta: John Knox Press, 1988).

Stibbe, M.W.G., *John* (Sheffield: JSOT Press, 1993).

Talbert, C.H., *Reading John: A Literary and Theological Commentary on the Fourth Gospel and the Johannine Epistles* (London: SPCK, 1992).

Westcott, B.F., *The Gospel according to St John* (London: John Murray, 1882).

B. *Articles and Monographs*

Aland, K., 'Eine Untersuchung zu Joh 1;3,4: über die Bedeutung eines Punktes', *ZNW* 59 (1968), pp. 174-209.

Ashton, J. (ed.), *The Interpretation of John* (Issues in Religion and Theology, 9; London: SPCK, 1986).

—*Understanding the Fourth Gospel* (Oxford: Oxford University Press, 1991).

Barclay, W., 'Great Themes of the New Testament: John 1.1-14', *ExpTim* 70.3, 70.4 (1958, 1959), pp. 78-82, 114-17.

Barrett, C.K., 'The House of Prayer and the Den of Thieves', in E.E. Ellis and E. Grässer, *Jesus und Paulus,* pp. 13-20.

—' The Prologue of St John's Gospel' in his *New Testament Essays,* pp. 27-48.

Barton, S.C., 'The Believer, the Historian and the Fourth Gospel', *Theology* 96 (1993), pp. 289-302.

Bauckham, R., 'Jesus Demonstration in the Temple', in B. Lindars (ed.), *Law and Religion,* pp. 72-89.

—'The Beloved Disciple as Ideal Author', *JSNT* 49 (1993), pp. 21-44.

—'Papias and Polycrates on the Origin of the Fourth Gospel', *JTS* 44.1 (1993), pp. 24-69.

Blakesley, J., 'Pictures in the Fire? Austin Farrer's Biblical Criticism and John's Gospel—A Comment', *Journal of Literature and Theology* 1.2 (1987), pp. 184-90.

Boers, H., 'Discourse Structure and Macro-Structure in the Interpretation of Texts: John 4.1-42 as an Example', in P.J. Achtemeier, *SBL 1980 Seminar Papers*, pp. 159-82.

Boer, M.C. de, 'Narrative Criticism, Historical Criticism and the Gospel of John', *JSNT* 47 (1992), pp. 35-48.

Boismard, M.E., *St John's Prologue* (ET: Carisbrooke Dominicans; London: Blackfriars Publications, 1957).

Borgen, P. *Logos was the True Light, and other Essays on the Gospel of John* (Department of Religious Studies; University of Trondheim: Tapir Publishers ['RELIEF'], 1983).

Born, J.B., 'Literary Features in the Gospel of John: An Analysis of John 3.1-21', *Direction* 17.2 (1988), pp. 3-17.

Botha, J.E., *Jesus and the Samaritan Woman: A Speech-Act Reading of John 4.1-42* (NovTSup, 65; Leiden: Brill, 1991).

Braun, F.-M., 'L'Expulsion des Vendeurs du Temple', *RB* 38 (1929), 178-200.

Brodie, T.L., *The Quest for the Origin of John's Gospel: A Source-Oriented Approach* (Oxford: Oxford University Press, 1993).

Brown, R.E., 'Three Quotations from John the Baptist in the Gospel of John', *CBQ* 22.3 (1960), pp. 292-98.

—'Incidents that are Units in the Synoptic Gospels but Dispersed in St John', *CBQ* 23.2 (1961), pp. 143-60.

—'The Problem of Historicity in John', *CBQ* 24.1 (1962), pp. 1-14.

—*The Community of the Beloved Disciple* (New York: Paulist Press, 1979).

Brown, S., 'The Beloved Disciple: A Jungian View', in R.T. Fortna and B.R. Gaventa (eds.), *The Conversation Continues*, pp. 366-77.

—'The True Light', *Toronto Journal of Theology* 1.2 (1985), pp. 222-26.

Bultmann, R., 'The History of Religions Background of the Prologue to the Gospel of John', in J. Ashton (ed.), *The Interpretation of John*, pp. 18-35.

Burge, G.M., *The Anointed Community: The Holy Spirit in the Johannine Tradition* (Grand Rapids: Eerdmans, 1987).

Buse, I., 'The Cleansing of the Temple in the Synoptics and in John', *ExpTim* 70 (1958), pp. 22-24.

Cahill, J.P., 'The Johannine Logos as Centre', *CBQ* 38.1 (1976), 54-72.

Carpenter, J.E., *The Johannine Writings* (London: Constable, 1927).

Carson, D.A., 'Historical Tradition in the Fourth Gospel: After Dodd, What?', in R.T. France and D. Wenham, *Gospel Perspectives*, II, pp. 83-145.

—'Understanding Misunderstandings in the Fourth Gospel', *TynBul* 33 (1982), pp. 59-91.

—'Historical Tradition in the Fourth Gospel: A Response to J.S. King', *JSNT* 23 (1985), pp. 73-81.

—'The Purpose of the Fourth Gospel: John 20.31 Reconsidered', *JBL* 106.4 (1987), pp. 639-51.

Charlesworth, J.H., *The Beloved Disciple: Whose Witness Validates the Gospel of John?* (Valley Forge, PA: Trinity Press International, 1995).

Collins, R.F., 'The Representative Figures of the Fourth Gospel', *The Downside Review* 94.1, 94.2 (1976), pp. 26-46, 118-32.

—'Jesus' Conversation with Nicodemus', *TBT* 93 (1977) pp. 1409-19.

—*John and His Witness* (Collegeville: The Liturgical Press, 1991).

Culpepper, R.A., 'The Pivot of John's Prologue', *NTS* 27.1 (1980), pp. 1-31.

—*Anatomy of the Fourth Gospel: A Study in Literary Design* (Philadelphia: Fortress Press, 1983).

—*John, the Son of Zebedee: The Life of a Legend* (Columbia, SC: University of South Carolina Press, 1994).

Culpepper, R.A., and F.F. Segovia (eds.), 'The Fourth Gospel from a Literary Perspective', *Semeia* 53 (Atlanta: Scholars Press, 1991).

Culpepper, R.A., and C.C. Black (eds.), *Exploring the Gospel of John: In Honor of D. Moody Smith* (Louisville, KY: Westminster John Knox Press, 1996).

Cullman, O., 'A New Approach to the Interpretation of the Fourth Gospel', *ExpTim* 71.1, 71.2 (1959), pp. 8-12, 39-43.

—*The Johannine Circle* (London: SCM Press, 1976).

—'The Theological Content of the Prologue to John in Its Present Form', in R.T. Fortna and B.R. Gaventa (eds.), *The Conversation Continues*, pp. 295-98.

Dahms, J.V., 'The Johannine Use of *Monogenes* Reconsidered', *NTS* 29 (1983), pp. 222-32.

Davies, M., *Rhetoric and Reference in the Fourth Gospel* (JSNTSup, 69; Sheffield: Sheffield Academic Press, 1992).

Deeks, D, 'The Structure of the Fourth Gospel', *NTS* 15 (1969), pp. 107-29.

Dodd, C.H., *The Interpretation of the Fourth Gospel* (Cambridge: Cambridge University Press, 1953).

—*Historical Tradition in the Fourth Gospel* (Cambridge: Cambridge University Press, 1965).

Dubarle, A.M., 'Le Signe du Temple', *RB* 48 (1939), pp. 21-44.

Duke, P.D., *Irony in the Fourth Gospel* (Atlanta: John Knox Press, 1985).

Dunn, J.D.G., 'Let John Be John: A Gospel for Its Time', in P. Stuhlmacher (ed.), *Das Evangelium und die Evangelien*, pp. 309-39.

Edwards, M., 'The World Could Not Contain the Books', in M. Warner (ed.), *The Bible as Rhetoric*, pp. 178-94.

Ellis, E.E., *The World of St John: The Gospel and the Epistles* (Grand Rapids: Eerdmans, 1984; London: Lutterworth Press, 1965).

Eppstein, V., 'The Historicity of the Gospel Account of the Cleansing of the Temple', *ZNW* 55 (1964), pp.42-58.

Eslinger, L., 'The Wooing of the Woman at the Well: Jesus, the Reader and Reader-Response Criticism', *Journal of Literature and Theology* 1.2 (1987), 167-83.

Evans, C.A., 'Jesus' Action in the Temple: Cleansing or Portent of Destruction?', *CBQ* 51.2 (1989), pp. 237-70.

Fortna, R.T. and B.R. Gaventa (eds.), *The Conversation Continues: Studies in Paul and John* (Nashville: Abingdon Press, 1990).

Green, H.C., 'The Composition of St John's Prologue', *ExpTim* 66.10 (1955), pp. 291-94.

Hamilton, N.Q., 'Temple Cleansing and Temple Bank', *JBL* 83 (1964), pp. 365-72.

Hanson, A.T., *The Prophetic Gospel: A Study of John and the Old Testament* (Edinburgh: T. & T. Clark, 1991).

Harrison, E.F., 'The Discourses of the Fourth Gospel', *BSac* 117 (1960), pp. 23-31.

Harvey, A.E., *Jesus on Trial: A Study in the Fourth Gospel* (London: SPCK, 1976).

Hayward, C.T.R., 'The Holy Name of the God of Moses and the Prologue of St John's Gospel', *NTS* 25.1 (1978), pp. 16-32.

Hengel, M., *The Johannine Question* (ET: J. Bowden; London: SCM Press, 1989).

Hiers, R.H., 'Purification of the Temple: Preparation for the Kingdom of God', *JBL* 90 (1971), pp. 82-90.

Hooker, M., 'John the Baptist and the Johannine Prologue', *NTS* 16 (1969-70), pp. 354-58.

Jonge, M. de (ed.), *L'Evangile de Jean: Sources, Rédaction, Théologie* (BETL, 44; Leuven: Leuven University Press, 1977).

—'John the Baptist and Elijah in the Fourth Gospel', in R.T. Fortna and B.R. Gaventa (eds.), *The Conversation Continues*, pp. 299-308.

—'Nicodemus and Jesus: Some Observations on Misunderstanding and Understanding in the Fourth Gospel', *BJRL* 53.2 (1971), pp. 337-59.

Käsemann, E., 'The Structure and Purpose of the Prologue to John's Gospel', in *idem*, *New Testament Questions of Today*, pp. 138-67.

Kermode, F., 'St John as Poet', *JSNT* 28 (1986), pp. 3-16.

—'John', in R. Alter and F. Kermode (eds.), *The Literary Guide to the Bible*, pp. 440-65.

King, J.S., 'Has D.A. Carson Been Fair to C.H. Dodd?', *JSNT* 17 (1983), pp. 97-102.

Kysar, R., *The Fourth Evangelist and His Gospel: An Examination of Contemporary Scholarship* (Minneapolis: Augsburg, 1975).

—*John's Story of Jesus* (Philadelphia: Fortress Press, 1984).

Lacan, M.-F., 'L'Oeuvre du Verbe Incarné: le Don de la Vie', *RSR* 45 (1957), pp. 61-78.

Lamarche, P., 'The Prologue of John', in J. Ashton (ed.), *The Interpretation of John*, pp. 36-52.

Lee, E.K., *The Religious Thought of St John* (London: SPCK, 1950).

Lindars, B., *Behind the Fourth Gospel* (London: SPCK, 1971).

—*John* (NTG; Sheffield: Sheffield Academic Press, 1990).

Martyn, J.L., *History and Theology in the Fourth Gospel* (Nashville, TN: Abingdon Press, 2nd rev. edn, 1979).

McCrae, G.W., 'Theology and Irony in the Fourth Gospel', in R.J. Clifford and G.W. McCrae (eds.), *The Word in the World: Essays in Honor of F.L. Moriarty* (Cambridge, MA: Weston College Press, 1973), pp. 83-96.

Meeks, W.A., 'Equal to God', in R.T. Fortna and B.R. Gaventa (eds.), *The Conversation Continues*, pp. 309-21.

—'The Man from Heaven in Johannine Sectarianism', in J. Ashton (ed.), *The Interpretation of John,* pp. 141-73.

Millar, E.L., 'The Logos was God', *EvQ* 53 (1981), pp. 65-77.

—'The Logic of the Logos Hymn: A New View', *NTS* 29.4 (1983), pp. 552-59.

—*Salvation-History in the Prologue of John: the Significance of John 1.3/4* (NovTSup, 60; Leiden: E.J. Brill, 1989).

Minear, P.S., 'The Original Function of John 21', *JBL* 102.1 (1983), pp. 85-98.

Moloney, F.J., *Belief in the Word: Reading the Fourth Gospel, John 1–4* (Minneapolis: Fortress Press, 1993).

Moody, D., 'God's Only Son: The Translation of John 3.16 in the Revised Standard Version', *JBL* 72 (1953), pp. 213-19.

Morris, L., *Studies in the Fourth Gospel* (Grand Rapids: Eerdmans, 1969).

Mussner, F., *The Historical Jesus in the Gospel of St John* (ET: W.J. O'Hara; London: Burns & Oates, 1967).

Neirynck, F., 'The "Other Disciple" in Jn 18.15-16', in F. van Segbroeck (ed.), *Evangelica*, pp. 335-64.

—'The Anonymous Disciple in John 1', in F. van Segbroeck (ed.), *Evangelica II*, pp. 617-49.

—'John 21', in F. van Segbroeck (ed.), *Evangelica II*, pp. 601-16.

Neufeld, D., 'Reconceiving Texts as Speech-Acts: An Analysis of the First Epistle of John' (PhD Thesis; McGill University, Montreal, March 1991).

O'Day, G.R., *Revelation in the Fourth Gospel: Narrative Mode and Theological Claim* (Philadelphia: Fortress Press, 1986).

Ogg, G., 'The Jerusalem Visit of John 2.13-3.21', *ExpTim* 56.3 (1944), pp. 70-72.

Olsson, B., *Structure and Meaning in the Fourth Gospel: A Text-Linguistic Analysis of John 2.1-11 and 4.1-42* (ET: J. Gray; ConBNT, 6; Lund: CWK Gleerup, 1974).

O'Neill, J.C., 'The Prologue to St John's Gospel', *JTS* 20.1 (1969), pp. 41-52.

O'Rourke, J.J., 'The Historic Present in the Gospel of John', *JBL* 93.4 (1974), pp. 585-90.

—'Asides in the Gospel of John', *NovT* 21.3 (1979), pp. 210-19.

Painter, J., 'Johannine Symbols: A Case Study in Epistemology', *Journal of Theology for Southern Africa* 27 (1979), pp. 26-41.

—*The Quest for the Messiah: The History, Literature and Theology of the Johannine Community* (Edinburgh: T. & T. Clark, 1st edn/2nd edn, 1991/1993).

Panier, L., 'Cana et le Temple: la pratique et la théorie. Une lecture sémiotique de Jean 2', *Lumiere et Vie* 41 (1992), pp. 37-54.

Phillips, G.A., '"This is a Hard Saying. Who Can Be a Listener to It?": Creating a Reader in John 6', *Semeia* 26 (1983), pp. 23-56.

Pryor, J.W., 'John 3.3, 5: A Study in the Relation of John's Gospel to the Synoptic Tradition', *JSNT* 41 (1991), pp. 71-95.

—*John: Evangelist of the Covenant People. The Narrative and Themes of the Fourth Gospel* (Downers Grove, IL: Inter-Varsity Press, 1992).

Quast, K., *Peter and the Beloved Disciple: Figures for a Community in Crisis* (JSNTSup, 32; Sheffield: Sheffield Academic Press, 1989).

Rand, J.A. du, *Johannine Perspectives: Introduction to the Johannine Writings*, I (Doornfontein: Orion, 1991).

—'Plot and Point of View in the Gospel of John', in J.H. Petzer and P.J. Hartin, *A South African Perspective on the New Testament*, pp. 149-69.

Redlich, E.B., 'S. John 1-3: A Study in Dislocations', *ExpTim* 55.4 (1944), pp. 89-92.

Reinhartz, A., *The Word in the World: The Cosmological Tale in the Fourth Gospel* (SBLMS, 45; Atlanta: Scholars Press, 1992).

Robinson, J.A.T., 'The Relation of the Prologue to the Gospel of St John', *NTS* 9 (1962-63), pp. 120-29.

—*The Priority of John* (J.F. Coakley (ed.); London: SCM Press, 1985).

Roth, C., 'The Cleansing of the Temple and Zechariah XIV 21', *NovT* 4 (1960), pp. 174-81.

Ruckstuhl, E., *Die literarische Einheit des Johannesevangeliums* (NTOA, 5; Göttingen: Vandenhoeck & Ruprecht, 1987).

—'Johannine Language and Style', in M. de Jonge (ed.), *L'Evangile de Jean*, pp. 125-47.

Saxby, H., 'The Time-Scheme in the Gospel of John', *ExpTim* 104.1 (1992), pp. 9-13.

Schlatter, F.W., 'The Problem of Jn 1.3b-4a', *CBQ* 34.1 (1972), pp. 54-58.

Schneider, H., ' "The Word was made flesh": An Analysis of the Theology of Revelation in the Fourth Gospel', *CBQ* 31.3 (1969), pp. 344-56.

Seeley, D., 'Jesus' Temple Act', *CBQ* 55.2 (1993), pp. 263-83.

Servotte, H., *According to John: A Literary Reading of the Fourth Gospel* (ET: London: Darton, Longman & Todd, 1994).

Smalley, S.S., *John: Evangelist and Interpreter* (Exeter: Paternoster Press, 1978).

Smith, D.M., 'The Sources of the Gospel of John: An Assessment of the Present State of the Problem', *NTS* 10 (1963-64), pp. 336-51.

Sproston, W.E., ' "Is not this Jesus, the son of Joseph. . . ?" (John 6.42): Johannine Christology as a Challenge to Faith', *JSNT* 24 (1985), pp. 77-97.

Staley, J. L., 'The Structure of John's Prologue: Its Implications for the Gospel's Narrative Structure', *CBQ* 48.2 (1986), pp. 241-64.

—*The Print's First Kiss: A Rhetorical Investigation of the Implied Reader in the Fourth Gospel* (SBLDS, 82; Atlanta: Scholars Press, 1988).

Stibbe, M.W.G., 'The Artistry of John: The Fourth Gospel as Narrative Christology' (PhD Thesis, University of Nottingham, 1989).

—*John as Storyteller: Narrative Criticism and the Fourth Gospel* (SNTSMS, 73; Cambridge: Cambridge University Press, 1992).

—' "Return to Sender": A Structuralist Approach to John's Gospel', *Biblical Interpretation* 1.2 (1993), pp. 189-206.

—'A Tomb with a View: John 11.1-44 in Narrative Critical Perspective', *NTS* 40.1 (1994), pp. 38-54.

Stibbe, M.W.G. (ed.), *The Gospel of John as Literature: An Anthology of Twentieth-Century Perspectives* (Leiden: Brill, 1993).

Tenney, M.C., 'The Footnotes of John's Gospel', *BSac* 117 (1960), pp. 350-64.

Tilborg, S. van, *Imaginative Love in John* (Biblical Interpretation Series, 2; Leiden: Brill, 1993).

Tolmie, D.F., 'The Function of Focalization in John 13-17', *Neot* 25.2 (1991), pp. 273-87.

Vawter, B., 'What Came to be in Him was Life (Jn 1, 3b-4a)', *CBQ* 35.3 (1963), pp. 401-406.

Wahlde, U.C. von, 'The Johannine "Jews": A Critical Survey', *NTS* 28.1 (1982), pp. 33-60.

Warner, M., 'The Fourth Gospel's Art of Rational Persuasion', in M. Warner (ed.), *The Bible as Rhetoric*, pp. 153-77.

Wead, D.W., *The Literary Devices in John's Gospel* (Basel: Friedrich Reinhardt Kommissionsverlag, 1970).

—'Johannine Irony as a Key to the Author–Audience Relationship in John's Gospel', in F.O. Francis (ed.), *American Academy of Religion: Biblical Literature* (Missoula, MT: Scholars Press, 1974), pp. 33-44.

Webster, E.C., 'Pattern in the Fourth Gospel', in D.J.A. Clines, *et al., Art and Meaning*, pp. 230-57.

Wendland, E.R., 'Rhetoric of the Word. An Interactional Discourse Analysis of the Lord's Prayer of John 17 and Its Communicative Implications', *Neot* 26.1 (1992), pp. 59-88.

Yee, G.A., *Jewish Feasts and the Gospel of John* (Wilmington, DE: Michael Glazier, 1989).

INDEXES

INDEX OF REFERENCES

OLD TESTAMENT

NEW TESTAMENT

DATE DUE

MAR 21 2002			
DEC 22 2003			
3/8/05			
			Printed in USA

HIGHSMITH #45230